D1614520

Religion and National Identity

Religion and National Identity

Governing Scottish Presbyterianism in the
Eighteenth Century

Alistair Mutch

EDINBURGH
University Press

This book is for Gwen Mutch, whose communion card triggered the whole project, and in memory of Alexander Mutch (1926–2013), elder, treasurer, entrepreneur

© Alistair Mutch, 2015

Edinburgh University Press Ltd
The Tun – Holyrood Road
12 (2f) Jackson's Entry
Edinburgh EH8 8PJ
www.euppublishing.com

Typeset in Ehrhardt by
3btype.com, and
printed and bound in Great Britain by
CPI Group (UK) Ltd, Croydon CR0 4YY

A CIP record for this book is available from the
British Library

ISBN 978 0 7486 9915 5 (hardback)
ISBN 978 0 7486 9916 2 (webready PDF)
ISBN 978 1 4744 0344 3 (epub)

Contents

Illustrations

Figures

Tables

Acknowledgements

I am aware, as I present what I hope is a distinctive approach to the history of Scottish religious practice, that I am entering on territory often marked by confessional commitments. There is a hint in my dedication of this book to the confessional context of my own shaping. I was brought up with the practices of the Church of Scotland, although their distinctiveness as practices only became apparent to me many years later. By then I had abandoned any commitment to the beliefs that animated them, although over time I have also become more aware of their positive social functions and impact. I also have to acknowledge the influence of my uncle, the Reverend Malcolm Peach, in triggering my enduring love for the parish churches of England and for explaining some of the mysteries of the Church of England. However, I approach the topic from a secular position, albeit one with respect for some aspects of the traditions I am examining.

Another great Scottish institution whose excellence in records management I like to think may have been shaped by some of the practices I examine is what is now the National Records of Scotland (NRS). I owe a particular debt to the work done on the digital imaging of the records of the Church of Scotland, and to the NRS for allowing me to be involved in the remote testing of the prototype online access system for church court records. This has made a dramatic difference to the practical feasibility of this project, enabling me to move from a focus on particular areas to a much broader approach. I am grateful to Sir Archibald Grant for permission to cite material from the Grant of Monymusk muniments in the NRS, as well as his guidance on estate history. I, of course, also owe a great deal to all those other libraries and archives that I have used: the National Library of Scotland, The British Library, Nottinghamshire Records Office, the University of Nottingham Special Collections, the Derbyshire Records Office and the Liverpool Record Office. But I want to say a special thank you for the excellent service provided by my own institution's library, where Nottingham Trent University is exceptional in its access to electronic resources and its inter-library loan service.

In a time of intense focus on research funding, where the palm goes to ever larger applications shaped by an obsession with the demands of big science, I am grateful to Nottingham Business School for funding aspects of this research. I hope that the return on their investment indicates what can be done with relatively small sums of money. For their support I thank in particular Baback Yazdani, Harry Barton, Simon Mercado, David Smith and Melanie Currie, as well as former colleagues Martin Reynolds, Paul Bowker and Tony Watson. I have benefited during this project from conversations with a number of people, none of whom is responsible for my ignoring of their sound arguments: Margaret Archer, Ewen Cameron, Carol Craig, Rick Delbridge, Philip Gorski, Roger Friedland, Alan McKinlay, Mick Rowlinson, Roy Suddaby and Robin Urquhart. For understanding the importance of allusions in the conclusion that have been developed in enjoyable conversations with him, thanks to Greg Walker. For hospitality in Edinburgh, combined with good questions about exactly what I was up to, Ellen Hair and Graham Smith. I am grateful to the eagle eyes of Belinda Cunnison for eliminating the errors I had hoped I had avoided; any which remain are my responsibility. My thanks as well to those at Edinburgh University Press who shepherded me through the process. For bearing with the project for what must seem like an inordinate amount of time, my biggest debt is to Kath, Adrienne, Andrew and Ella.

Introduction

In Linda Colley's much acclaimed account of the construction of British identity in the eighteenth century, considerable stress is placed on the importance of a shared Protestantism in drawing together the peoples of the island in a struggle against the Catholic 'other' of France and other European powers.[1] This enabled Scots in particular to play a significant role in creating the British Empire, as soldiers, administrators and merchants. Such participation, in turn, reinforced loyalty to the British state, certainly among the country's elite. There is much that is persuasive about this account, but J. C. D. Clark points to some dangers in glossing over important distinctions. Colley, he argued, 'treated "Protestantism" without further discussion as essentially one thing, where the reality was much more complex'.[2] In particular, he pointed to differences in ecclesiastical polity between the component parts of the country. His account is developed very much from an English perspective and on the basis of elite writings; this book seeks to examine these differences from the perspective of Scotland through a detailed examination of practice.

In one account, which combines religious and social history, Jeremy Gregory has speculated on the degree to which the Book of Common Prayer might have fostered a sense of national identity, in being used routinely across the country over long periods of time.[3] This is, of course, a matter of English, Anglican identity; the attempt to impose the Book of Common Prayer on Scotland in the early seventeenth century was a factor in the religious conflicts, which created some potent Scottish traditions. What we often sense in such accounts, for all their value, is a conflation of the English experience with Britain. In this book, contrasts with English practice will be important and will help to point up the distinctiveness of practice in Scotland. It was to preserve the distinctive Presbyterian polity that eventually triumphed after the conflicts of the seventeenth century that so many associated with the Church of Scotland came to support the Union of the two countries of 1707. One of the conditions of that Union was the affirmation of the Presbyterian theology and polity of the Church of Scotland. That such commitments were fairly soon broken by Tory, Anglican-dominated Houses of Parliament reimposing patronage provoked a further round of disputes across Scotland throughout the eighteenth century, this time usually fought out primarily at local level. The eruption of these conflicts at a national level, through appeals to the General Assembly on both sides, has been one of the key motifs of Scottish religious history.[4] Connected with this, and associated with the fissiparous tendencies of Presbyterian theology, were various secessions from the Church of Scotland.[5] These developments were, of course, of considerable significance, but they tend to overshadow other more mundane practices that, arguably, have had more enduring consequences. Debates over patronage and theology, that is, have often been cast in terms of institutional history, drawing on printed disputations (of which there was no lack). By contrast, the account presented here, while always mindful of these debates, focuses on some rather more taken-for-granted practices.

The nature of these practices is pursued in more detail later in the book, but for now the key point is that rather than seeing organisations as a static endpoint, a focus on practices looks at them in terms of the processes of organising. That is, the achievements represented in more institutional accounts had to be put into effect through a great deal of effort. One obvious form of practice in the context of religion is the ritual, but beyond the ritual were further organising practices or routines that enabled the ritual to take place. One of the better known of such practices was the distribution of tokens to enable the faithful to undertake the central ritual of communion, but behind such practices lay others, such as the construction of communion rolls. Central to such routines in Presbyterian polity was attention to the detailed recording of transactions. Such records have often been used, to great effect, to explore questions such as poor relief, the status of women and the nature of educational experience.[6] Such accounts are illuminating, but they use the records as a source of evidence. By contrast, much of this book is based on using the very form and existence of these records as a type of evidence in their own right. Doing this enables us to consider some possibly enduring effects. A key contention of the book is that practices that had their origins in theological belief came to be relatively detached from belief. That is, adherents did not have to share or understand all the finer points of Presbyterian theology to engage in the practices that made its central rituals possible. Over time, such practices, such as detailed record keeping and forms of accountability, might become available for application in other domains.

There is a danger in considering mundane practices in this way that we detach them completely from the broader context of belief, which gave them their meaning. In particular, not only were there theological arguments of considerable importance during the period under examination, but also those arguments were also inextricably entangled with wider political considerations. At all levels of the church there were debates about the level and appropriateness of contact with secular authorities. The highest levels of the church, in its debates at the General Assembly, were particularly susceptible to political manipulation. Powers of patronage and presentation were used to insert candidates into the church that would be loyal to those of a particular political camp, often despite the wishes of large sections of those to whom they would minister.[7] These factors have to be borne in mind as the ever-present backdrop to the administrative practices examined here. At a number of points we will see their influence. However, these topics have been ably dealt with elsewhere; the present study is seen as a complement to these accounts and their content is not reproduced here. Rather, the focus is on the potential impacts of particular emerging administrative routines, both within the church and in other domains.

One of those domains is that of economic activity. In considering the explosive economic development towards the end of the eighteenth century in Scotland, Christopher Whatley suggests that Scots had to tackle 'two serious and interconnected problems'. One was the control of labour; the second was that of 'managing sizeable organisations'.[8] The lessons they learned, he argued, meant that 'before the end of the eighteenth century, and increasingly so in the nineteenth, Scots – who had hitherto been drawing hard on English (and other) expertise – were making contributions to the industrialisation process in England and Ireland and on the continent of Europe'.[9] There is rather more in his treatment of labour control than what we might term 'middle management' – but it is arguably here that Scots made their biggest contribution. One symbol of this contribution was Scottish preeminence in the development of accounting, from their writing of the leading textbooks in the eighteenth century to the founding much later of the first professional accounting association. This took an embodied form in the widespread employment of Scots as clerks and bookkeepers, the most famous being Robert Burns. He was bound for employment as a bookkeeper on a Caribbean plantation, where he would have joined many other Scots, before the success of his poems kept him in Scotland. A much less famous example outside the ranks of management scholars is James Montgomery, Glasgow cotton mill manager, devout Presbyterian and author of what has been termed 'the first management text' in 1832. These examples, and others, will be returned to much later, but it is argued that they are the product, in significant part, of a culture of accountability produced by Presbyterian governance practices.

Managers and accountants, of course, are hardly the stuff of myth and legend. They could scarcely make the nation 'secure in valour's station', as Burns has it. But arguably their contribution to the enduring nature of what it is to be Scottish is a significant one. This is to enter upon dangerous territory, where the myths and legends are ones of romance and heroism, not careful record keeping and attention to detail. But the figure of the Scottish banker in the film *Ned Kelly* can act as a counterweight to *Braveheart*.[10] Indeed, if we return to Burns we can see this tension at the heart of Scottish identity. Often remembered for his infractions of Presbyterian discipline and his humiliation at the hands of the church, he is seen as part Jacobite-inspired Scottish patriot, part advocate of the universal rights of man. But Liam McIl-vanny has shown just how important aspects of Presbyterianism were in the formation of Burns' ideas, especially 'the man o' independent mind'.[11] This sense of sturdy independence is one of the legacies of Presbyterianism; connected to it are habits of thought that another creative Scot, the novelist James Robertson, alludes to when considering the impact of his Presbyterian upbringing:

> The framework remains. I still find it a useful framework for coping with life – there was an intellectual rigour to the way I was taught to confront ideas of moral behaviour and spiritual belief, and even after the belief has gone the rigour remains.[12]

An author who has pursued the implications of this more than others is Carol Craig. In her stimulating *Scots' Crisis of Confidence*, Craig draws upon a wealth of examples from history and literature to seek to outline what is distinctive about Scottish life. She shows quite convincingly how some familiar tropes, especially the notion of the divided self, the famous Caledonian Antisyzygy, which owes a great deal to the activities of Hugh MacDiarmid, are not distinctively Scottish at all but can be found in many other contexts. She suggests that if we are looking for answers, then Presbyterianism is one of the key places to look. 'It is almost impossible to say anything about Scottish culture or character', she argues, 'without making constant reference to the influence of the Kirk'.[13] She adduces a number of characteristics to this influence, notably a focus on system and rationality. Here it is interesting to note that the contrast she makes with English characteristics is built into the very approach she takes to her subject. We can see this if we contrast her anatomy of Scottish character with that essayed by the English anthropologist Kate Fox in her book *Watching the English*.[14] Apart from a question of tone – serious in the case of Craig, humorous in the case of Fox – the key difference is in how the two authors approach their subject. Fox builds from empirical observation, piling up a host of illustrations and seeking to draw conclusions from them. Craig, by contrast, seeks to work from first principles and to deploy theories to build explanations. Craig's work is intriguing and many of her themes will be returned to and explored throughout this book, but in one aspect this book departs from her contrast between Scotland and England. Here she argues that:

> English culture is more introverted than Scottish culture – more interested in the inner, rather than the outer world. That is why English culture does not have the oral, energetic and active quality which is so apparent in Scotland. The combination of introversion and sensing has certain undoubted strengths. An individual of these preferences is usually dutiful and hardworking, down to earth, and very good at attending to detail. Hence this type is good at creating and maintaining administrative systems.[15]

By contrast, I am going to argue that a detailed examination of Presbyterian church governance indicates precisely the opposite. It indicates that Scottish practices favoured a systemic form of authority based on detailed record keeping, where the English relied much more on the personal qualities of those in positions of leadership. This carries through, it will be argued, to aspects of running business and other organisations.

If the work of Craig, and others, points to the need for a reassessment of Presbyterianism's contribution, then it seems useful to examine aspects of that faith in more detail. As will become clearer when we look at the historiography in detail, much of the existing work has a particularly confessional context. That does not prevent it containing a great deal of value, but it does mean that the focus is often on belief, with assumptions about the associated practices being based on rather slim evidence. Those assumptions are then carried forward into works concerned with more general arguments. In focusing on religion as a social practice, and especially on the routines that were necessary to put beliefs into effect, I want to complement some of these wider arguments and suggest that the impact of these taken-for-granted practices might be much wider. The sociologist David McCrone has pointed out 'that emphasizing your Scottishness is associated with social democratic values'.[16] This association is often related to some foundational myths, notably that of Red Clydeside, but also at times with the shadowy figures of the Covenanters in the mists of time. These are powerful myths that cannot be ignored, but perhaps adherence to collectivist values, as Craig suggests, owes a good deal to the distinctively Scottish institutions of the church, law and education that were preserved at the Treaty of Union. McCrone goes on to suggest that:

> people think of themselves as Scots – and they do, in increasing numbers, over being British – because they have been educated, governed and embedded in a Scottish way. It is a matter of governance, not sentiment; and, if anything, the latter derives from the former. In other words, people think of themselves as Scottish because of the micro-contexts of their lives reinforced by the school system.[17]

These micro-contexts, the taken-for-granted practices that form the ever-present context for action, are what are explored for the eighteenth century in this book. While the focus is firmly on religious practices, connections will be made as appropriate to the law and education because, it is argued, a dense set of interconnected practices that endure despite changing commitments to the core institutions shape what it is that we take to be key dimensions of Scottishness.

For those unfamiliar with the organisation of the Presbyterian Church of Scotland, there follows a brief sketch of its main features as they obtained in the eighteenth century. This sketch will be filled in during the book and is intended at this point just as a means of introducing some key terms. At the root of the system were the parish, the minister and the kirk session. The minister was the clerical incumbent, supported in his spiritual duties by the session composed of a number of elders. These men (and they were always men) were selected by the minister and session and ordained to office for life. They were to support the minister in his spiritual duties, especially in bringing sinners to discipline, and to run the financial affairs of the church, in particular in regard to the relief of the poor. The minister's stipend, his house (the manse), the church building and the school were the financial responsibility of the heritors, the landowners who possessed the tiends (tithes) in their rentals. The minister and an elder were members of the presbytery, which was at the heart of the church polity. Comprising a group of about fifteen parishes, this body monitored local activities and translated national policy into local effect. It was concerned with maintaining the provision of ministers and ensuring their correct behaviour. It also acted as a court of appeal for those complex cases that could not be resolved at a local level. It had powers of inspection of local records and activities. Meeting generally monthly, it sent members to the synod, which met twice a year and consisted of a regional collection of presbyteries. Presbyteries sent their registers to the synod for approval, appealed to it in cases involving their members and particpated in discussions on matters of national policy. Presbyteries also selected several of their number, both ministers and elders, to attend the General Assembly, which met annually in Edinburgh. This was the supreme policymaking body of the Church, but its 'overtures' were sent out to presbyteries for discussion and approval before they were ratified as 'Acts'. The General Assembly was the forum for debates over contentious matters, the most salient of which during the eighteenth century were those over patronage. This was the right of landowners to present a minster to a vacant parish, something bitterly resisted by significant numbers in the Church. The moderator of the Assembly was chosen each year and was the chair of the meeting, rather than an executive. There was also no executive body to act in between Assemblies, although a commission was appointed to follow through resolutions. The entire structure, that is, had sets of built-in checks and balances that distinguished it from more conventional hierarchies.

This system relied on a whole set of routines to make it work; specification of the nature of these routines is the theme of Chapter 1. The historian Alan Megill has observed:

> [the] more that one knows, through the experience of having argued with them, about how the practitioners of other disciplines argue, the less likely one is to think that the different modes of argument are compatible enough for any one person to practice them at the same time.[18]

As this work straddles the boundary between history and another discipline, that of organisation theory, it is likely to fall foul of this incompatibility. Chapter 1 engages in rather more theoretical discussion than might be to the taste of many historians and so they might want to pass over the earlier sections. However, it also considers the existing historiography and the evidence base. The more abstract discussion is useful in examining what historians have tended to take for granted: that is, the mundane practices that put organisations and ideas into effect. Such practices are importantly linked to the very richness of the surviving material for Scotland, access to which has been dramatically improved by technological advance. The real history, then, starts with Chapter 2, which draws on the existing historiography to point to the development of administrative practices, almost hidden from view by the more turbulent events of the seventeenth century that, rightly, have occupied historians. This forms the context for the consideration of one distinctive aspect of the Scottish experience: the attempt to lay down blueprints that outline governance in a systematic fashion. It is necessary to understand this ambition in order to measure it against practice, which is the task of the following three chapters. Chapter 3 takes as its focus the work of the presbytery, seeking to show how some of the ambitions in the organisational blueprints were wildly unrealistic. It looks, in particular, at the fate of the parochial visitation, tracing its operation and eventual disappearance through a sample of presbyterial records across the southern Lowlands. However, other mechanisms for monitoring local activities, such as the 'privy censure' and the 'revision' of church records, were also significant and are considered in some detail.

This review of the work of presbyteries forms the background to an examination of local practice. Chapter 4 looks at how the main actors – the minister and the elders –were selected and what their key activities as a session were. In this chapter, one key focus is on record keeping, especially in the context of a practice that was central to the local church year, the annual communion 'season'. This ritual required a number of organisational routines to make it work, including distinctive artefacts (the communion token) and recording practices. The session also had other important records, especially those concerned with the relief of the poor, and these are examined in Chapter 5. Examination of the surviving records suggests that detailed practices of recording financial activities long predated two court cases at mid-century, Cambuslang in 1752 and Humbie in 1751, which have featured in the broader historiography. These accounting records were at the heart of routines of reconciliation that fostered a particular form of accountability. Chapter 6 summarises the evidence for this systemic accountability and considers some temporal and regional variations in its operation. It is also related to other important aspects of the Scottish context, notably education and the law. These are seen to complement and reinforce a distinctive Scottish focus on system. The operation of this system at the end of the eighteenth century is then considered in some detail through the experience of one Aberdeenshire parish, Monymusk. A rather neglected and long-running court case that turned on tensions between a heritor and his local kirk session offers valuable insights that help to summarise this part of the discussion.

This material is of considerable interest in its own right and adds to our understanding of the interaction between church and society in this period, but its distinctive nature is pointed up further if we contrast it to practices elsewhere. The contrast in Chapter 7 is with English practice at the same time. A contrast with governance practice at local level in the Church of England reveals a very different form of accountability, one that rested on the personal characteristics of the office holders. This contrast is then used to frame some consequences of the Scottish system for economic activity. At the local level, the corporate form that the kirk session took enabled it to accumulate financial resources that were then lent out at interest to provide poor relief. In some cases this led kirk sessions to be investors in nascent commercial concerns, especially in the activities of Glasgow merchants. This had a direct impact on economic development; a rather more indirect, but perhaps more lasting impact, was in the authoring of works on accounting and management. Accounting texts produced by Scottish authors, who in turn had strong links to the church, dominated the market on both sides of the Atlantic. It is in North America, especially in the United States, that the long-term impacts of the Scottish focus on systemic accountability might have been felt. These implications are followed up in Chapter 8, where contrasts are made with the evidence, admittedly sketchy, about practices in other major belief systems. Attention then returns to the potential impacts on Scottish identity and so to the questions raised by Craig's discussion. The enduring impacts of the practices we have examined, and the tensions they might point to, which are disguised by a focus on 'shared Protestantism', give another dimension to ongoing debates about Scottish identity in questioning the nature of Britain.

CHAPTER I

Looking for Practices

In his exploration of the roots of the early modern state in Europe, Philip Gorski has pointed to the importance of Calvinism.[1] He suggests that this was one of several elements in the production of the modern bureaucratic state. In so doing, he raises some doubts about a very famous historical thesis: that of the relationship between the rise of Protestantism and that of capitalism proposed by the German social theorist Max Weber. We will return to this important thesis later, but what is significant about Gorski's work is his focus on the importance of practice as well as belief. Much of the debate about the putative impact of Protestantism, that is, has been cast in terms of the inferred impact on psychological states of doctrines such as that of predestination, that is, the idea that only a small elect has been selected by God for salvation and that earthly actions can have no impact on this election. Such effects are notoriously difficult, if not impossible, to evidence. What we *can* examine, however, argues Gorski, are the effects of such beliefs, in the forms of practices that might be adopted to translate the consequences of the beliefs for the faithful. In this way Reformed Protestantism was the laboratory for devising new forms of governance practice. This means that we need to explore the connections between bodies of belief and the practices that were needed to put them into effect. Over time, it will be argued in this book, such practices became taken for granted and relatively detached from (although always given their meaning by) bodies of formal beliefs. In the process they could become available for transfer to other domains. In Gorski's case this was for state formation; this book will pay particular attention to the economic domain. This chapter looks in a little more detail at the literature on the nature of practice in order to give us some orienting concepts. We then examine the existing historical literature on Scottish church governance with a view to drawing together the hints about such practices, before considering how to expand such hints using the evidence available to us in the archives.

The Protestant Ethic and practice

First published in 1905, Weber's *The Protestant Ethic and the Spirit of Capitalism* has spawned an enormous body of work.[2] Much of this work seeks to dispute the supposed direction of the relationship between religious belief and capitalism, although arguably this was not Weber's main concern.[3] We will return to this concern with the formation of subjectivity later, but the core thesis, of an elective affinity between certain forms of Protestantism, notably Calvinism, and the valorisation of economic activity as a good in its own right, has particular resonance for Scotland. As the most thoroughgoing instantiation of Calvinism in Europe, it formed a useful site for the investigation of the links. This is what was essayed by Gordon Marshall in his 1980 book *Presbyteries and Profits: Calvinism and the Development of Capitalism in Scotland, 1560–1707*.[4] Here he found interesting examples of the attention to business that Weber suggested, but discovered that they were constrained by the objective circumstances of Scotland at the time. It was the timing that troubled historians. Thus, as Christopher Smout had earlier observed, 'few countries were more completely Calvinist than Scotland, yet it is hard to see how any support can be found for Weber's thesis from the situation in this country between 1560 and 1690'.[5] Given that Scotland's take-off as a fully-fledged capitalist economy is generally accepted to have been in the later years of the eighteenth century, any formulation that looks at capitalism seems flawed. As McCrone puts it:

> it might seem that the Scottish case does refute the thesis because, while no one can deny that Scotland was infused with Calvinism as early as the late sixteenth century, that it was a theocracy, it was not until at least a century or more later that it became in any meaningful sense a capitalist country.[6]

In addition, Todd has pointed out that in the circumstances of the earlier years of the new church, 'eldership was an onerous burden on men with businesses to run'.[7] Attendance at weekly meetings of session as well as at weekday sermons would require extensive commitments of time on the part of the most conscientious of the faithful. Although these demands might relax with the passage of time, particular aspects of Scottish church practice, such as the extended communion season, might legitimately be seen as eating into the time available for economic activity. However, this has not stopped others returning to the thesis.

For example, in a detailed examination of the Edinburgh firm of papermakers Cowans, McInstry and Ding point to the devoutly held beliefs of the family through a number of generations.[8] They use, in particular, a remarkable diary of Charles Cowan, third-generation owner and manager. His diary provides an extraordinary example of detailed accounting for time, using a printed template produced by his own company to break down weekly activities into categories of business and both public and private spiritual duties. Such examples could be multiplied. They could, for example, have cited the Kintyre shipowner Sir William MacKinnon. The firm's 'resident partners were invariably elders or deacons in the Free Church in Calcutta, and sat on its Financial and Corresponding Board. MacKinnon Mackenzie & Co as a firm was the church's treasurer.'[9] However, there is a two-fold problem here. One is that the timing, again, is wrong. These examples are drawn from the nineteenth century and show an undoubted contribution of Presbyterianism to the forms of enterprise in that period. This is, however, in the context of a mature capitalist economy. Given that the roots of this economy are, arguably, in the agrarian enterprises of England in the fifteenth century, spreading to the trading networks of the Low Countries, then the Scottish example is of little assistance. The second problem is with the reasoning from individual cases, no matter how interesting their detail. It ignores the work done by Jeremy whose prosopographical work on business leaders in Britain (although, again, for a later period) suggests that the majority of business leaders were Anglican in declared religious affiliation.[10] Systematic surveys of this nature do point to the dangers of working from illustrative examples.

We can, however, find value in the Weber thesis if we moderate both the link to the rise of capitalism and the focus on belief.[11] There are hints in Marshall that point to an alternative approach that might be fruitful. This is a focus on taken-for-granted organisational practice. Marshall has an extensive discussion of the Newmills Cloth Manufactury, established in Haddington-shire in the 1680s by a group of merchants:

> There were at least four general meetings each year at which company policy was decided and accounts were examined, all decisions being arrived at on the basis of binding majority vote. At the meeting in May five members were elected as 'managers' and, after the first election, two remained in office and three new ones were elected each year. The managers met at least once a week, electing among themselves a 'praeses' (chairman) for each meeting. A quorum of three was necessary for business to proceed. The day to day running of the factory was, however, entirely in the hands of the 'Master', that is (in modern usage), 'paid manager'.[12]

This organisational structure seems to borrow elements from church practice, especially the institution of the kirk session, suggesting that a further exploration of such elements is merited. Where Weber is useful here is in some relatively little-used passages in his work on religious sects. For one commentator this work is an essential complement to the *Protestant Ethic*.[13] In it, Weber relates membership of sects to business success because of the certification of moral quality that membership tests provide. Two important facets here are the existence of membership and the denial of sacraments to any other than fully qualified members. So Weber notes that:

> The tremendous social significance of admission to full enjoyment of the rights of the sectarian congregation, especially the privilege of being admitted to the Lord's Supper, worked among the sects in the direction of breeding that ascetist professional ethic which was adequate to modern capitalism during the period of its origin.[14]

Weber goes on to note, although only in passing, some organisational concomitants of this restriction of sacraments, such as the circulation of certificates among congregations. This presupposed, as we will see later, further organisational practices such as the recording of membership. It also required specific roles to maintain discipline, and the importance of lay elders is stressed. However, he continued even here to return to the central importance of the internalisation of ascetic values:

> The church discipline of the Puritans and of the sects was vested, first, at least in part and often wholly, in the hands of laymen. Secondly, it worked through the necessity of one's having to hold one's own; and, thirdly, it bred or, if one wishes, selected qualities. The last point is the most important one.[15]

Hennis points out that for Weber 'in all social phenomena it is the non-everyday that interests him, that which bursts through everyday life'.[16] The hints he provides, therefore, remain just that, but they can be explored in the work of a much later social theorist who was centrally concerned with the formation of subjectivity in modernity, Michel Foucault. Recognising this agenda, Hindle has observed its top-down nature and argued that 'Such analyses arguably ignore, or at least overlook, the extent to which order and authority did not merely "trickle down" but "welled up" within society itself'.[17] This is a fair criticism of the most influential of Foucault's earlier work, notably *Discipline and Punish*, but his later work on governmentality has a much closer focus on mundane practices.[18] In particular, his concern to examine how populations come to be governed is initially based on the exploration of what he terms 'pastoral power'. Foucault's focus here is on religion as social practice. He argues:

> it seems to me that the history of the pastorate has never really been undertaken. The history of ecclesiastical institutions has been written. The history of religious doctrines, beliefs, and representations has been written. There have also been attempts to produce the history of real religious practices, namely, when people confessed, took communion, and so on. But it seems to me that the history of the techniques employed, of the reflections on these pastoral techniques, of their development, application, and successive refinements, the history of the different types of analysis and knowledge linked to the exercise of pastoral power, has never really been undertaken.[19]

The specific practice for his focus in his initial discussion of pastoral power is the confessional within the Roman Catholic church.[20] He points to the importance of manuals about how to conduct the confessional as well as the importance of artefacts such as the confessional box in cementing the practice and thus, he argues, consolidating the power of the individual priest. This echoes our focus above on the importance of artefacts, but also poses some problems. His method was to examine accounts prescribing the proper conduct of the self and here we face another problematic area, that of the relation of such texts to practice. In his work on the confessional manuals, for example, he acknowledged that '[t]hey were effectively put to work in the formation of confessors themselves, rather than in the average faithful among the people'.[21] This suggested a need to examine the sites of such formation, notably the seminaries, and raises questions about how to explore such relations – questions that send us back to primary sources in a way not pursued by Foucault. As Gorski notes, 'one would expect a brief overview of the various disciplinary mechanisms invented by Protestant and Catholic religious reformers and of the ways in which territorial rulers utilized them as part of their strategies of domination'. However, on 'the concrete social mechanisms through which this power operated, the central concern of so much of his work, Foucault is strangely silent'.[22] Gorski speculates that this might be because such an investigation would throw into question Foucault's focus on the eighteenth century as the site of the disciplinary revolution, which Gorski persuasively argues needs to be shifted back to the early seventeenth. Be that as it may, the investigation outlined in this book seeks to elucidate just some of those concrete mechanisms of Protestant pastoral power and their wider influences.

To do so, it is worth considering a little further what we mean by 'practice'. Existing work on religious organisations is not of great help here. A common theme in a volume of essays that sought to examine the nature of religious bodies as organisations was that there was little consideration in the sociology of religion of the mundane practices of organising. In one contribution, Peter Dobkin Hall observed:

> First, the historical precedence of large-scale bureaucratic enterprises in religion is indisputable. Second, the influence of these religious organizations both as models for bureaucratized secular organizations and as institutions that provided individuals with the values and skills needed for building and working in bureaucratic organizations, though circumstantial, points to the need for more detailed examination of the religious backgrounds of the founders of the modern economic order.[23]

This echoes an earlier work, *Clergy, Ministers and Priests*, in which Ransom, Bryman and Hinings drew attention to some of the structural characteristics of three organised Christian faiths – Roman Catholicism, Methodism and the Church of England – pointing out that 'theological beliefs are rooted in their denominational context rather than independent and free-floating'.[24] However, with its focus on how these factors impacted on the clergy, aspects of lay practice remain implicit. The early lead given by this book has had little impact. A comprehensive handbook on the sociology of religion has only three index entries for 'organisation' and here differences within Christianity are sketched out in terms of three forms of religious polity.[25] At one pole are the hierarchical churches, Catholic or Episcopalian, in which authority is centralised and flows through the central figure of the bishop. At the other pole is Congregationalism, in which control is at the local level and vested to different degrees in members of the congregation. The 'middle way' is that of Presbyterianism, with its structure of regional councils or 'presbyteries'. We will encounter a similar tendency in historical work, if churches are considered as organisations at all, to focus on them from the top down.

The nature of practice

For Demerath and Schmitt, religion can be conceived of as 'any mythically sustained concern for ultimate meanings coupled with a ritually reinforced sense of social belonging'.[26] One of the practices that we need to consider therefore is the ritual. The lineages of this approach can be traced back famously to Durkheim, but beyond him, interestingly, to the Scottish theologian William Robertson Smith.[27] Smith was an adherent of the Free Church who drew on contemporary biblical criticism to examine a number of topics that resulted in his being tried by the church for heresy in 1877. This saw him lose his lecturing position and move to Cambridge, where he produced his most influential work, *Lectures on the Religion of the Semites*.[28] The type of Reformed Protestantism that Presbyterianism represents has often been seen as relatively free of ritual, with a focus instead on preaching and the power of the Word. However, rituals remain important in their performance. For Friedland:

> Religion appears to us as a distinctive kind of institution, replete with rite, that is, with practices – prayer, penitence, piety, pilgrimage, sacrament and charity – that have a non-arbitrary relationship to what they signify, that is, symbolic actions, as well as with performative forms of speech, where use of language is a form of action, referring to the reality it itself produces. Both cleric and laity literally speak and act God's presence into existence, an ontological substance that can never be reduced to its attributes, nor to the practices that access or evoke it.[29]

Weber, Friedland suggests, shaped by his Protestant preconceptions, tends to downplay ritual and so material practice. Eric Schmidt has shown that while Protestant rituals were indeed different from Catholic ones, in particular being less in number and more focused on the Word, they still lacked nothing in intensity.[30] His examination of the centrality of the sacrament of communion, as embodied in the Scottish 'Holy Fair' or communion season, which acted as the template for the development of American revivalism, provides a reason for the focus on this particular ritual in what follows. The detailed evidence to support this initial sketch is provided in Chapter 4, but for the present the focus is on the interaction between rituals and routines.

Work drawing on anthropology and cognitive psychology in the 'modes of religiosity' approach provides us with some useful resources for considering further the nature of ritual. Whitehouse defines rituals as practices that display an excess over technical motivation and so invite exegesis. However, 'procedural competence is, therefore, somewhat disconnected from people's explicit concepts of why rituals take the form that they do'.[31] As Asad suggests, 'apt performance involves not symbols to be interpreted but abilities to be acquired according to rules that are sanctioned by those in authority: it presupposes no obscure meanings, but rather the formation of physical and linguistic skills'.[32] That is, in many cases it is perfectly possible to take part in rituals successfully and give accounts of that performance, 'constrained more by commonsense principles than by the kind of complex theoretical knowledge available to experts'.[33] This gives rise to the danger of seeking to construct ritual performances and their meanings from formal bodies of theology alone.[34] Ritual is also important in making connections – connections that come from shared performance rather than, necessarily, shared values. So, observes Whitehouse, 'what it means to be a regular churchgoer is not to be part of a particular group but to participate in a ritual scheme and belief structure that anonymous others also share'.[35] In turn, the rituals that are shared can become a powerful indicator of identity. Whitehouse observes that although 'people who attend church regularly do not need to have quasi-theoretical knowledge of the links between standing and singing, kneeling and praying, and sitting and listening, such knowledge is bound to emerge over time'.[36] That knowledge can then articulate particular identities, which are shaped more by the common performance of the ritual than by more abstract theoretical considerations. In his study of the religious influences on the cities of Boston and Philadelphia, Baltzell recounts the story of an eminent Boston Unitarian commenting to an Episcopalian friend, 'Eliza, do you *kneel* down in church and call yourself a miserable sinner? Neither I nor any member of my family will ever do *that*!' (emphasis in original).[37]

This discussion of ritual, therefore, indicates some important dimensions of practice. However, what are missing from this account are the practices that enable the rituals to take place in their particular form. This can be illustrated by returning to the Presbyterian form of the sacrament of communion. In Christianity, a sacrament is a particular practice that is sanctified as a sign of belief. A key dividing point between the Roman Catholic church and Protestants was over the nature and number of sacraments. While the Roman Catholic church recognised seven – baptism, communion, penance, confirmation, marriage, ordination and the last rites – the Reformed Protestant tradition recognised only two – baptism and communion.[38] Communion was the symbolic consumption of bread and wine in imitation of the Last Supper that Jesus took before his crucifixion. In the Presbyterian tradition (and this is a point of difference from other Protestant traditions, such as Anglicanism), communion was only to be taken by those considered fit to receive it. This meant that criteria had to be laid down, which required examination. In turn, this meant that routines came to be established for such examinations. Over time, this turned from the annual examination of the faithful by the minister and his elders to the scrutiny of lists of communicants. Having done this, some means of identifying those who qualified had to be devised. This came in the form of small metal tokens, which were distributed following the examination of the lists and which governed access to the communion table (as described in more detail below). A ritual, that is, had to be accomplished in more ways than through performance of the core ritual itself. Resources had to be mobilised in such a way that entailed the development of routines that in turn shaped the nature of the governance of the church. Accordingly, it is appropriate to consider the nature of routines in more detail.

By the very name, routines have the connotation of the mundane and the taken-for-granted. This can lead us to underplay their importance in shaping organisational life. Such has been the argument presented by Feldman and Pentland in a series of articles, where they have advanced the case for seeing organisational routines as 'generative systems'.[39] Their work has stressed the potential for change that lies within organisational routines, drawing attention to the fact that routines have to be performed and that the variations and connections inherent in such performances give the possibility of change. They define routines as 'repetitive, recognizable patterns of interdependent actions, carried out by multiple actors'.[40] A key focus in their various articles is the stress on agency. Routines are not just abstract sets of instructions; they are performed. This means that they are 'not only effortful but also emergent accomplishments. They are often works in progress rather than finished products.'[41] Given this perspective, those who perform the routines, it is argued, are not blind rule followers but active selectors from a menu of possibilities, 'from which organizational members enact particular performances'.[42]

If one examines repeated cycles of the records of the Church of Scotland one sees a distinct pattern to the ritual year, one that triggered not only rituals but also their supporting routines. So at a point in the year the minister and elders settled on the date for the annual celebration of communion, a date usually fixed in relation to tradition and the practices of neighbouring parishes. The minister then announced his circuits for examining the spiritual knowledge of his parishioners. In the session, lists of communicants were examined before tokens were issued to those considered worthy. The church was then prepared for the event itself, with elders occupying the roles of gate-keepers, only allowing approach to the communion table in return for the surrender of tokens. These routines operated on an annual basis, but if one looks more closely, prompted by a sense of the importance of the routines that enabled the church to function, then one sees evidence of other routines, notably those to do with accountability. Such routines are embedded in particular forms of recording, which leads us to consider another aspect of practice, that of genre.

In their study of organisational communication, Yates and Orlikowski define a genre as 'a typified communicative action invoked in response to a recurrent situation'.[43] Genres in this context are 'social institutions that both shape and are shaped by individuals' communicative actions'.[44] What is important here is the focus on the way in which genres, because of their taken-for-granted and to-hand quality, shape action. This makes them more than just carriers of other practices but makes them important practices in their own right. For example, Stinchcombe refers to 'standard report forms put out by people who specialize in printing them' as a key source for the transfer and adoption of new routines.[45] The genre contains particular assumptions that have been given material form and make new actions possible. In the context of Reformed religion, Wuthnow draws our attention to the evolution of the genre of the sermon, the public exposition of the faith by ministers:

> Although it depended heavily on advances in literacy, demands for preaching in the vernacular, and the revival of biblical scholarship, insofar as Scripture was its most tangible symbol, it was also the reformers' most creative contribution. In pitting the godly, spiritual, and scriptural against the temporal world of institutional practice, they opened up an ideological space, as it were, in which to pose alternative forms of conduct and thought.[46]

Such sermons were enthusiastically consumed by the faithful, diaries indicating rounds of sermon attendance and reflection.[47] However, genre also interacted with routine and ritual in other ways. The Scottish church was distinctive in seeking to set out, at considerable length, the ways its activities were to be carried out and recorded. As well as specifying the particular details of what was to be recorded and the form of that recording, the language of that guidance, replete with Latin tags and legal terms, generated a particular genre, heavy with seriousness and formality. As an illustration, in the parish of Rayne in 1750 the minutes record:

> And then proceeding to revise the treasurers account & having diligently collated and compared them with the accounts kept by their clerk and finding them to agree in omnibus found that the hail money intromitted with by him from the Day of last clearance (vide page 61 & 62) amounts to the sum of Ninety six pounds ten shillings & Eight pennies Scots money.[48]

Not only does this bear Latin tags (as well as the vernacular Scots 'hail' for 'whole'!) but also this passage shows the interconnection of the written records with another genre: that of the accounting record. Accounting routines were central to enabling the ritual life of the church to proceed, and from an early date (1608 being the first recorded set of separate accounts to have survived), the Scots church was marked by detailed accounting records. We will see the impact of this below, but first we need to examine the fourth dimension of practice: that of artefacts.

Material performance is not limited to the artefactual; as we have seen, the embodied performance of rituals with symbolic intent is also a key aspect of material practice. This consideration of the material relates not just to specific artefacts but also to their arrangement in time and space. An interesting example drawn from English church history is supplied by Steve Hindle, when he notes that in the late sixteenth century:

> Whereas manor courts did not meet in parish churches (even though they were

almost certainly the only buildings large enough for the purpose), vestries
almost invariably tended to do so. The simple fact of this relocation rendered
the presence of the state all the more tangible in the local community, for if
Elizabethan vestries met in parish churches they did so in the presence of the
royal arms.[49]

This contributed, he argues, to the consciousness of local parish officials that
they operated under the aegis of the state, thereby inculcating that remarkable
social depth to the English state that Hindle argues develops in this period.
As we have seen, developments in printing enabled the production of standard
report templates, which could diffuse genres and their associated routines
across a wider audience. In the context of religion, Wuthnow points to the
importance of the relatively new innovation of printing in facilitating the
emergence of a new genre, the pamphlet, and its impact on religious dispu-
tation in the Reformation. Printing also facilitated not only the lively contro-
versies over doctrine that marked Scotland in the late seventeenth century,
but also the production of guidance for local action. Our example of communion
also illustrates the importance of artefacts and their arrangement in shaping
action. Communion in the Church of Scotland in the eighteenth century was
taken infrequently, generally annually, and required particular spatial arrangements.[50] It was taken collectively seated at a table, with the vessels containing
the bread and wine blessed by the minster passed from communicant to
communicant.[51] This required the construction of tables and so the arrangement of space, usually in the church but, if numbers demanded, outdoors.
That space also had to be enclosed so that another key artefact, the communion
token, could be collected. The effective performance of ritual, therefore,
required the accomplishment of particular routines, facilitated by material
artefacts and shaped by particular genres.

Logics, therefore, can be represented in different forms of practice. At the
most abstract level, religious logics are developed in documents held to be of
sacred origin, the foundation for textual exegesis and the articulation of
systematic bodies of knowledge. However, such theologies, while themselves
an important symbolic form and requiring particular material practices, do
not contain or exhaust the practices that sustain faith. In many cases, theological disputations remain the province of a small group of adepts, and the
tensions between scholarly and popular conceptions of a notionally shared
religious belief have been a source of considerable attention from both sociologists and historians.[52] So we may be looking for the articulation between
formal bodies of knowledge and other practices.

One source of such practices, one that might be regarded as something of
a mediating hinge between theological practice and what we might term local
practice, is the organisation. That is, religions are often also organisations:
organisations that produce guidance on how tenets of belief are to be put into
operation. However, such procedure manuals can neither anticipate all

circumstances nor ensure that their strictures are put into operation in a faithful fashion. The scope for interpretation that this leaves means that we also need to consider how practice operates on the ground. Here, forms of knowledge may often be more tacit and come to be embedded in material practices. As we have seen, one example might be in how key rituals, such as prayer, are performed. It is here that symbolic meanings and material performance are fused: where, for example, a particular bodily position or gesture in a particular spatio–temporal context acquires a meaning that reaffirms and performs the logic. Such performances cannot be simply 'read off' more formal theological statements. But, in turn, it will be argued, such performances also need to be accomplished and this brings in other forms of practice, which are to do with the routines that make the more sacred achievements possible. There is also not a simple one-way causal relationship between formal bodies of knowledge and embodied practices, in which believers simply replicate laid-down formulae. Rather, practices can themselves generate more abstract ideas. An example that has some relevance for our later discussion is given by Withrington, when he discusses the widely held view that Scottish higher education possessed particular virtues as summed up in the phrase the 'democratic intellect'. This view that Scottish universities had adopted a generalist philosophical basis for study arose, Withrington argued, not from some fundamental values, but from a response to the poverty of Scottish universities and the need to take students (who paid the fees of the professors) with low levels of initial education. Thus the late eighteenth-century professors:

> hereby pulled off a very clever trick indeed: for they converted a new practice into an ideal, and found it then transformed for posterity into a tradition. To have created an educational tradition which happened so neatly to coincide with their own economic advantage was a truly remarkable feat.[53]

In similar vein, Charles Camic points to changes in educational practice, notably the shift from regents to professors in Scottish universities, as producing the educational setting for many of the key figures of the Scottish Enlightenment.[54] What this suggests is the need to combine attention to belief as articulated in theological statements with practice, sensitive to the interplay between both.

What we are investigating, then, is the dynamic and unfolding relationship between formal theological belief and organisational practices. Theological belief, especially when, as in the case of Scottish Presbyterianism, it asserts the necessity of an organised church, needs to be put into effect. This means the generation of rituals, enacted in particular material spaces and inscribed in specific genres, which also entail the creation of routines to put them into effect. Such routines can, over time, become taken for granted and so relatively detached from their theological origins. The rituals and routines become simply just what the faithful do. Given this, they can become also taken-for-granted templates for organising in other domains. They can form, that is, the elements of a 'culture of organisation', a source of routines and meanings about what organised activity looks like. Aspects of these can be traced in existing work on the history of religious bodies, but it tends to be subordinated to considerations of belief. This existing literature, and what it says about religion as a social practice in the Scottish context, is the focus of the next section.

Scottish religious practice

Some support for Foucault's assertion can be found in the literature on religious history in Britain generally and Scotland in particular. David Jeremy, in a volume considering the relationship between business and religion, presented 'an anatomy of sects, denominations and churches in Britain in Britain 1750–1950' against four dimensions: theology, liturgy, local leadership and organisation/polity.[55] This is useful in drawing some broad contrasts, but it tends, as does much of the traditional literature on church history, to concentrate on either formal theological pronouncements and debates or the organisation seen from the top down. A number of voices draw attention to some problems with this. Jeremy Black has observed, 'there is a danger in concentrating on themes found in metropolitan print culture' and thereby a need to examine 'the relationship between print culture and actual practice'.[56] In his study of the Church of England in Wiltshire in the late seventeenth and early eighteenth centuries, Donald Spaeth points to the need to 'distinguish between religious belief, knowledge, experience, practice and secular impact'.[57] Most members of congregations, he argues, had little interest in the more abstruse theological debates that featured in print. For an earlier period, Hindle suggests the need to 'think less of government as an institution or as an event, than of governance as a process, a series of multilateral initiatives to be negotiated across space and through the social order'.[58] These observations are useful as we approach a more detailed consideration of religion as a social practice in eighteenth-century Scotland.

Here again, much of the focus has been on debates at the national level, whether about theology or organisation.[59] There are, of course, exceptions, such as Callum Brown's detailed study of the practice of pew renting in Glasgow in the nineteenth century, in which changes in practice are related to social class.[60] A similar focus on the social basis of changes in church organisation is found in Alan Maclaran's study of the Disruption in Aberdeen, which saw the departure of many ministers and adherents of the Church of Scotland to form the Free Church in protest against patronage. In Aberdeen, he suggests, these events can be seen to rest on the rise of a successful business class.[61] However, both these examples are from the nineteenth century; in the eighteenth century the dominant focus is on questions of patronage and the rise of the Moderate Party, both topics that tend to be treated at a national level and are often based on debates at a refined level.[62] This literature will be valuable when we consider the broader context in the next chapter, but it is to literature with a more confessional bent that we must now turn for some consideration of the more mundane practices that lay behind the more visible and memorable events.

History always mattered to the Church of Scotland, not least in cementing its claims after the settlement of 1690. Presbytery minutes are littered with exhortations to their members to purchase Robert Wodrow's two-volume *The History of the Sufferings of the Church of Scotland from the Restoration to the Revolution* published in 1721–2.[63] This drew on church documents to present an account designed to sustain the faith of Church adherents. In the following century the minister of the Secession Church, Thomas McCrie produced monumental biographies of John Knox and Andrew Melville, also drawing on extensive archival materials.[64] However, their strict confessional tone fell out of favour, and indeed contributed to a later turning away from the austere view of Presbyterianism that they promoted. By the time Andrew Edgar, the minister of Mauchline, Ayrshire, came to present a series of lectures on *Old Church Life in Scotland* many of the practices and beliefs that both Wodrow and McCrie would have endorsed could be regarded as historical curios to be excavated. Published in two volumes, Edgar's lectures drew not only on the records of his own parish but also on those of neighbouring parishes and the presbytery of Ayr.[65] In their recognition of the immense value of these records the book is a precursor of other works. It contains a good deal of valuable material, some drawn from records that are not now available, which complement the detailed account presented later. It is also of significance as a major source for a far more influential work, Henry Graham's *The Social Life of Scotland in the Eighteenth Century*, published in 1899. Another minister of the Church, Graham had a particular distaste for many of the practices that his more enlightened times had escaped. So he writes of presbyterial meetings: 'in those tedious, useless, pedantic, solemn assemblies time was freely spent'.[66] He draws on a number of sources, including Edgar, but he is not averse to exaggerating some of what he finds there. For example, when discussing parochial visitations (which we will examine in much more detail in Chapter 3), of which he thoroughly disapproved, he cites Edgar to the effect that such practices were revived in the presbytery of Ayr in 1750.[67] However, this cannot be found in Edgar (whose discussion relates more to the years before the Disruption of 1843), and there is no trace of the practices in the presbytery minutes.[68] So Graham's accounts have to be taken carefully, vivid and insightful as they might be about other aspects of Scottish life at the time. This matters, because later writers have drawn upon Graham, such as Camic, who refers to his passages on visitations. In looking at the detailed records, which is far easier for us than for Graham, we will have occasion to temper some of his claims.

A much calmer tone can be found in another important source, G. D. Henderson's *The Scottish Ruling Elder*, published in 1935. A Church of Scotland minister and Professor of Church History at the University of Aberdeen, Henderson located his work firmly in the context of the reunification in 1929 of the Church of Scotland with the majority of those whose predecessors had left in 1843. Noting that the reunited church could claim over 30,000 elders, he thought that 'these ought to have some acquaintance with the history of their office generally'.[69] He drew on kirk session records from eighteen parishes across Scotland to give illustrative examples of the ways in which the role of the elder had developed and changed across time. This gives us a valuable insight into specific practices, such as the ability of the session at Yester in 1728 to draw up a budget for its spending for the forthcoming year. However, not only was Henderson restricted in the archives he could access, but his purpose was to examine such practices in the context of a better definition of the nature of the eldership. Another book in 1929, *A History of Church Discipline in Scotland* by Ivo Mcnaughton Clark, also has to be set in the context of debates about the meaning of discipline in the twentieth-century Church. Clark's concern as a minister of the Church was to rediscover a sense of discipline as being about the guiding of spiritual development. He dated the growth of a legalistic conception of discipline to the early eighteenth century, when he argues that discipline became 'largely the work of a court, instead of a human soul pleading with another soul'.[70] Again, the book provides us with some useful indications of practice, albeit that its focus is mainly a confessional one.

Finally in this group of works with origins in the Church that give us insights into ongoing practices there is J. M. McPherson's *The Kirk's Care of the Poor, With Special Reference to the North-East of Scotland*, published in 1945. This was anxious to rescue the reputation of the Church at local level from its perceived obsession with discipline by focusing on what he saw as its more positive achievements. In commenting on the response of local sessions to harvest failures, such as the catastrophic one that struck the northeast in 1783, he asserted that 'the Church was never more Christ-like than in the stand it took on behalf of the defenceless poor'.[71] His book draws on session records and gives a good sense of practices in this particular part of Scotland, albeit that these seem at time to jump from period to period. This collection of rather neglected works contains much that suggests the value of returning to their careful work among the original sources.

The relative neglect of these sources may owe something to the divorce between social history and church history that Gregory bemoans.[72] It may also be due to a rejection of the confessional tone of such works, in a more general turn away from the ethos of Presbyterianism more generally among the generation of historians that emerged in the 1960s and 1970s.[73] Often inspired by the idea of 'history from below' such historians switched their focus away from institutions to those who were subject to their ministrations. Sometimes this could lead to a rather exaggerated and misplaced critique, as in Wormald's mocking of the failure of the faithful to achieve godliness. This raised questions, she argues:

> [about] the insistent and sometimes strident claims for an unreally high level of godliness by the Kirk, by those offshoots which set themselves up when the Kirk was not godly enough, and by historians who bought into these claims.[74]

But for historians the point is surely not the success of the claims for godliness, but what was done to mobilise such claims and what their enduring impacts (if any) might be. In some ways the rejection of Presbyterianism in this form represents just a mirror image of those strident adherents. Rather more measured responses can be seen in the examination of claims about the impact of Scottish education, in the nature of poor relief and in the treatment of women.[75] In all these cases, the records of the church are used to good effect as a source of evidence. In passing this also tells us something about the practices that were involved, but this is incidental to the main purpose. It does mean, however, that the records are used primarily for their *content*. It will be argued below that it can also be possible to use their *form*, indeed the very fact of their existence, as evidence of important and enduring practices.

The potential of these sources to give a more rounded picture of the impact of Presbyterianism at local level is best realised in the rich and powerful consideration by Margo Todd of *The Culture of Protestantism in Early Modern Scotland*. With a firm focus on the activities of the kirk session, she examines the records to argue that:

> Where the life of the community could be organised around sermons and Bible-reading, and where the most ordinary could be regularly held to a public recitation of their faith, Calvinism became genuinely a religion of the people. Where the institution of the kirk session was available, its combination of close oversight, rigorous enforcement, commitment to teaching and persuasion, and co-operation with neighbouring parishes did, indeed, serve to achieve the Reformers' goal of a religion of the word.[76]

For the late sixteenth through into the seventeenth century she establishes the success of the Reformed church, at least in many Lowland districts, in establishing not only its polity but also a broader adherence to the rituals and sacraments of the church. In doing this she makes a number of obser-vations about governance practices that, while not her main focus and for an earlier period, suggest a focus for exploration in the eighteenth century. She notes for example, that 'good record-keeping is a hallmark of Scottish communion seasons, with lists of those eligible and those who actually appeared at the table routinely compared to ensure that no one had commu-nicated unworthily'.[77] Another account that also has a valuable focus on a particular locality and so examines local experience in some depth is the

account provided by John McCallum of the progress of the Reformation in
Fife. Here he notes, although not in any developed form, the genesis of practices that were to become more widespread in the eighteenth century. So,
for example, he notes the rough scrawl of the early pages of the minutes at
Markinch but the 'scribe's tendency to record every financial detail'.[78]
These works refer, of course, to a very much earlier period than that under
review here. One work that uses parochial records to good effect to examine
a particular parish over our period is Alison Hanham's examination of *The
Sinners of Cramond*.[79] This uses kirk session records to examine the impact
of the kirk's activities on its local context and provides valuable material
for our explorations.

What can be drawn out of this brief survey is that much of the useful work
that looks at the practices of the kirk is based on the earlier period. The local
life of the church in the eighteenth century is relatively neglected, but it can
be argued that it played a vital role in the consolidation of Presbyterian
hegemony in Scotland in the period.[80] Even an approach that seeks a balanced
assessment of the impact of Presbyterianism during the years following 1690,
such as that essayed by Whatley, depends on printed sources at the national
level.[81] However, what such accounts point to is the importance of the period
following 1690 as crucial in the formation of certain important features of
Scottish life in later years. Here the salience of 1707 and debates about the
Union with England can be misleading, for they cause us to neglect the
important developments that happen before that date. Some of these will be
considered in the following chapter and they will form an ever-present
backdrop to our detailed consideration of local practice. For now, however, it
is important to consider some questions about the nature of the evidence that
can be used to excavate such practices.

When sociologists and anthropologists look for evidence about the nature
and meaning of practices, they generally advocate intensive means of inquiry
such as participant observation. Practices, the argument runs, by their very
nature, cannot be explored through research techniques that are distancing
in character, such as questionnaires. Indeed, research subjects may not
recognise the practices that they use because they are so deeply immersed in
them. Gorski, however, argues that on the basis of his explorations we need,
in examining practices, to look at 'distributions rather than cases'.[82] The
nature of the evidence available in Scotland, as explored below, means that it
is possible to estimate distributions in some cases, and the desire to do so is
a guiding principle. However, this always has to be in the context of the nature
of the evidence, given that this is limited to the traces that practices leave
behind, rather than direct evidence of the practices themselves. We have
already noted the gap between what is written in books that seek to lay down
practices and the practices themselves, and that it makes written testimony
unreliable. This means that we need to look for markers, which might

indirectly reveal practices. An intriguing example can be found in the work of Keith Snell on the sense of place in England in the nineteenth century. He uses inscriptions from over 16,000 gravestones in eighty-seven burial grounds. Given the expense of carving memorial stones, he argues, what was recorded must have been considered to be of importance. He tracks how details of place vary over time, showing that it was considered important to record locations until the end of the nineteenth century, after which place becomes unremarked. As he concludes, 'people were once described, given an identity, and their behaviour even accounted for, by their place and their occupation in it, however parochial that might be'.[83] As his broader project was 'to infuse cultural meaning into administrative history', it has some parallels with the present project.[84] His attention to overlooked sources of evidence suggests that we might give attention to the very existence of particular records, to the form as much as to the content of the archives that we use.

Part of his project, therefore, is to make the familiar strange in order to bring to the fore mundane practices, which are so taken for granted that they are obvious and so invisible. In his work on the practice of writing history, Paul Veyne suggests the importance of comparative treatments in facilitating this process. He argues:

> If in order to study a civilization we limit ourselves to reading what it says itself – that is, to reading sources relating to this one civilization – we will make it more difficult to wonder at what, in this civilization, was taken for granted.[85]

This contrast can take place in a number of ways. We can contrast temporally, to look at how practices change and develop over time. In this account, what we see in the historical record for the eighteenth century will be contrasted with what we know from secondary sources about earlier practices, for the contrast points to roads not taken. This is a key task of the next chapter. However, it also necessary to contrast what happened in one part of the country against what is taken for granted in another. We will see that the richness of the surviving material from the Church of Scotland enables us to do that. The basis for the selection of such comparisons is given below. Finally, a particularly useful contrast can be obtained by looking at the experience of England. Under the veneer of shared Protestantism were significant differences in practice that will be alluded to in the detailed discussion of Scottish practices and returned to in more detail in concluding comments. Here, however, we are limited by the restricted attention that has been paid to the administrative history that Snell refers to. This means that the contrasts can only be suggestive ones, but, in lieu of more detailed work, that is the best that we can do.

Sources

What these comments suggest is that it is worth paying detailed attention to the form of the archival resources that are used here. This is because their existence in itself tells us something distinctive about the Church of Scotland. The National Records of Scotland (NRS) is the official repository for all of the records of the Church. It estimates that these records add up to over five million pages. Since the General Assembly passed an act authorising the transfer of records into the custody of what was then the Scottish Records Office, documents at all levels of the Church have been transferred. NRS has had authority to transmit records to local archive offices if thought appropriate. However, the NRS maintains a central catalogue to all Church records. Further, it has been a pioneer in the digital imaging of Church records so that researchers consult its Virtual Volumes system rather than the original records. This means that records retained in local archives are generally available for scrutiny in Edinburgh (with the future possibility of broader access). This development has had an impact on the transfer of the catalogue to electronic form. It means that the catalogue itself has the potential to be a source of evidence in its own right, as we will see in our discussion of the emergence of separate books of account. However, the sheer scale of the material available has deeper roots. In 1696 it was suggested:

> That registers of all Judicatories may be better Preserved, it were fit, that every Session deliver their fair Register to the Presbytery every 10 Year; and every Presbytery theirs, and the Sessions in to the synod, every 15 Years; and that every Synod, every 20 Year, order all these, and their own fair Register, to be laid up in the publick Library of that University, which is next adjacent to them; where they may be safely kept from Accidents, for the future benefit of the Church.[86]

Clearly such a suggestion had practical limitations, not least that many areas were at a considerable distance from their nearest university. However, the very nature of the suggestions indicates the centrality of the written record to the church's conception of itself. We will pay some attention to the development of this conception in the next chapter, but for now we will consider the nature of the records that have survived in a little more detail.

The sheer volume of available records means that some degree of selectivity was essential. Because of the relative low penetration of Presbyterian organisational structures into the Highlands until the late eighteenth century, the study was limited in scope to the Lowland areas of the country. It was also decided to focus on areas that were mainly rural in complexion. This, in part, was to avoid the confounding influences of urban mercantile practices. If, as suspected, practices of careful record keeping could be found in predominantly rural areas then this might suggest the religious, rather than the economic, roots of such practices. In addition, the rural parishes of

Scotland were often seen as the ideal type of Scottish Presbyterianism, the places where Presbyterian discipline could be seen in its purest form. Of course, all of the areas examined had some urban settlements, but a conscious decision was taken to avoid the larger burghs, with their rather more complex organisational structures and practices that might owe a good deal to that complexity. Within this area, five presbyteries were selected for closer attention to local records. They were selected in part because of links to other material that could shed further light on governance practices. Linlithgow, on the western outskirts of Edinburgh, for example, was shown from the analysis of separate accounting books to be a forerunner of this practice, connected, perhaps, to the participation there of the key writer on church procedure, Walter Steuart of Pardovan. Two court cases concerning the parishes of Cambuslang in the western presbytery of Hamilton and Humbie in the eastern presbytery of Haddington have been cited as potential influences on accounting practice.[87] A similar dispute, although one not as widely noticed, occurred in the parish of Monymusk in the presbytery of the Garioch, Aberdeenshire.[88] Finally, Edgar's early historical examination of governance practices in the parish of Mauchline suggested attention to the presbytery of Ayr.[89] These areas can also be mapped onto persistent differences in the flavour of belief. The two western presbyteries of Ayr and Hamilton had rich Covenanting traditions and contained considerable strongholds of Evangelical commitment. The presbyteries of Linlithgow and Haddington, lying as they did on the west and east of Edinburgh respectively, were more likely to contain adherents to the Moderate Party in the church. In contrast to both, Aberdeenshire was long a stronghold of Episcopalianism, although over the course of the century the particular character of the Aberdeen Enlightenment confirmed the success of Presbyterian polity. The areas also had differing economic characteristics. All were broadly rural, although having significant market towns, often the seat of the presbytery at their hearts. Linlithgow and, in particular, Haddington were advanced centres of 'improved' agriculture, with large tenant farms. The western presbyteries were more pastoral in nature, with smaller farms producing, in particular, dairy products. The Garioch, although a naturally fertile area, was slow to adopt new farming practices and remained a mixed farming area with a high degree of subsistence farming. It was also an area that continued to fall victim to subsistence crises during periods of adverse weather, particularly in 1782–3.

The electronic catalogue gives us an indication of the volume of records available and trends in their production. Table 1.1 shows the number of parishes in each of the presbyteries, the number of parishes for which a run of records is available, the total number of pages in those records and finally the number of pages in the presbytery minutes themselves.

Table 1.1 Parishes and records available

	Parishes	Records	Pages	Presbytery pages
Ayr	28	11	6,387	2,483
Garioch	15	12	7,713	2,435
Haddington	16	11	6,176	1,689
Hamilton	15	10	1,988	1,525
Linlithgow	17	11	7,219	3,344
Total	91	55	29,483	11,476

Source: Calculated from NRS catalogue, CH2 Church of Scotland records.

These are crude figures: the number of pages occupied by minutes depends, of course, on a number of variables – the nature and size of the handwriting, the size of paper used and the use or not of margins, for example. Only an analysis by words, which would require electronic transcription, would counter these factors. In addition, some other factors might explain variances. Some presbyterial minutes (those of Linlithgow, for example) have complete copies of synodial minutes inserted, which will increase their length. It might only take one complex disciplinary case or a lengthy dispute between session and heritors (such as will see in Cambuslang, Humbie and Monymusk later) for minutes to be swollen beyond their usual size. We will consider these factors in more detail in subsequent chapters. However, despite their crude nature, these counts of pages give both some indication of the volume of records available and some pointers towards areas for explanation. On the face of it, for example, record keeping in the presbytery of Hamilton appears as noticeably sparser than that elsewhere. Table 1.2 shows how many years the surviving records cover, in bands of twenty-five years for parishes and for the presbytery as a whole.

Table 1.2 Record survival

	Number of parishes with records for:				Number of years for which Presbytery records survive
	25 years	26–50 years	51–74 years	75–100 years	
Ayr	1	3	3	4	87
Garioch		1	4	7	98
Haddington	1	1	3	6	100
Hamilton	4	4	1	1	95
Linlithgow	1		2	8	100
	7	9	13	26	

Source: Calculated from NRS catalogue, CH2 Church of Scotland records.

In two parishes, Bolton in Haddington and Dalrymple in Ayr, records survive for the full hundred-year period. It can be seen that almost half of the parishes examined had surviving records for over three-quarters of the century. It is also clear that Hamilton has a low rate of record survival relative to other presbyteries. Again, this focuses some of the later discussion, but the important point here is the impressive rate of record survival in general (something that stands in stark contrast to the picture for Church of England records).

What appears distinctive is that records are considered to be the property of the Church as a body with continuing existence, rather than their survival depending on the actions of the individual who happened to be in possession of them at any particular time. This is a point that will be further elaborated on when we consider the composition of the session, but for now it is worth considering further what the records tell us about their own format and preservation. The custody of papers could be a source of disputes. When the session clerk of Keithhall, one Chalmers, left in 1777 he took the records with him. The session resolved not to pay him fees owing until he returned them.[90] Presbyterial records suggest that minutes were very often not contemporary recordings of discussions. The desired practice was as follows:

> In the Minute Book, which should be a bound Book, and not loose sheets of Paper, the Clerk at every Meeting, and in presence thereof, is to record the names of the Members of that Sederunt, and mark the Absents, and the Meetings Determination in every Affair, before they proceed to any other business; and in Affairs of any moment or difficulty, he is to read what is minuted, before the Meeting proceed to any other.[91]

This guidance then imagined that:

> in the fair register, the Clerk is betwixt and the next Meeting of the Judicatory, to have extended in ample Form, and recorded all the acts, Votes and resolutions of the former Meeting; and that without any interlinings, or erasing of Words or pages.[92]

Some of the working papers that the clerk used have survived. As Edgar noted of the records of his parish, Mauchline, 'some of these volumes, too, are very tiny, and scarcely deserve the name of volumes; some are unbound and incomplete; some are scroll books and are headed "Brulie Minutes"'.[93] The records themselves suggest that there could be considerable delays in transcribing minutes from loose sheets to the bound register. In 1777 the session of Insch 'strictly required the present Sess Clerk to be exact & faithful in writing down the minutes & preserving them till they are transcribed into the Register'.[94] Problems could occur during this process of transcription. The session clerk of Chapel of Garioch apologised in 1783 because 'in filling up the book from the separate minutes he had neglected to charge the treasurer in clearance of December seventy-five with eight shillings and four pennies Scotch'.[95] Such problems led the session at Insch to resolve that:

every day's minutes shall be read Coram and then inserted in the Session book against their next meeting at wc time they appoint ye Clerk to have the book wt him that they may have knowledge of his diligence & faithfulness there anent.[96]

Despite such resolutions, presbyterial visitations are replete with admissions that registers were often hopelessly behind time. For example, at the visitation of Edelstoun in the Presbytery of Peebles in 1709 the minister, being asked:

> If he had a session book, answered he had; but in regard that there were many years yet to be filled up in it, and he having the Communion now before his hand, it would take some time before it could be filled up, but should labour to have it done as soon as possible.[97]

In this process, it was not necessarily the case that minutes were a complete, verbatim report of proceedings. The delay in filling up registers could enable decisions on what might be recorded, and not just at local level. The presbytery of Hamilton, for example noted in 1710 that their register had not been filled up since 1707. One of their members, Mr Wylie, took the opportunity to state that:

> That being unwilling to retard the filling up of the Register he had offered of his own accord more than a year ago to pass from the recording of the affair. And now though he had not obtained what he thought was reasonable to demand, yet that it may be no stop upon the account of what concerneth him, he consents that the Representation, Proposal and Protestation given in by him to the Presbytery 24 June 1707 with all that hath followed thereupon in the Presbytery and the Committees may be left out in filling up the book or Register.[98]

What the discord was about, therefore, we do not know. Forty years later the presbytery of Ayr noted that, because of the ill health of their clerk, their register was several years out of date. They took the opportunity to seek the advice of synod: 'in as much as there are in the Minutes several incidents not necessary to be filled up in the Register', whether 'the Presbytery may not fill up in the register only matters of importance'.[99] Thus the minutes might be extraordinarily comprehensive, but we have to cautious in their use given these practices.

However, as well as using the records for their content, we are also interested in what their form tells us. Because of the sheer volume, this requires sampling of the records to test, for example, for accounting formats. The basis for this selection will be explained when the particular concerns are being addressed. At times the selection is a cross-sectional one, where records for a particular year are contrasted across a full range of parishes. In other cases individual parishes are selected for examination in more detail longitudinally. The desire is not just to provide interesting illustrations, but also to give some indication of how general particular practices were. Here, the excellence of the archive enables this type of systematic survey in a way that was simply not open to previous historians.[100] In addition, the tools for comparative analysis that we now possess make systematic comparisons more feasible.

However, the account presented also draws on other sources. Being able, for example, to examine presbyterial records across the country means that hints picked up from the parishes examined can inform the scrutiny of the presbytery records in other areas. This is particularly the case when examining practices of parochial visitation, where the availability of records enables us to test claims such as those made by Graham on the basis of practice in a very narrow part of the country. There are also other rich sources, which supplement the archival sources. Here the *Old Statistical Account* (*OSA*), whose compilation itself rested heavily on the efforts of Church ministers, is invaluable in providing context at the end of the century.[101] It has been consulted in detail for the presbyteries considered. The extraordinary detail supplied in the biographical material supplied by the *Fasti Ecclesiae Scottianae*, with its lists of minsters parish by parish, enables us to locate some of the key actors in their social and educational context.[102] Finally, the printed *Acts of the General Assembly* and other contemporary printed material helps to provide the national and 'official' context. As well as this material, the existing historical work is invaluable in setting the practice-based approach in its wider setting. In order to understand the situation in the eighteenth century, we need first to understand both the material and the historical factors that shaped it. It is to this that we turn in the next chapter.

CHAPTER 2

The Emergence of a Governance System

In September 1710 the presbytery of Meigle in Perthshire received a petition from the heritors and session of Glenisla. Having been without a minister for some time, they sought to divert the unpaid stipend to 'pious uses within the paroch'. As well as the provision of essential items such as communion cups, this importantly encompassed the building of a bridge

> over the Impetuous and frequently impassable water of Isla, the want whereof is of unspeakable loss to the paroch, not only in respect of their worldly affairs, and traffique, which att sundry seasons is wholly interupted; but also, in that many who would attend ordinances are many times hindered from coming.[1]

The frequent mention of infrastructure projects such as bridges, harbours and roads in the minutes of church courts serves as a reminder of the practicalities that shaped church governance. This chapter outlines the material and historical factors shaping the operation of governance practices in the eighteenth century. It starts with an outline of some of the material factors, as these are perhaps too easily forgotten when considering the activities of church members. This is followed by an outline of the structures of the church in order to provide background to a more detailed discussion in later chapters of their operation. These structures emerged from and were shaped by the events of the late sixteenth and seventeenth centuries, and these are interwoven with a more detailed consideration of the evolution of detailed practices, derived from the existing historiography. This enables us to examine the attempts at codifying practice at the end of the seventeenth century, and to recognise that they were built on substantial foundations.

Structure of the church

Table 2.1 gives an indication of the organisational structure of the church in the eighteenth century. The numbers of parishes should be taken as a broad guide; there were some changes at the margin as parishes were either combined or divided, but the real movements came later as the church struggled to cope with the growth of population.

What these figures indicate is the weight of the two major synods based in Glasgow and Edinburgh in the affairs of the church. However, it is useful to delve a little deeper into the material characteristics of both presbyteries and parishes, as these could shape their operation. Parishes in the more

Table 2.1 Structure of the church

Synod (16 in total)	Presbyteries	Parishes
Aberdeen	7	89
Angus and Mearns	7	76
Argyll	5	34
Caithness and Sutherland	3	22
Dumfries	4	48
Fife	5	69
Galloway	3	36
Glasgow and Ayr	8	134
Glenelg	5	42
Lothian and Tweeddale	7	104
Merse and Teviotdale	6	67
Moray	6	48
Orkney	2	14
Perth and Stirling	5	63
Ross	3	24
Shetland	1	4
Total	77	874

Source: NRS catalogue CH2 Records of Church of Scotland.

remote areas were often of considerable size, with scattered populations. This was not just a feature of Highland presbyteries; Lowland presbyteries also contained parishes of great extent. Table 2.2 shows this in more detail in the presbyteries selected for more detailed examination.

Table 2.2 Parish sizes

	Number of parishes	Average size	Total area	Maximum	Minimum
Ayr	28	19,001	513,018	75,000	3,052
Garioch	15	7,500	112,506	13,117	4,446
Haddington	16	6,316	94,741	17,000	740
Hamilton	15	15,029	210,400	35,000	2,283
Linlithgow	17	7,721	131,260	20,000	200

Source: Samuel Lewis, A Topographical Dictionary of Scotland, 1846.

The presbytery of Ayr stands out both as having an exceptionally large number of parishes and for covering the largest area. This was because of the size of some of the parishes with extensive areas of moor in the south of the area fringing on Dumfriesshire. However, all of the presbyteries contained some large parishes. At the other end of the scale, the very small parishes in Haddington and Linlithgow were atypical, being coastal burghs with no landward area. It was in this area that there were smaller parishes with more concentrated settlement patterns, especially as the century wore on and agricultural improvement took hold. Parishes here were more likely to feature kirks relatively close to lairds' houses, where these kirks were of some antiquity. Here the presence of landed power was often represented in burial aisles, featuring, as in the case of Abercorn, elaborate galleries or 'lofts' where the landed families could observe services.[2] Such material features were not entirely absent in other areas, and the loft in Monymusk kirk in Aberdeenshire will feature later. However, in these more northerly parishes especially, but also in the more pastoral west, settlement was scattered, with small clusters of dwellings or 'fermtouns' surrounded by extensive tracts of moor. Here the pre-Reformation church was often ruinous and inadequate, with a great wave of rebuilding taking place towards the end of the eighteenth century. Here kirks were relatively plain preaching boxes, dominated by the pulpit on their south wall (Glenbuchat in Aberdeenshire being a fine surviving example). Such kirks were often centred in their parishes for maximum accessibility, often with only a small kirktoun accompanying them.

These factors demand consideration, because they conditioned the working practices of both ministers and sessions. In his *Statistical Account* of Midmar in Aberdeenshire, for example, the minister complained that:

> [because of the] road from these parishes to the Presbytery seat, and higher parts of the presbytery, being, by the hill of Fare, at all times unpleasant, and, in winter, commonly impassable, these ministers are often precluded from supplying occasional vacancies and from attending the meetings of Presbytery, even on the most urgent occasions.[3]

The presbytery of Biggar took these factors into account when responding to an attempt by the synod of Lothian and Tweeddale to enforce attendance in 1740. The framers of the resolution, being based in Edinburgh, had not recognised the difference in circumstances between 'those absents who are on the Spot, or at a little distance and those who are in the outmost bounds of the Synod'.[4] These factors were important given the monitoring of the conduct of both ministers and elders. Ministers, for example, were expected to visit all the families in their parish at least once a year for the purpose of examining their spiritual health, as well as visiting the sick in times of more bodily infirmities. Given the poor state of roads in many areas, a frequent cause of complaint in the *Statistical Accounts*, this itself represented a considerable challenge in the bigger parishes. In Fetteresso in Fordoun, complaints were brought against the minister that he had neglected his visitation duties. In response he argued that:

> [he had] often told you that his parish is so large being about ten miles long

from North East to South West & in many places above six miles in breadth, & lyes at such a distance from the Church, that he will have sometimes fourteen miles travell, to visit one sick person, so that the largeness of his congregation necessitated him to take the above method [that is, combining visits with catechising].[5]

He had, he further observed, always been clear about his practice with members of the presbytery and it had always been approved in the past. The minister was cleared of any wrongdoing, the allegations appearing to spring, in the judgement of the presbytery, from a vexatious complainant. The size of parishes could also be used as an excuse by elders for difficulties in exercising their duties, especially the unpopular position of treasurer. So Macpherson reports that when a new treasurer was need in Auchterless, Aberdeenshire, in 1735, the elders 'asserted they all lived at a considerable distance from the Church', and so asked to be excused.[6] Similar excuses can be found at later dates in, for example, Insch, Aberdeenshire in 1768 and Saltoun, Lothian, in 1775.[7] These material considerations need to be borne in mind when thinking about the often considerable gap between the desired practice enacted in Edinburgh and the realities on the ground.

This forms the basis for an outline of the basic components of the polity of the Church of Scotland in the eighteenth century. Aspects of this will be elaborated on in what follows, but it serves as a basic orientation and explanation of some of the terms that will be used as we explore the emergence of the system. At the base of the system were the kirk sessions. These were always chaired by the minister as moderator; in the absence of a minister, the presbytery might supply a stand-in to allow essential business to be transacted. The session consisted of a number of elders, selected according to the particular features of the parish. In rural areas their numbers varied from about six to fifteen; in urban areas sessions were often larger, with representation from other bodies such as guilds. Elders were responsible, with the minister, for ensuring adherence to the discipline of the church and facilitating its operations. In some parishes they were supplemented by deacons, who had responsibility for poor relief, but in many sessions the two functions were combined in one. From their number they selected a treasurer to handle their financial transactions. Elders were appointed for life. Their activities were supported by a session clerk, who kept the minutes of their meetings and was, by convention, also the schoolmaster.

Sessions were subject to the oversight of the presbytery. As noted above, this generally consisted of fifteen or so parishes. It was staffed by all the ministers of the constituent parishes and by representative elders from each. It selected its own moderator from among its clerical members on a rolling basis, as well as one to act as clerk for a longer term. It met generally monthly and had a number of functions: the spiritual development of its members; recruitment and placement of ministers; handling complex cases of discipline as referred to them by sessions; monitoring the activities of sessions; and transmitting the instructions of the synod. It also selected members for the synod, which generally met twice a year. As well as being a body of appeal, this checked up on the activities of the presbytery and framed larger questions of policy. Presbyteries also selected commissioners to attend the General Assembly, an annual meeting that by the eighteenth century was always held in Edinburgh. This body was the supreme law making body of the Church, as well as its ultimate court of appeal. It selected a moderator annually from among its number and appointed a commission to oversee the implementation of its decisions between its meetings.

An emerging system: the seventeenth century

Such were the broad outlines of the mature system as it operated during the eighteenth century. However, its creation was a process that spanned a number of years and took a form that did not spring intact from the original activities of those who led the Protestant Reformation in Scotland. The success of that Reformation, argues Alex Ryrie in a comprehensive account, owed much to a particular conjuncture of factors and events. As he notes, '[u]nexpectedly, almost accidentally, Scotland had stumbled into a new world'.[8] That new world involved questions not only of theology but also of church polity. We will examine some of the features of that polity in more detail later in this chapter, but it is important to note at this stage that for the reformers the two questions were intimately linked.[9] Drawing on the work of Calvin and experiences in Geneva and France, the committee that drew up the constitution for the new church took advantage of the technologies of printing to promulgate their *Book of Discipline*, which was suggestive in two respects. One was that it marked from the outset a concern to lay out detailed blueprints for the structure and practices of the church. The second was its concern with discipline as the mark of a true church. However, how that discipline was to be enforced was not originally clear, with particular ambiguity and debate surrounding the status of bishops.

Presbyteries as a central part of the system of discipline were not, therefore, on the agenda of the reformers until the *Second Book of Discipline* in 1570, a work particularly associated with the figure of Andrew Melville. This saw not only the transition from the eldership as a matter of annual selection to a lifelong office, but also the emergence of the presbytery from the 'exercises', or regular meetings, of 'ministers with some elders for interpreting scripture in the main town of the district'.[10] What this meant was that the church assumed a commitment, in Kirk's words, to the position that 'unity in doctrine and discipline might best be safeguarded by assemblies presided over, for order's sake, by a moderator among colleagues, and not by a distinct office of bishop as such'.[11] Although this position was an emergent one, it became hardened with the passage of time after an Act of 1592 established presbyteries. In particular, bishops became associated with practice in the Church of England and through this with what were seen as dangerous popish tendencies. In particular, the embedding of bishops in the politics of the English state threatened the distinctive Presbyterian emphasis on two states – one spiritual, the other secular – which were mutually reinforcing, but maintained their own distinct spheres of operation.

The establishment of a distinctively Presbyterian form of church polity was, therefore, a process rather than a one-off event. However, it is worth examining some of the founding documents of the new church in a little more detail for what they tell us about the governance practices that they adopted. These formed the basis for the mature system that we will examine for the eighteenth century. The documents that emerged at the end of the seventeenth century were an attempt to codify the efforts of those who went before. We will look at the turbulent events of that century shortly, but it is important to note that underneath these events was the submerged evolution of rather mundane practices that gained significance in a period of greater stability. These practices have to be seen in the context of the commitment of the reformers to the institution of a church, a commitment that flowed from ultimate theological beliefs. The first, which is clear in the Scots Confession of 1560, is that discipline flows from the absolute necessity of the existence of a church.[12] While the theological focus may be on God's intentions as revealed in His Word in the Bible, this did not mean that each believer should be free to go his or her own way. 'We utterly abhor', thundered Knox, 'the blasphemy of those that affirm that men which live according to equity and justice shall be saved, what religion soever they have professed'.[13] The core characteristics of a church rightly established were true preaching, right administration of sacraments and discipline: 'the strict observance of Church discipline in accordance with what God's Word prescribes, whereby vice is suppressed and virtue promoted'.[14] It is of significance that these were developed in works titled *Books of Discipline*. The word 'discipline' has a number of connotations in this context. The one that springs to mind immediately is the disciplining of members of the church, to ensure that they adhere to its beliefs and rules. This is the image of discipline most strongly associated with the Scottish church, with its disciplining of sinners in public view. But discipline also relates to the need for a church, a need which goes back to the focus in Calvin, drawing on Augustine, on the fall of man and his [sic] essential depravity. This bleak view of human nature means that a church, as a collection of believers, needs forms of organisation in order to counter its essential nature as the fallible creation of fallible humans. Calvin, perhaps because of his legal training, had much to say about the form of the church, and what he said was laid out in orderly and systematic form, both features that would be carried on into the Scottish church.[15] All human activity, Calvin argued, needed some form of government to preserve order, and churches were not exempt from this. From Paul he drew the injunction, 'that all things be done decently and in order'.[16] This could be said to be the leitmotif of the Scottish reformers and their successors. But such order could not be left to chance. It would not spontaneously emerge but needed the creation of 'ordinances'. It was such ordinances or rules that were the constituent parts of a system of discipline, here being the constitution or polity of the church.

This produced what Kirk describes as a series of 'concentric courts'.[17] As Weatherhead puts it:

> the distinctive thing about the presbyterian system is that the Church's authority, received from Christ, is vested in church courts and not in individuals. It is a conciliar system, in which legislative, judicial, and administrative decisions, and supervisory actions, are taken corporately.[18]

It is important to see that this was developed in opposition to what were seen as the fundamental flaws of the Roman Catholic church: flaws that were seen by the reformers as having produced the abuses that had brought them to revolt against its authority. In returning to the constitution of the primitive church, Calvin argued that '[to] the government thus constituted some gave the name of Hierarchy – a name, in my opinion, improper, certainly not one not used by Scripture'.[19] This attempt to trace models of church polity founded in Scripture was an enduring feature and meant that there was resistance to the notion of a formal hierarchy, even if in practice an informal one might emerge. So, for example, those who chaired church courts, the moderators, were selected annually (with the exception of the kirk session, where the minister was always the moderator). This dispute about the relative authority of church courts was to be an enduring one with echoes into the eighteenth century, as we will see when we consider the relative stances of the Moderate and Popular parties on the authority of the General Assembly. However, this concern to avoid the dominance of any particular group runs through the earlier formulations.

One concern was to avoid the emergence of a priestly caste, something that was at the heart of the reformers' quarrels with Rome. To this end, the religious officials of the church should be under surveillance. Once a year, the *First Book of Discipline* laid down, officials from each local church should report to the ministers in the supervising church (this being before the institution of presbyteries), 'the life, manners, study, and diligence of their ministers, to the end the discretion of some may correct the levetie of others'.[20] Ministers should be selected by their congregations and subject to annual visitations, which should 'examine the life, diligence, and behaviour of the ministers, as also the order of the kirkes, the manners of the people'.[21] The people in turn are to be subject to the public examination of their faith annually by the minister and elders. The elders, who are a central part of this system, are not, however, to be entirely trusted. They are to be elected annually, 'lest, of long continuance of such officers men presume upon the liberty of the kirk'.[22] This is linked to the concern that secular influences will intrude into the church and, in particular, subvert its financial resources away from the maintenance of its activities and the poor. Accordingly, elders are to be supplemented on the session by deacons, who are to husband the money. They 'shall be compelled and bound to make accounts to the Minister and Elders of that which they have received, as oft as the policie shall appoint'.[23] In this way, as we will see in more detail later, accounting systems are implied right from the outset.

How this influenced practice can be seen in the surviving records of the kirk session of Perth, transcribed by Margo Todd. Here she notes extensive and detailed record keeping from 1577. Elders were elected annually and, indeed, she notes a complete turnover of members of the session in one year. She suggests that as they were almost without exception members of either a merchant or a craft guild and thus 'already experienced in self-government, the "nitty-gritty" of administration', they were 'well equipped to do the work of the new protestant kirk'.[24] This led them, she argues, to the keeping of detailed minutes and the evolution of distinct practices. In particular, the clerk's 'development of quite specific forms of marginalia for quick reference is noteworthy'. He used this, she suggested, to see at a glance from the register whether the sentences of the session had been followed. This does rather assume that the register was filled up immediately which, as we have seen, was not always the case. Be that as it may, her observation that 'Perth's session clerks deserve a place in the history of early modern bureaucracy, and those who would understand the pervasiveness and efficiency of Reformed discipline would do well to attend to bureaucratic convention, not just theology and preaching'[25] is an important one in the context of this book's focus on just such practices.

What one does note from the minutes, however, is that practices appear to develop but they fade away. For example, in August 1585 the session appointed that their treasurer should give account of his collections every Monday. There were three records of such accounting in the following months but then, with the election of a new set of elders, the practice disappeared. New treasurers were appointed in December, but there was no trace of any accounting through to the constitution of the new session in the following year.[26] Adherence to the annual selection of the session thus prevented the emergence of a set of practices. This would change with the institution of presbyteries following the *Second Book of Discipline* in 1592. Emerging from meetings of ministers for collective worship, they formed, argues Kirk, a pragmatic solution to the practical problems of church administration. They were to be the focus for monitoring the conduct of ministers, although these were still to be subject to the same scrutiny of their sessions. Now, however, annual election was to be replaced by eldership in perpetuity: 'Thir offices ar ordinarie and aucht to continew perpetuallie in the kirk as necesarie for the government and policie of the same'.[27] These two institutions, the presbytery as the key body for ensuring church discipline, and perpetual eldership, were to become central articles of faith for the faithful, to be defended resolutely against alternative polities.

The focus on detailed record keeping was continued, but now these institutions could form the basis for the monitoring of conduct, rather than relying on the elders to produce an annual report. In one of the new bodies, the presbytery of Stirling, it was laid down in 1587 that every minister was to produce their 'buikis of disceplein' before their colleagues so that they might 'be sein and considderit be thame'.[28] There is no evidence that this actually happened, and we will see later how difficult it was to adhere to this practice, but the statement is interesting for its assumptions about what records the kirk session ought to be keeping. Their records ought to include registers of marriages, baptisms and deaths, together with, 'the almus collectit for the pure at their kirk duris with the rollis of the distribitone thairof'.[29] This stress on financial transactions is also seen in the parochial records of Fife.[30] Todd has provided the most comprehensive and stimulating account of this period, which lays particular stress on the careful keeping of records at the local level, where the participation of a wide range of laity in church affairs led, she argues, to widespread acceptance of the Reformed religion. 'It required,' she contends, 'lay elders and deacons to take on remarkably onerous duties at the parish level, and these men were not only lairds and wealthy merchants, but also craftsmen, tradesmen and farmers who worked for a living'.[31] It was this parochial administration that counted for most people. The social, as well as religious, function of the session in keeping local order meant that it proved remarkably enduring, despite the extreme turbulence of events at national level.

That turbulence was caused in part by the poor fit between a presbyterial system of governance and the ideas of the Divine Right of Kings entertained by Stuart kings. While he was pleased to get away from the country of his birth and the dour Presbyterian upbringing he had endured, James VI and I was sensible enough not to confront the Scottish church head on. Bishops were reintroduced after 1606, but operated in concert with the Presbyterian system. His son, Charles I, enjoyed no such sensitivities. Influenced by the High Anglicanism of his Archbishop of Canterbury, William Laud, he sought to introduce the English Book of Common Prayer into Scotland, prompting an angry response. This took organised form with the signing of the National Covenant in 1638. Widely signed across Scotland, this affirmed the distinctiveness of Presbyterian polity and rites as well as connecting with the idea of Scotland as a 'covenanted nation' with a particular mission to fulfil the law of God. Drawing on the many experienced military veterans who returned from their participation in European conflicts, the Covenanters were able to raise effective armed forces that held off Charles' attempts to quell Scottish rebellion. This in turn helped to trigger the events leading to parliamentary revolt against his rule in England. Covenanting military success led to their intervention on the side of parliamentary forces, based on the Solemn League and Covenant of 1643. The price for military aid was to be the exporting of the Scottish Presbyterian model to England.[32]

However, the Covenanters were faced with opposition at home and the growing success of the New Model Army in England, reducing their negotiating power. Their troops withdrew from England in 1647 and splits in the government led to a disastrous invasion of England in support of Charles. Military defeat in England led to a radical Scottish political regime, initially backed by Cromwell and dedicated to creating a godly state in Scotland. This Scottish regime reacted in horror to the execution of Charles in 1649, declaring his son as Charles II under the condition that he adhered to the covenants. This led to the invasion by Cromwell and the crushing defeat of the Scottish forces at Dunbar in September 1650. The fighting ability of the Covenanting forces was impaired by the radicals' insistence on purging all but the most godly. Their power was lost for good in the following year when Charles' forces were defeated at the battle of Worcester; many Scottish prisoners were transported to the West Indies. Scotland was under full-scale Cromwellian occupation.

Through all this, presbyteries persisted as an organisational form. Indeed, it could be argued that they were to thrive under Cromwellian administration, forming as they did a to-hand administrative structure. Not long after the calamity of Dunbar, the synod of Aberdeen issued a 'platform for ordering session books', which it ordered to be copied into local records.[33] It is worth exploring in some detail as an example of the development of mundane administrative practices that carried on during turbulent times, which was to form the template for later developments. It points to the enduring status of the session and the presbytery and the vital role that record keeping played in securing this for both.

The guidance extended to over 1,500 words and was rather a jumble of advice on form and content. The first injunction, for example, was to do with the material nature of the records to be kept, followed immediately by one to do with the opening and closing of meetings by prayer.[34] The advice on content, that is, was also split between things the session should do in conducting their meetings and the ways in which they should record them. To start with the form of record keeping, the guidance laid down that each session should keep five books: a register of discipline (including money collected); one for penalties imposed by civil magistrates (showing the closeness of the religious and secular authorities in conceptions of the godly state); and separate registers for marriages, baptisms and burials.[35] The book

of discipline should be 'ane weell bound book of good paper, paged throughout, keeping a fair equable margent for the compend of acts'.[36] The value of
the index in the margin for the speedy identification of decisions echoes the
earlier practice in Perth. The head of each page should bear the year and every
session recorded should show the day of the month. The register should be
kept by the session clerk as distinct from the minister, but if 'the clerk has
Littell scriwand dexteritie, let the moderator help him in formalie framing
and dextrous wording of acts'.[37] The register should be carefully written up,
without blot or blank. This point was repeated twice, suggesting the importance placed on a clear set of records. After injunction number 9 gave a simple
warning, injunction 20 reinforced it thus:

> That ther be no acts blotted out, nor cancellit, in whole, nor in part, in the
> register, nor inter-lyning, nor acts written in whole nor in part in margin. That
> no adition be with another hand, or with other ink.[38]

All the decisions of the session were to be fully and carefully recorded. Any
outcomes of presbyterial visitations were also to be noted.

Much of the guidance was concerned with the processes of the session,
rather than with their records. For example, they were instructed, 'That discipline be impartiallie exercised, and no mans publick confessing of sin (how
great soever he be) be sould for money, or be redeemable that way be compen-
sation'.[39] However, there was also very specific guidance given on the language
to be used for recording decisions and processes, the detail of which is
perhaps instructive in itself. Sessions were to 'abstain and amend basse and
unseamlie expressions' and the synod then gave a list of suggestions, which
perhaps tells us much about their obsessions:

> as for his partie, to say his whore, for Laick elder (which is popishe), to say
> ruling elder, and for, ane ruling elder was chosin, or, such a man was chosen
> ruling to attend the presbitrie and prowenciall assemble, to say such a man of
> our ruling elders was chosen to attend, &c.[40]

Much more followed in the same vein. There was a concern, then, with
formal language in place of the everyday, down to the use of names, and with
the blunt, if not the downright misogynist as in 'whore'. A commitment to
strict doctrinal orthodoxy was displayed by the objection to terms like 'laick',
that is 'lay' elder, given the position that elders were ordained members of
the church and so not strictly 'lay'. There was also a distinctly pedantic edge;
what we will see as a legalistic obsession with precise formulations is thus
present in this guidance. It is fair to observe that this guidance was probably
the work of a godly minority, given the rather conservative nature of
Aberdeenshire, later an area of Episcopalian strength. Whether any of the
guidance was followed would require detailed study of the records. However,
this is perhaps not as important as the attempt to supply such guidance, which

indicates a tradition that would re-emerge with the confirmation of Presbyterianism forty years later.

Before then, however, Scotland would have to endure considerably more turbulence in her governance, both civil and religious. In 1660 Charles II was returned to the throne, but the dominant players were English, and Scotland from that time was subject to many initiatives with an English flavour.[41] One was the reintroduction of bishops from 1662, which accentuated the splits in Scottish life that had characterised the later years of the rule of the Covenanters. Those who adhered to the strict letter, as they saw it, of the Covenant, notably in southwest Scotland, adhered to those ministers who had been expelled from their livings because they refused to sign an oath of allegiance to the new monarch who endorsed the reimposition of episcopacy. Worshipping in illegal outdoor conventicles and listening to itinerant ministers, they took up arms to defend themselves against increasingly strong government repression. This resulted in the 'killing times' of 1685 in which a significant number were killed. Although a relatively small number in the broader context, this formed the basis for a tradition of persecution. However, such outright resistance was limited in relative terms. Some who could not stomach the new regime went into exile in the Netherlands, which was to become an increasingly important centre for agitation against the Stuart regime, especially under the reign of James VII and II. Others took advantage of a number of Acts of Indulgence, which allowed them conditional tenure of their charges. The revocation of the Act of Indulgence of 1679 increased the numbers seeking a safe home in the Netherlands.[42] While here they joined in the predominantly Calvinist confessional life of their hosts, and plotted their return.

During this time, however, presbyteries and sessions continued to function. We have noted already the use of the visitation as a means of ensuring the right conduct of sessions. This continued under episcopacy, with an interesting example being contained in a register of visitations between 1677 and 1688.[43] This is introduced as flowing from the orders of the Archbishop of St Andrews, but used the existing presbyterial machinery as its key vehicle. As with the platform for ordering session books examined above, it is worth examining for what it tells us about how visitations were conducted and how it foreshadows later practice. The book, which appears to be the only survivor of its type, contained details of sixteen visitations. Each used a standard format and set of questions, with reports extending to about three pages for each visitation. The account developed here is a composite one, as the document is damaged in some places.

Visitations commenced by asking if the meeting had been duly intimated to heritors, elders and heads of families. The former often did not attend dutifully, perhaps because of their responsibility for paying for the church, the manse and the minister's stipend – all issues that would be covered during

the visitation. The visitation started with the removal of the minister and all
but two of the elders (perhaps selected by seniority, but the minutes give no
indication of this). They were then asked twelve questions about their
minister's life and work, with a particular focus on his exercise of his duties.
These questions will be presented in more detail below when we contrast
them to those laid down at national level in the early eighteenth century, but
they concerned his family life, his attention to parochial matters and his
personal conduct – seeking to know, for example, if he frequented taverns.
Having obtained their answers, the remaining members of session were called
in two by two and confirmation sought of the initial picture they had arrived
at. When it had been filled up and presented in advance the register of discipline was 'revised' by two members of presbytery who gave their report:

> they had visited the said book and yt they found both the minister and session
> were careful to censure the Scandelous in the place and zeal in his adminis-
> tering of discipline & found them both zealous and impartiale the book was
> approven and the clerk appointed to subscribe it in testimony yrof.

This points to the continuing importance of the written record in supporting
oral testimony.

Having returned, the minister was then questioned in some detail about
his practice, such as how he expounded the gospels. This is where the more
spiritual aspects of his conduct were examined, perhaps because it was felt
that the session was not in a position to judge. The minister was then asked
about the conduct of his session. Here there were no detailed questions, but
rather a general inquiry as to 'their Diligence in Delating of Scandals and ...
zealous assistance in ye exercise of Discipline and whither [their conversation]
was grave and were sure and becoming office bearers in ye cause of God'.
There then followed questions about the church officer and schoolmaster,
about the money they had for the relief of the poor and the utensils they
possessed for the administration of the sacraments, and about the stipend of
the minister. The visitation concluded with an inspection of the fabric of
church and manse, often with a recommendation that the heritors should
repair them. We will see that the broad thrust of these practices was to form
the basis of later guidance, but this guidance had to wait on the outcome of
further momentous events at national level.

Consolidating the Revolution settlement

The register closed with the visitation of Dunnottar in 1688; in the same year
William of Orange invaded England to overthrow James VII at the invitation
of Whig notables. His acceptance in Scotland in the following year was accompanied by his confirmation of Presbyterianism as the polity and doctrine of
the Church of Scotland. He was lukewarm about this, despite the dominance

of Calvinism in the Netherlands, as he preferred one form of religious polity across his new domains.[44] However, he was surrounded by Scottish advisers drawn from the émigré community who were confirmed Presbyterians – notably William Carstares, who was to become Principal of Edinburgh University. Also among their number was a rather more obscure exile, Walter Steuart, laird of the small estate of Pardovan on the outskirts of Linlithgow. He was to play a significant part in the consolidation of Presbyterian governance. He was a commissioner for the burgh in the parliament of 1690 that voted supplies for the new king, and passed an act confirming Presbyterianism. Brother-in-law of the Principal of Glasgow University, John Stirling, and a correspondent of Robert Wodrow, he was well connected to adherents of the Revolution settlement.[45] Ordained as an elder for the landward parts of Linlithgow in 1691, his contribution to the codification of church governance is explored in more detail below.[46] The ratification of Presbyterianism by parliament paved the way for the General Assembly to meet again for the first time since 1653, when Cromwell had banned them from meeting. The Assembly thus had a good deal of business to consider, not least the staffing of parishes with convinced Presbyterians. In some places, notably in the southwest, the job of removing Episcopalian incumbents was done for them by the 'rabbling' of ministers by mobs of parishioners anxious to restore Presbyterian incumbents. In other parts, especially north of the Tay, the mobs acted in the opposite direction to resist the expulsion of their Episcopalian ministers.[47] The General Assembly were also acting against the backdrop of the failed rising in favour of James by John Graham of Claverhouse, Viscount Dundee. Although Dundee was killed at the moment of his victory at Killiecrankie in 1689 and Jacobite forces had been heavily defeated at the Haughs of Cromdale in the following year, the security of the Presbyterian settlement was still precarious. The church had to reestablish its governance infrastructure and to restock its ministerial ranks. It is in this context that the Assembly of 1696 was presented with *Overtures Concerning the Discipline and Method of Proceeding in the Ecclesiastick Judicatories in the Church of Scotland: humbly tendered to the consideration of the several Presbytries, and to be by them prepared for the next, or some ensueing General Assembly.*[48]

The *Overtures* extended to sixty printed pages. A foreword reminded readers that '[what] put a stop to Our Worthy Fathers going on, in giving a Compleat Directory for the discipline of the Church, and the Methods to be Used in Ecclesiastick Judicatories in their proceedings, some yet alive may Remember'. It observed that with 'a Young Generation rising', there was value in providing detailed guidance on church governance. The book was split into three chapters, with the observation that a further three chapters were wanting, 'to render the whole a Compleat Book of Discipline', but that these were still in preparation.[49] The first chapter of the material that was presented was concerned with general directions that might apply to any court of the church, the second with matters specific to kirk sessions and the third with the operation of presbyteries. Each chapter was further subdivided into headed sections dealing with a particular aspect. Within each section were short numbered paragraphs, with echoes of Stair's *Institutions* and beyond that Calvin's *Institutes*. There is the sense of the logical structuring of topics with a particular focus on the definition of process, although, as we will see, this did not prevent the breaking through of more idiosyncratic opinions. The concern with the written record runs throughout and is given prominence in the third section of the first chapter. In an echo of the practice noted above, the clerk is enjoined to maintain both a book of minutes and a 'fair register' into which decisions should be copied. The *Overtures* laid down:

> This Register is to be paged, and a large margaine; Whereon the title or subject of the Acts and Orders, are to be indexed, for the more speedy finding anything; As also there ought to be a fair Index, and the end of each Book, of all the contents, and that Alphabetical.[50]

As we have seen, this is a recapitulation of advice and practices stretching back to the late sixteenth century. Further continuity can be found in the emphasis on the procedures to be followed in visitations, which we will return to below. Much of the content was concerned with the detailed operation of church courts, with a decidedly legalistic cast. However, this was mixed up with rather more idiosyncratic passages, where the book takes on more of the attributes of a guidance manual. This is particularly the case in the passages about chairing meetings. So, for example, moderators are urged:

> He would likewise prevent the Members, their making long Harangues (savouring of mens loving to shew their Parts) or deviating to matters alien from the present Affair; he would keep them closs to the business, and to use few Words to gain time; and he will be called sometimes to interrupt talkative Members.[51]

Similarly, after hearing witnesses in cases before them:

> the Members of the Judicatory are to reason the Affair calmly, speaking alwise to the Moderator, one after another, without interrupting one another; using no reflecting Language to, or of one another, nor long Harangues, or Digressions.[52]

Such passages are redolent of somebody who has sat through such meetings, and of proceedings which one suspects, having read extensive extracts of court minutes, were all too common in the Scottish church.

The 1697 Assembly appointed the *Overtures* to be sent to presbyteries, asking for their observations.[53] Considering the scale of the work, the Assembly in the following year appointed a committee to consider revision. This committee consisted of the principals of Glasgow and Edinburgh universities, six ministers and, of significance in the light of discussions below,

Sir James Stewart, his Majesty's Advocate, Adam Cockburn of Ormiston, Lord Justice-Clerk, and Sir Colin Campbell of Aberuchle, one of the Senators of the College of Justice, as Ruling Elders.[54] By 1703, this committee reported that they had carried out revisions and obtained comments from some presbyteries. They recommended a further revision to be carried out, adding a further two chapters to the work. This was to be done by a further committee drawn from members of the Synods of Lothian, Glasgow and Fife. Their numbers still included legal representation with the Lord President of the Session, Sir Hugh Dalrymple, joining Stewart and Campbell.[55] In the following year the Assembly 'taking into their consideration that all the former endeavours about the bringing the printed Overtures of Discipline to a period, have not had the desired effect' advised their committee:

> the Assembly considering that albeit the printed Overtures for Discipline be not so succinct as need were, yet that the same, as now amended, may be very useful, do, therefore, recommend to the Commission to cause again revise the said whole overtures, with the amendments, and cause reprint and transmit the same to the several Presbyteries.[56]

In their Acts the Assembly adhered to the project of producing a complete guide to process, noting:

> Seeing there are several things wanting in the overtures now printed, to make the same a complete Book of Discipline, Presbyteries are entreated to continue in adding and amending, and to send their thoughts there anent in writing to the Clerk of the General Assembly, in order to the perfecting of this work.[57]

This process indicates a key problem in the presbyterial system, that is, getting a sufficient number of church bodies to respond to initiatives. We will see that the sheer weight of business that presbyteries were faced with often prevented them from giving longer-term projects their full attention. Without a clearly defined executive branch business could be long delayed, unless it was triggered by an external event of some urgency. One such event was the treaty negotiations for Union with England, which certainly concentrated the collective mind. The impact of this is considered below, but before then it is instructive to consider the evolution of the *Overtures*, by examining the changes made between 1696 and 1704.

One major alteration they made was the addition of new chapters on proceedings and methods in Synods and the General Assembly. This had always been the aim of the original authors and the new version came with the explicit warning that:

> as to the two last chapters, concerning Synods and General Assemblies, &c., they were never before in print nor transmitted, and so the opinions of Presbyteries were not given thereupon; and besides were not so narrowly examined by the Committees as the other chapters were, so that it can only be looked upon as coming from a private hand.[58]

Particular attention was paid to the section 'Of Proceedings in all Church judicatories and the members' Behaviour therein'. Here we can see the elimination of the experience that clearly animated the original writer with the substitution of the cooler language of a committee. So, for example, paragraph 10 of the original, which gives guidance to courts to think carefully about charges being brought lest they fall foul of 'the Passion, Imprudence, Malice, or Self-designs, or mistaken Zeal of the Informers or Delators', has no direct equivalent.[59] By contrast sections on the calling of witnesses (sections 14 and 18 in the 1704 document) are given far more elaboration, suggesting the influence of the lawyers on the committee. Other sections that underwent substantial revision were those on admission to communion and those on the licensing and ordination of ministers.

One area of particular interest is the evolution of the questions to be asked at visitations. Appendix 2 compares the questions asked at the visitations in the presbytery of Fordoun between 1677 and 1688 with those suggested in 1696 and 1704. What we can observe is considerable continuity in the initial questions that were to be asked, with a strong focus on the minister's personal conduct, not just in public but also in his family life. Being a role model for his congregation meant that most of his time should be spent on parochial duties, and here there is strong continuity between the questions asked in practice in the Mearns and those suggested in both later lists. Where the difference in emphasis comes in the 1696 document is the greater focus on the doctrinal conduct of the minister. Where the 1677 questions are further concerned with the minister's social behaviour, such as his drinking habits, the later suggestions drop this in favour of a focus on how he preaches. In 1677 these questions had been matters between the presbytery and the minister: that is, between ministerial peers. In the opening up of these questions to the session we can observe a desire to enhance the role of elders as ordained members of the church and so fit to pronounce on matters of doctrinal performance. We could also link this to the ascendancy of Presbyterian loyalists, anxious to reinforce ministerial conformity to key tenets. This might also be seen in the much wordier formulations of the 1696 list, anxious to specify in detail just what ministerial duties might comprise ('Reading, Meditation, and Prayer, and study of the Holy Scriptures'). The 1704 document removes much of this wordiness, favouring tighter formulations but also adding material. This is largely to do with Acts that had been passed since the original formulation, and no material elements were removed. What we can see from this comparison is that the *Overtures* were building on existing practices, but were revised to add a much stronger focus on the minister's exercise of his doctrinal responsibilities.

The process of visitations was also broadly consistent with what had gone before. The ambition expressed in the 1696 *Overtures* was that there should be an 'ordinary' visitation (that is, not one occasioned by some special event), 'once a year, if it can be attained'.[60] There should be a rota established, so that each parish was visited in turn. At each visitation advance warning should be given, with heritors, elders and heads of families to meet after sermon. Having pronounced on their assessment of the sermon, the assembled members of the presbytery should then review any minutes of prior visitations. Then, as in the Fordoun records, the minister was to withdraw and the questions were to be posed to the elders. For the framers of the 1696 *Overtures* such questions were to be posed to the whole body of the session and the heads of families, as opposed to questioning pairs of elders in turn, as had been the practice in Fordoun. They also laid out in much more detail questions to the minister about his session. What had been a broad question was developed into five questions in 1696 and further elaborated in the 1704 proposals into a set of eleven specific questions (as reproduced in Appendix 4). These developments again suggest an increased emphasis on the importance of elders and their conduct. An extended set of questions for minister and elders about the state of the parish were then posed, together with questions about the kirk officer and schoolmaster. Just as in Fordoun, these were followed by questions about material matters: the state of money held for the poor, the utensils and books held by the session, the adequacy or otherwise of the minister's stipend and the state of repair of both manse and kirk. One area that was added to the 1696 *Overtures* by the revision committee but harked back directly to the earlier practice that we saw in the Fordoun visitations returns us to the importance of the written record. 'The session registers', they specified, 'are to be produced to the Presbytery before the visitation, and given to some brethren to be revised, and they to report at the visitation'.[61]

Of course, producing detailed guidance and having it followed are two different matters. The 1704 document provides us with a useful yardstick against which to measure the detailed examination of local practices that will follow later, but it was never adopted as church policy. In part this was because it was being debated against the looming shadow of a far greater issue: incorporating Union with England. The concern of church leaders was to preserve the distinctive Scottish church polity in the face of anglicising threats, especially from High Church Anglicans. Securing the status of the church was a key factor in swinging the majority of Presbyterians away from opposition to the Union, if not towards whole-hearted advocacy of it.[62] A key focus then for the Assembly became clarifying the ways in which the church would operate, which included extracting from the previous work all the elements of church proceedings in discipline cases, which formed a *Form of Process*, adopted in 1707.[63] This took something of the momentum out of the drive to adopt a full-scale approved governance manual. Not that the Assembly stopped trying. In 1708 presbyteries were reminded to send in their observations about the larger project and in the following year the Assembly repeated its injunction in more detail, drawing the attention of presbyteries to specific passages.[64] In 1710 a further committee was appointed to revise the *Overtures* and present them to the following Assembly.[65] However, perhaps because of the perturbations represented by Jacobitism, the *Overtures* once again disappeared from view, to re-emerge for the last time in 1718. The Assembly of that year,

> considering the necessity of having a complete system of rules for the procedure of the judicatures of this Church in matters of discipline, and that the framing of this is one of the most proper works of the General Assemblies of this Church, from which they have been long diverted by other incidental things, and not having time now to overtake this necessary work,

once again requested the views of presbyteries.[66] However, the momentum had been lost, perhaps best reflected in the observation of the presbytery of St Andrews in 1710:

> As to the Larger Overtures for Discipline Reserved by the General Assembly to the several Prebyterys to give their opinion thereanent, the Presbytery considering that the form of Process already approven by the general Assembly anno [1707] doth contain the substance of what is contained in the said larger overtures, and that it may be a work of time and difficulty to obtain unanimity in the several other particulars in the said overtures from all the Presbyterys in this church, They are of opinion that these larger Overtures may be by the first compiler, or some other fit person further digested into an historical Narrative of the Presbyterial constitution of the church of Scotland, and of the manner of procedure in her judicatories, and that it be not published by the authority of this church but as the work of a Private hand.[67]

What they may well have had in mind was the work of Walter Steuart of Pardovan, who we met briefly above. In what follows he is frequently referred to, as he was by contemporaries and others who used his work, by the honorific of his estate, that is as 'Pardovan'. It is time now to consider his contribution in more detail.

Steuart of Pardovan

Pardovan was one of the exiles in the Netherlands, where he was friendly with the eminent Presbyterian soldier John Erskine of Cardross, who had studied law at the University of Leiden. Together, according to Drummond, the two studied Dutch religious institutions, being influenced by the 'close, accurate study of Presbyterian polity' by Pastor Koelman. 'With clarified conceptions', argues Drummond, 'they returned home to re-examine the worship, discipline and polity of the Church of Scotland, with reference to continental conditions'.[68] Both opposed the Union, and Pardovan moved an overture for a fast in the parliament of 1706 that was designed to split church and parliament, albeit without success.[69] Pardovan opposed the Union in his service in parliament representing Linlithgow from 1700. Both were elders of the church and it is this capacity that Pardovan produced his *Collections and Observations Methodiz'd; Concerning the Worship, Discipline, and Government of the Church of Scotland* in 1709.[70] Although there is no direct evidence, some features suggest that Pardovan had at least a partial hand in the original *Overtures*, and that seems to be hinted by the presbyterty of St Andrews in the passage cited above. He shows no evidence of this in his introduction to his work, however, representing that he had drawn on material scattered in a variety of sources.

His ambition was that his book would form a text for considering matters of church polity in university courses, which he felt had been much neglected. His fear was that 'except this subject be studied and understood by ministers and elders, their memories may well be burdened with their duty, but their judgements, till then, shall still remain ignorant and unsatisfied about it'.[71] The work is split into four books. The first deals with the governance of the church, the second gives guidance on the nature of worship, the third details the nature of sins and scandals and the fourth suggests how such sins and scandals are to be disciplined. For the purpose of the present discussion, the main focus will be on the first book and, within this, on the presbyterial visitation. This is because this book bears the greatest relation to those portions of the *Overtures* that were left over after the sections on process had been filleted out. While the chapter on parochial visitations by the presbytery in Steuart had only ten sections, in contrast to the twenty-two in the 1704 *Overtures*, this is not because the discussion was shortened. Many of the original questions were combined and the logic and structure of the chapters was identical. Indeed, some text, such as that on the church officers, was also identical in both texts. The key difference between the two texts lay in the attention given to the questions to be asked about the minister and session. In both, these questions lay at the heart of the visitation, but whereas the text recommended to the General Assembly contained nineteen questions directed at the conduct of the minister, Steuart had only eight but these were expanded at considerable length. Thus, while the 1704 questions used 428 words, Steuart extended to over 1,000 words. A flavour of his approach can be seen in the following extract from the first question:

> Hath your minister a gospel walk and conversation before the people? And doth he keep family worship? And is he one who rules well his own house? Is he a haunter of ale-houses and taverns? Is he a dancer, carder or dicer? Is he proud or vain-glorious? Is he greedy, or wordly, or an ursurer? Is he contentious, a brawler, fighter or striker? Is he a swearer of small or minced oaths? Useth he to say, Before God it is so; or in his common conference, I protest, or, I protest before God. Or says he, lord, what is that? All of which are more than yea or nay? Is he a filthy speaker or jester? Bears he familiar company with disaffected,

profane or scandalous persons? Is he dissolute, prodigal, light or loose in his carriage, apparel, or words? How spends he the Sabbath after sermon? Saw ye him ever drink healths?[72]

What we can see in this passage was a return to the concerns of the earlier visitations with the personal conduct of ministers. This opportunity to expound on the ills that Steuart evidently saw as threatening to ensnare ministers can also be seen, if to a lesser degree, in the questions to be asked about the conduct of the session. Here he used 372 words to frame his eight questions, in contrast to the 187 words that the 1704 committee used for their eleven questions. By contrast, the passages on questions about the congregation were nearly identical in both. One gets a sense here of the perspective from an activist, pious ruling elder, concerned to maintain a tradition of discipline over ministers.[73] It is interesting to note that one element that is removed from the discussion about the requirements of the visitation is the need to inspect the poor's box, and there is a sense that Steuart is seeking to return the focus to a more religious one. So, for example, in an observation about seating he suggests that it would be best if 'Church Members would take their seats in the Church without respect of their Civil Character, as they do at the Lord's Table'.[74]

Steuart's conservatism in this regard can be seen in his extensive discussion of the role of deacons. The role of the deacon was to take care of church funds, especially as they pertained to the poor. In the *First Book of Discipline* there is a persistent use of the formulation 'deacon or treasurer', and in practice the office seems to have been subsumed under the latter heading. That is, rather than there being two classes of members of the session, elders and deacons, each with their own prescribed roles, in practice (no doubt due to the difficulty of finding sufficient candidates) sessions were composed of elders alone. This is a topic to which we will return in a subsequent chapter, but, despite the frequent exhortations of presbyteries, in practice many sessions combined the two roles. Certainly the 1704 *Overtures*, while mentioning deacons in passing, do not seek to specify a specific role. By contrast, Steuart spends a good deal of space on precisely such a definition. His reasoning, again, was a conservative one based on what he argued was a strict reading of Scripture:

> Where it follows that, seeing this office is divine institution, it is an unwarrantable omission in some congregations, that either they put no difference betwixt elders and deacons, or else they neglect to appoint any to the office of a deacon.[75]

His subsequent discussion on the role of deacons focuses on their fundraising work for the benefit of the poor, applying them and then accounting for them. This focus on the role of the deacon perhaps explains why he omits the poor box from an otherwise faithful copy of the 1704 *Overtures* on the items to be produced at visitation, and why he does not mirror the suggestions about half-yearly accounting to be found in that document. Steuart is at one, however, with the *Overtures* in stressing the importance of the recording of decisions. He discusses extensively the need for the revision of registers at different levels in the church, and includes guidance that extends to the full detail that we noted being advocated in Inverurie in 1650. So for example:

> All sentences and acts are to be filled up in the records, as all other things should be, according to the priority of their being voted or agreed unto, and that although no extract hath been, or perhaps ever may be called for. And when any thing is omitted in the body of a record, it may be written on the margin, which the moderator and clerk must subscribe again. When anything is delete, let it be marked delete on the margin, and subscribed as the other, counting the lines or words blotted out.[76]

Referred to by Drummond as a 'classic', Pardovan's work was reprinted throughout the eighteenth century and remains a source for Presbyterian church polity. In 1841 the author of a compendium on church law in Scotland considered it to be 'a work of great and unquestionable merit', which 'accordingly has been deemed a standard authority and guide in the church'.[77] It was also widely adopted by church bodies, which might indicate why the momentum for an officially sanctioned version dissipated. In July 1709 the minutes of the presbytery of Hamilton report the purchase of 'Twenty copies of a book upon Church Discipline published by the Laird of Pardovan'.[78] The presbyteries of Irvine and Lanark in the following year also both urged their members to subscribe for copies.[79] Much later in the century, in 1786, the kirk session of Gladsmuir, Lothian, noted their ownership of a copy of 'Pardovan's Collection'.[80] The book continued to be referred to as a source for Presbyterian church law. It also framed subsequent discussion of practices such as the visitation. Deploring the legalistic tendency of the documents we have been examining, for example, Clark observed of Pardovan's questions, 'to pass in all of which successfully should have qualified him for canonisation among the saints. The system was an encouragement to men to show up one another's faults'.[81] In a similar vein, Graham drew on Pardovan's account of the visitation, claiming that, 'in some districts they took place every year, for the design was to promote peace and order in the parishes, and to secure diligence in fellowship in all various parts of the congregation and faithfulness in the minister'.[82] Graham was hostile both to the visitation and to those who he thought supported it: 'As the century went on these old visitations were gradually dropped, as they were found to be mere sources of trouble and discontent, interesting only to busybodies in the Church courts and grumblers in the pews'.[83]

Of course, there is often considerable variation between what is prescribed in guidance manuals and what happens in practice. The next chapter looks at visitations in particular and presbyterial oversight of their parishes in general through a detailed examination of such practice. We will see that there was both a gap between prescription and practice and a need to revise judgements such as those of Clark and Graham. However, it is worth emphasising the distinctive nature of the efforts that we have reviewed in this chapter. By 1709 the Church of Scotland possessed a considerable body of work that presented its governance system in a structured, systematic fashion. Already we can see a distinctive approach that sets it off against other church polities.

CHAPTER 3

Presbyterial Business

In July 1740 members of the presbytery of Kirkcudbright arrived in the parish of Kells.[1] Despite the miserable weather, a crowd of some 200 parishioners met them in the church. The occasion was the moderation of a contested call for their new minister, a call that occasioned extensive debate. That debate does not surface in the pages of the *Fasti*, where we learn simply of the ordination of the successful candidate. Thanks to the detailed minutes taken by the clerk we can trace the events of the day and in so doing appreciate the sheer volume of business that a presbytery could be faced with, even when questions of patronage were not at issue. This enables us to frame the trajectory of visitations and the other governance mechanisms at the disposal of presbyteries. It helps us to measure practice against the prescriptions set out in the guidance manuals and come to a more balanced assessment.

The events at Kells commenced with the death of Andrew Ewart, minister since 1691, in January 1739. He had had a young assistant in the later years of his ministry, Robert McMorran, who seems to have been highly regarded by his session and many of his parishioners. Certainly, by July that year a petition arrived at the presbytery signed by thirteen elders and a heritor asking for a trial for McMorran. However, signs of impending tensions were provided by a counter petition from Sir Thomas Gordon of Earlstown and his son requesting that others might be heard 'so that Man might not be imposed on the Parish by a few leading Men in the Session'.[2] At this distance in time and without other sources, it would appear that in part the tensions that were to be revealed lay between a number of heritors in the parish, with others being rather at their mercy. The presbytery appointed several of their members to talk to each side to see if a harmonious solution could be reached.

However, those who adhered to McMorran were not to be moved from their commitment. What appears from the minutes is a determination on the part of both some in the parish and some in the presbytery to pay particular attention to the wishes of Lord Kenmure. This might have seemed odd in some ways, as Kenmure not only was not in communion with the Church of Scotland but he was the son of a prominent Jacobite who had been executed for his part in the rising of 1715. Kells was a parish under the patronage of the Crown, so it was not that he had any particular right, but his status as the leading landowner carried weight. It is perhaps also significant that Sir Thomas Gordon was selected as the elder to attend the General Assembly in the following year. In all events, it appears to have been their pressure and some unspecified objection to McMorran that led to the affair being appealed to the synod in April 1740.

The synod considered an appeal from Kenmure and others that McMorran be set aside. Despite strong arguments from McMorran's supporters that Kenmure was not in communion and so his objections should not be considered, the synod found that because of the 'opposition to Mr McMorran By Such numbers and Such persons of Distinction in the parish of Kells', McMorran should be removed as a candidate and that both presbytery and parish should endeavour to find another candidate. In this, they were 'to pay all due regard to the honble Family of Kenmuir and to use all prudent methods in order to gain the Concurrence of the Honble Gentlemen on both sides'.[3] McMorran's supporters, notably David Newall of Knockreoch and William Newall of Barskeach, appealed immediately to the General Assembly. In June they appeared before the presbytery to announce that the commission had ruled that McMorran should not be excluded.[4] They therefore requested that his candidacy be considered. It was at this stage that Gordon proposed Peter Yorstoun, who had been licensed by the presbytery of Edinburgh in 1735 and at thirty-three was just three years older than McMorran. Perhaps his education at the University of Glasgow and his time in Edinburgh made him a more appealing candidate to the more substantial heritors of the parish and to the town council of New Galloway (which was the creation of the Kenmure family in the seventeenth century). Both men were appointed to preach in the parish; it was these events that lay behind the meeting of the committee in July who arrived to moderate a call.

There are clear suspicions that the presbytery was at the very least inclined towards Yorstoun before the meeting and that such leanings may have influenced their conduct of the meeting. However, that meeting is recorded in remarkable detail, extending to eight pages in the presbytery minutes.[5] The meeting was opened with a sermon from the moderator, who had a substantial audience of elders, heritors and heads of families. The presbytery was also faced with John Dalziell, Collector of Customs, and Alexander Gordon as advocates for the adherents of Yorstoun and John Dun, writer in Wigtown, as representing the supporters of McMorran. The adversarial nature of proceedings became clear from Dun's immediate challenge of the committee's first decision, that of hearing from heritors first. Dun protested that the committee should register the votes of elders first. The committee overruled this objection and started to record the votes of the heritors. Dun started to challenge their voting credentials, when, following discussion between all the advocates and the committee, it was decided to record votes first and then consider objections later. This unusual form of proceeding was to cause some further disagreements, but a poll was taken. From this it would appear that Yorstoun had a slim majority – 99 votes, against 95 for McMorran. However, more of McMorran's supporters were present at the meeting (94 against 93) and the composition of the voters was revealing. More heads of families (77 against 71) recorded support for McMorran, who also had the support of eight elders and two deacons (while Yorstoun had just two elders). Yorstoun had more support from heritors and from members of the town council. As we will see, the way was open for McMorran's supporters to argue that much of this support came from pressure.

Having taken this poll, the committee 'adjourned to the manse in compassion to a vast Multitude of people who could not be turned out of the Church under a heavy rain & who had no oyr place to shelter ymselves'. Having met for some time, they returned to the church to announce that they had decided to recommend to the presbytery to sustain a call to Yorstoun. This caused immediate uproar, with Dun complaining that no call could be made until objections against the right of people to vote had been heard. He led the supporters of McMorran to the other end of the church in order to subscribe a call to their candidate; meanwhile the committee had their own call to Yorstoun subscribed. While they were doing this, the committee ordered anybody 'who had any objection agt the Subscribers were required to attend and Object immediately as the voters were called'. In the chaos of this scene and as McMorran's supporters (understandably) objected that the call could not be made until voting qualifications had been scrutinised on both sides, only Dalziell's objections were heard. Dun protested that 'we did not imagine the Committee would had proceeded to receive or judge in Objections', and appealed to the full presbytery. By this time the meeting was adjourned, it was 'now past four o clock in the Morning'. The business was taken up again when the committee reported to the meeting of presbytery on 5 August.

Brushing aside Dun's objections to the committee's proceedings, they nevertheless sought to see if both sides could reach an accommodation. The members who attended the meeting reported, in another example of the attention paid to Kenmore's wishes, that:

> Ld Kenmore according to his Usuall and laudable Manner Declared tho it was exceeding hard to him to part with a Gentleman of Such a Character whome he had brought upon the field and was not sure if the people of Newgalloway and oyrs concerned would easily part wt him yet yt he was willing for his part if both parties agreed to lay the present Candidates aside and Submitte the Nomination of a third to the presbr or if a third could be named and agreed to by parties this night before they parted he was willing to acquiesce therein.[6]

However, no such agreement could be reached and at 8 o'clock at night the presbytery proceeded to hear objections to voters on both sides. The minutes here occupy twelve pages. Nineteen of McMorran's supporters were objected to, including those carried forward from the parish meeting. Dun was far busier, objecting to twenty-six of Yorstoun's voters. The grounds for these objections are revealing of the faultlines in the parish. John Dalziell, in his objections, focused his attention on the elders, deacon and session clerk, these being seven of his nineteen objections. His objections to them were on the grounds of their conduct which, he argued, rendered them unfit to have a voice in proceedings. For example, he alleged that the deacon James Gordon, 'was convicted before the Magistrates of Newgalloway of Selling Salt and oyr things by fals measure', and so should be barred from having a vote (although Dun argued that this was a mere allegation and that no church censure had been imposed at the time of the vote). Several of these objections did, it would appear, seem to rest on rather shaky ground. Certainly, Dun's objections seemed to rest on surer ground. He was able to show that two who claimed rights as heritors had actually sold their properties in the parish and had moved elsewhere. His main focus, however, was on those voting as heads of families, where he challenged the credentials of eighteen. Much here turned on employment status, with Dalziell protesting that in the case of John Donaldson, evidently a young man, 'if the hiring and Maintaining Servants and by his own personal Industry Supporting an Aged Mother will not Entitle John Donaldson to be the head of a Familie the Respondent does not know what will'. More seriously, Dun raised the spectre of coercion, arguing that five tenants of the Gordons of Earlstown had been forced to record their votes for Yorstoun or they would be fined for cutting wood. Unfortunately, the presbytery gave no decision on the validity of these objections, but, 'after long reasoning upon them the Presby agreed wtout entering upon a Decision of the Sevll objections agt voters on both sides, to this State of a Vote'.[7]

This is frustrating for our understanding of the grounds for participating in a call, but what is important for our appreciation of presbyterial functioning is the recording that, in adjourning their meeting, '[c]onsidering how long they had Sat it being now twelve of the Clock next day'. There is a clear tension in these proceedings between the presbytery's tender consideration of the status of Lord Kenmure and their adherence to an inclusive approach to participation in the call. Their desire to support Kenmure's candidates led them to some unusual forms of proceeding, which then laid them open to extensive challenge. The lack of clarity about qualifications for voting meant that a determined lawyer like Dun could find plenty of grounds for objection, which extended proceedings. It is this extension of proceedings that is important for our topic. That is, much of the guidance material assumed the smooth functioning of presbyteries, with none of the conflicts that the call at Kells indicated. In addition, their focus on legalistic forms simply invited further debate about exactly what the laid-down procedures meant. It is worth remembering that this was not a case of disputed patronage of the type that figures so much in accounts of the time. Indeed, when we examine the future careers of both candidates we will see that these events were put behind them. However, before that stage there were still more processes to be endured. In October Dun appealed on behalf of McMorran's supporters to the synod.[8]

When they sustained the presbytery's decision, he appealed in turn to the commission of the General Assembly. It was only in December 1740, when the commission rejected this appeal, that the whole process was exhausted and Yorstoun could proceed to ordination.[9]

Yorstoun was eventually ordained minister of Kells in March 1741, with no objections being recorded. (The session minutes of Kells, which are very perfunctory, also record no dissent.[10]) That the new minister was not universally popular is indicated by a story in the *Fasti* that some parishioners, aggrieved by proceedings, started to attend another church. To reach this they had to cross a river. On hearing of this, the *Fasti* recounts, Yorstoun:

> told the boatman to make no charge, and to send him the account, which he would pay. It is said that the people were so pleased at this that they resumed attendance at the parish church, and when he left the parish much regret was felt.[11]

He further consolidated his local position by marrying Agnes, the daughter of the previous minister. He served for twenty-two years before being called and translated to the parish of Closeburn in 1763. Here he was succeeded by his son; a further two sons became ministers of Hoddam and Totherwald. Meanwhile Robert McMorran had to wait another three years before obtaining a post. Ordained to Kirkpatrick-Durham in August 1744, he served as minister there for thirty years.[12] One of his sons became minister of Caerlaverock. Both men died within two years of each other (in 1776 and 1774 respectively) after long years of service to the church and in eminently respectable circumstances. There are only faint traces of the conflicts that marked their start on the ministry.

Similar patterns can be found elsewhere. In Kirkcaldy, for example, in 1740 a meeting whose record extended to four pages considered objections to the qualifications of heritors. In this presbytery the votes of heads of families were not counted, but their consent was requested. However, the 'Committee considering it was late and the Church dark & crowded found they could not propose to know distinctly by calling to the Heads of Families which of them declared their consent'.[13] At Abdie in the presbytery of Cupar, a disputed call took three meetings to resolve, with many objections to voters being made. In an echo of Kells, 'James Rymer one of the Elders protested that several of the Heritors not being hearers nor of the Communion of this Church, can have no right to vote in choosing a Minister'.[14] These examples are not developed at the length that the clerk of Kirkcudbright gave us, but they do support the sheer volume of work that was occasioned by the ambiguous nature of this fundamental part of presbyterial work. It is this volume of work that is important to appreciate when we come to a fuller consideration of the success or otherwise of the guidance on visitations that we outlined in the previous chapter.

Business as usual in the presbytery

The example of Kells was drawn from a review of the surviving records of all the Lowland presbyteries south of Aberdeen for the years 1710, 1720, 1730 and 1740.[15] This review was undertaken to examine the evidence for presbyterial visitations. It complemented the more detailed examination of the presbyterial records for the five areas looked at in more depth for this study – that is, the presbyteries of Ayr, Garioch, Haddington, Hamilton and Linlithgow. Together these records enable us to construct an overview of presbyterial business before examining the practice of visitation and other monitoring practices in more detail. It is difficult to do this in the sense that there is no 'typical' year for such work. The possibility always exists of an issue erupting out of the normal course of events and skewing the patterns we can identify. However, such patterns can be identified in a broad sense. Quantifying these patterns would be difficult, for different presbyteries, as we have seen, recorded their proceedings in varying levels of detail. The sheer length of the minutes, anyway, is not a reliable guide to the time that might be taken over proceedings. A brief mention of 'privy censures' having passed satisfactorily might record a whole day's proceedings.

Some attempt will be made later to indicate how the patterns here shifted over time, but it is worth starting with the observation that for all the talk of 'courts' and 'judicatories', presbyteries had the spiritual development of their members at their heart. At least two meetings in the year were normally reserved for prayer, usually followed by the 'privy censures' that we will consider in more detail later. All normal meetings started not only with prayer but also usually (unless sickness got in the way) with the 'exercise and addition' of one of the members. To take one example at mid-century from a well-recorded presbytery, at the first meeting of Ayr presbytery in January 1750, 'Mr Richard Cunninghame [minister of Symington] Delivered the Exercise and Addition from Matthew 5th and 16th and [was] Approven'.[16] Of course, some of the categories discussed here had blurred boundaries with, for example, aspects of this spiritual development being connected with the surveillance activities of the presbytery, but broad indications are useful.

One broad area is what would now be called 'human resource management'; that is, the recruitment, approval and placement of ministerial candidates. Most presbyteries administered bursaries at universities to support students training for the ministry. They tested and selected appropriate candidates, received reports on their progress and collected the money needed for their support. In 1740, for example, the presbytery of Garioch chose between Robert Forbes, schoolmaster at Insch and James Taylor, schoolmaster at Inverurie to hold their burse, which they awarded to Forbes 'for his encouragement in the prosecution of his studies in Divinity'.[17] Once students had passed their courses successfully, they were then licensed by presbyteries. In preparation for this they were put to a test of their knowledge. In 1740, for example, John Faichney, having preached before the presbytery of Perth, was ordered to prepare the following tasks for their next meeting:

> for his popular Sermon verse fifth of the forty seventh Psalm God is gone up with a Shout, the Lord with the Sound of a Trumpet and for Lecture the said forty seventh Psalm per totum. For the Tryall of his Knowledge in the Hebrew Psalm fifty first, and for Tryall in the Greek to expound a Portion of the New Testament ad aperturam Libre. For Tryal of his Knowledge in Chronology the last half of the first Century. Likewise they appoint him to sustain his Theses, and to answer Catechetick Questions that may be put to him.[18]

Having studied at St Andrews, receiving his MA in 1728, Faichney was licensed by the presbytery in 1733. Although what he did while waiting for a call is not recorded, it was usual to act either as a schoolmaster or a private tutor. Faichney was called to be minister of Collace in 1739 and, after passing the trials listed, was ordained in March 1740.[19] As we have seen the process of getting a candidate to this stage was often time consuming (and there had been objections to the call to Faichney, although none of the scale of Kells). Once accepted, a new minister was ordained by the presbytery in their parish.

Activities concerned with the spiritual health of the ministerial cadre intersected with the role of the presbytery in the spiritual welfare of their parishes. They had to make sure that absence, whether temporary (for example, when ministers attended the General Assembly) or more permanent (through, for example, ill health) was covered. They could direct ministers to supply cover, which was needed in particular to ensure that kirk sessions could continue to function. A particularly tricky question for them was the provision of assistance to ministers failing through age or infirmity. Ministers, who were ordained for life, guarded their status and position in their parish jealously. This could extend to attempts both to make their life easier and to provide for the spiritual and pastoral needs of parishioners. Ministers, for example, were expected to visit families on a regular basis, especially those where sickness obtained. Given the size of parishes and the nature of transport, this often posed real problems for sessions faced with a minister reluctant to call for help. In September 1740, for example, the presbytery of Jedburgh received a deputation from the session of Minto. Together with Sir Gilbert Eliot they had, they said, waited for their minister, John Ritchie, 'who is in a bad state of health and has been for some time very Infirm, In order to Represent to him Somethings tending to his own Ease and the advantage of the Congregation of Minto, but without any Success'.[20] For assistance, they appealed to the presbytery, who sent a committee of their number to converse with Ritchie. This secured a letter of demission, provided that he was granted an annuity payable out of the stipend while he lived. Before accepting this offer, the presbytery decided to hold a meeting in the parish, to consult with parishioners there. Unsurprisingly the offer was accepted, but again this indicates the amount of time that might be consumed in routine business.

The concern with the spiritual health of parishes also overlapped with a major area of work, that of ensuring that the material aspects of the parish were in order. Specifically, they were concerned with the state of repair of the kirk, the manse and the schoolhouse, as well as with the minister's glebe. These issues were generally handled through the mechanism of a visitation, usually by a committee of the presbytery. This is to be clearly distinguished from the parochial visitation to be considered in more detail below, although sometimes the two could overlap. Here we are concerned with those visitations which were concerned solely with the inspection of property. These could be triggered by a number of requests. The most common was the request from a new minister demanding the repair of his manse or, in some cases, the provision of one. It was the responsibility of a minister, once his manse had been declared free and legal, to maintain it and, if translated to another parish, he might request a visitation to confirm its condition. Such a request might also be submitted by a minister's widow.[21] These requests were generally to do with either the manse or the glebe; requests to repair the church tended to come from the session. Occasionally, however, they might come from heritors who were anxious to have a division of the kirk and needed the presbytery to act as a broker of their competing demands. In 1740, for example, the presbytery of Stirling had to deal with the complaints of Lady Shaw about the intrusion, as she saw it, of the pulpit and elders' seat into her husband's aisle.[22] Once a visitation was agreed, intimation would be given to interested parties from the pulpit and by letter to non-residing heritors. On the day, those invited would meet with the committee and with tradesmen who had been appointed to attend. Tradesmen were sworn to give accurate assessments of the work needed. Their estimates are generally contained in considerable detail in the reports of visitations, offering a great source for building practices and prices of the time. Once agreed upon, heritors were generally expected to stent or assess themselves for the cost of the work. Once the work was done, especially on a manse, a return visitation was needed to certify that the presbytery's instructions had been carried out.

Such a process would have taken up a good deal of the presbytery's time even when matters ran smoothly, but they frequently did not. In some cases heritors were unable or unwilling to take on the task of stenting themselves and so, in frustration, the presbytery would undertake this task, often using the latest valuation of the parish for cess or land tax. Extensive lists of these valuations, running to several pages, can be found in presbytery minutes. Sometimes the problem was that heritors disagreed among themselves as to the work that was needed. In 1740 the presbytery of Penpont had to consider plans for the rebuilding of the ruinous church at Closeburn. They had reached agreement with the majority of heritors but one, William Dalrymple of Waterside, presented an alternative plan. A simpler church, he felt, would be entirely suitable:

any Heritor having a mind to put up Lofts or Seats or Beautify it any manner of way than by plain work it may be done at their own expenses and not at the Expense of any of the Rest of the Heretors.[23]

The plain nature of many Scottish kirks, especially the preaching boxes of the eighteenth century, thus reflects not just theological niceties but also the concern for frugality among heritors, especially when there were several in a parish.

These matters of what might seem rather mundane business often took up a large part of presbytery time, rather more in some cases than the disciplinary role for which they are perhaps better known. The presbytery was the court of appeal when local sessions found cases too complex for their adjudication. Often these might be when cases concerned those of higher rank in society, such as the extensive attempts to bring the Marquis of Lothian and his mistress to a realisation of their offence by the presbytery of Dalkeith in 1720. This required consultation with the synod about a 'person of quality' and numerous attempts to broker a private settlement. Eventually the presbytery wrote to him in July 1720 expressing disappointment:

> that after all the pains they have been at with you by private conferences, letters and Committees sent to your Ldsp from them, with concurrence of others from the Synod, you will come into no measures for removing the scandal you have given.

Still achieving no success in September the same year, they had him formally summoned to attend their meeting, 'but that the Marquis and that woman being gone to London', they were unable to proceed further.[24] As the Marquis died in early 1722 it appears that he was able to avoid the ministrations of the presbytery, but it had consumed a large amount of their time.

All this pressure of business meant that often a further area of their activity, that of debating and promulgating policy, was squeezed for attention. Overtures proposed to and accepted by the General Assembly were forwarded to presbyteries for their debate and assent. Frequently, as in the case of the 1704 proposals (often referred to as the 'Larger Overtures for Discipline' by contemporaries), we see such matters being adjourned because of the pressure of other business. In January 1710, for example:

> considering that at their last meeting they Resolved to take the Larger Overtures for Disciplin under consideration this day, But in regard of their throng of business, and the Circumstances of some Brethren throw indisposition, [the presbytery of Meigle] thought fit to delay the said affair at this time.[25]

The upshot was that in many cases the Assembly did not receive sufficient responses and had to appeal for attention to these matters. In 1708, for example, they observed:

> finding that many Presbyteries have not as yet returned their opinion about the large overtures concerning the method of procedure in ecclesiastical judicatories, which were transmitted to them by former Assemblies; they do

hereby, of new, require the several Presbyteries forthwith to take these overtures under their consideration, and send in their opinions about the same to
the Commission of this Assembly, to be by them prepared against the next
Assembly.[26]

It should be emphasised that all the areas we have been considering – spiritual
development, staffing of parishes, upkeep of the physical estate, disciplinary
affairs, policy – were in the normal run of business. The pressure of business
we have observed could only be exacerbated by the rather more visible and
spectacular eruptions of patronage dispute. These could rumble on for many
years and involve numerous appeals. At St Ninians near Perth, for example,
a presentation over the determined opposition of the presbytery rumbled on
from 1767 to 1773.[27] However, even without these, presbyteries could
struggle to meet their obligations. 'The Presbytery being Straitened for time',
complained the minutes for Lanark in September 1710, 'having had much
business before them to Day adjourns their Dyet for prayer and privie
Censures till their next meeting resolving then to stay all night for that end'.[28]
This is an important context for our consideration of the success or otherwise
of the methods for monitoring parochial affairs, which were the other
important part of presbyterial duties.

The parochial visitation in practice

We have seen in the previous chapter how central parochial visitations were
to the framers of guidance for the operation of church discipline. We need to
distinguish them from both the visitations we have already touched upon and
other means of monitoring. Although there could be some blurring (parochial
visitations, for example, often moved onto the inspections of building fabric),
the two were quite distinct practices, as will be explored below. We also should
note here that the framers of the guidance also envisaged a degree of
inspection of the state of the parish at ordination. We have already noted early
attempts to use session registers as a means of regulating conduct; their use,
and that of 'privy censures' later in the century were also important practices.
However, our initial focus on parochial visitations is conditioned by their
appearance in the later literature, especially that influenced by Graham's
Social Life of Scotland in the Eighteenth Century. Graham was harsh on many
aspects of the eighteenth-century church, but none more so than on the
parochial visitation. He argued:

> These inquisitions did vastly more harm than good. They were dangerous
> weapons to put in the hands of every malcontent who had a grudge to gratify
> or a fanatical grievance to express, with the risk of making a clergyman's life a
> burden to him and his congregation a terror.[29]

His assertion, drawing on Pardovan, that such visitations took place annually has later been drawn upon by others. Stephen, for example, suggests that 'visitations were a regular occurrence for all parishes regardless of whether or not a minister was under a process'.[30] Unfortunately, Graham is not always a reliable guide. His work was heavily dependent on a limited range of sources and was coloured, Withrington argues, by an anti-clerical bias.[31] So it is worth examining the records in a little detail (and to be fair to Graham, we now have both much better access to sources and much better means for their analysis).

The summary in Table 3.1 is drawn from the surviving records of the presbyteries south of Aberdeen and the Highland line for each of the years 1710, 1720, 1730 and 1740. It was considered that the more northerly presbyteries were still in a state of recomposition in these years and so unlikely to be concerned with visitations. The ten-year intervals were selected to cope with the sheer volume of material. Four presbyteries had no surviving minutes at all for the period, and six had years missing. For the period a total of 149 records were inspected, against an expected total of 172 if all records had survived. With over 86 per cent coverage, this is comprehensive, with only the synod of Dumfries being particularly poorly represented (only 45 per cent of records survive). While, therefore, Table 3.1 is not a complete representation of parochial visitations, it is a good indication of the main patterns and throws some light on the gap between guidance and practice.

Table 3.1 Parochial visitations in Lowland presbyteries, 1710–40

	1710	1720	1730	1740
Angus and Mearns	1	2	0	0
Dumfries	2	0	0	0
Fife	2	3	1	0
Galloway	1	1	1	0
Glasgow and Ayr	6	10	3	2
Lothian and Tweeddale	4	0	0	0
Merse and Teviotdale	0	1	0	0
Perth and Stirling	1	1	0	0
Totals	17	18	5	2

Source: Presbytery minutes.

Table 3.1 shows the pattern of visitations in the decades following 1710. In 1706 the General Assembly, 'considering that frequent Presbyterial Visitation of Parishes would be of great advantage to the Church, and might tend much to promote piety and holiness and suppress sin', recommended that presbyteries, 'be more frequent and conscientious in visiting parishes'.[32] In 1713 they required those inspecting synodal minutes to check if presbyteries were carrying out regular visitations.[33] There were attempts, that is, to follow up on the procedures laid out in guidance manuals. However, these attempts met with mixed success. The figures indicate that presbyteries were a long way from fulfilling the vision of a visitation of each parish each year. They also indicate a distinct geographical split, with the exhortations of the Assembly being most faithfully complied with in the south and west, especially in the synod of Glasgow and Ayr – which is just where much of Graham's evidence emanated from. Indeed, if we dig into this further we find that the presbytery of Glasgow supplied five of the visitations in 1720. By contrast it is perhaps instructive that another influential synod in the national affairs of the church, that of Lothian and Tweeddale never managed any visitations in the area it covered after 1710. Of course, these figures are just snapshots; they may give a misleading picture of the pattern of parochial visitations if they happened to fall outside the sampled years. According, a review was carried out for four of the presbyteries that had been selected for closer examination of the minutes between 1700 and 1740. The results are in Appendix 2. What this confirms is that the attempt to make visitations was a regular feature in the early years of the century. It does indeed indicate that the surprising lack of parochial visitations in the presbytery of Linlithgow in the sample years was misleading for at least the early period, but it also confirms the way in which these practices fizzled out in the eastern presbyteries in the second decade of the century, with the last visitation in Haddington being the outlier of a visitation at Gladsmuir in 1723. It also suggests that visitations were adhered to on a regular basis in western districts, with the presbytery of Ayr managing the highest number of visitations in one year, six in 1722, of all the sampled years. Unfortunately the volume of minutes covering the years between 1733 and 1745 is missing, so it is not possible to confirm just when visitations ceased there. As will be seen below, visitation reports for this presbytery are fairly standardised and brief, but they are the presbytery that attempted consistent visitations. However, it is difficult to discern a pattern: Coylton parish received five visits in the period, New Cumnock and Mauchline four, while some parishes, including the presbytery seat, only one. All the parishes had been visited by 1722. As well as examining these presbyteries, the broader patterns suggested the need to look at the presbyteries of Irvine and Dumbarton more closely, both having the only parochial visitations in 1740. This does seem to suggest that the last parochial visitation may well have been that at Kilwinning in 1742; its outcome, examined in more detail below, does seem to support at least part of Graham's argument for the demise of the practice.

The passing of parochial visitations was not from want of encouragement from synods, whose attestations of presbyterial registers often exhort them to more frequent visitations. Thus the presbytery of Haddington, having been enjoined to carry out more visitations in 1705, were reminded in 1707 'that they have more frequent parochial visitations'.[34] A similar pattern of exhortation can be found, although with a singular lack of success, in Dunfermline.

In 1720 and 1730 it is noted, respectively, 'they had no parochial visitations for several years', and 'that they have parochial visitations more frequently'.[35] The reasons why these exhortations were relatively unsuccessful is considered later; for now, however, we can examine the extent to which visitation practices conformed to what was imagined as best practice by the framers of the guidance. These observations are based on the detailed examination of the visitations carried out in 1710 and 1720: a total of thirty-five. In the case of the presbytery of Glasgow records for 1710 (two visitations) only fragments can be gleaned because of the state of the records, but in all the other cases it is possible to match the records of visitations against the procedure and questions laid down in the 1704 *Overtures*. Indeed, we see those *Overtures* being referred to frequently. Of course, what we are examining here are the traces left by the clerk, so what we might be measuring is the completeness of the minutes as opposed to the experience of the visitation itself, but the contrast between different styles of recording over time is instructive in itself. As well as yielding useful material for discussion in later chapters, the records of visitations over time supplement the bare numbers obtained from the sampling of the records.

The 1704 *Overtures* suggested that visitations were either 'ordinary' or 'extraordinary', that is, where they were called to deal with a special item of business. Ordinary visitations ought to be part of a designed programme, in which all churches were to be visited once a year, or 'at least this ordinary visitation should be going round all the parishes in order, till they be visited, before others be revisited in ordinary'.[36] We have seen that no presbytery, not even the remarkably energetic Glasgow presbytery in 1720, got anywhere near the first aspiration. Indeed, given a typical figure of fifteen parishes per presbytery and the depth of the intended inquisition, this was never likely to be achieved. Some presbyteries did, however, attempt to establish a regular programme of visitations. In 1710 the presbytery of Dalkeith, 'taking to their consideration the necessity of parochial visitations do appoint their Clerk to bring an account of the paroches within the bounds that falls next to be visited'.[37] In considering how to order such a list, the presbytery of Linlithgow in 1706 decided to begin with the home church, 'and so downwards according to the antiquity of the kirks within the presbytery'.[38] An order of visitations for Glasgow parishes can be inferred from the observation of the minister of Govan that a suggested visitation of his parish was out of turn.[39]

However, there could be other motives for visitations. In 1710 the presbytery of Lanark, 'designing a Course of visiting of the several paroches within their Bounds', decided to start with the parish of Dunsyre.[40] This plan coincided with a letter from a leading heritor expressing some concerns about the minister. The subsequent visitation revealed dissent in the parish emanating from this heritor that the presbytery judged to be without foundation.

An examination of the other visitations in this year reveals other examples of visitations being sparked by concerns raised within the parish. In the

presbytery of Lochmaben, both visitations addressed concerns about ministerial conduct: in Ruthwell allegations of the minister's fondness for the drink,
in Dalton his inadequate delivery of sermons.[41] At Lundie, the presbytery of
Dundee had to address concerns about the impact of extra-ministerial work
on the ability of their minister to perform his duties adequately.[42] Four of the
seventeen visitations in 1710 seemed to be prompted by such concerns; their outcomes will be considered later. As far as can be ascertained from the records,
none of the visitations ten years later was prompted by such concerns.

In all of the recorded visitations the clerk is careful to note the details of
how the meeting had been intimated and those of rank who attended. Major
heritors often sent a representative; in some cases heritors failed to appear at
all. In Dunsyre for example, despite the concerns that had been received, no
heritors appeared. None of them resided in the parish, and the use by the
dissenting heritor of a proxy in the form of Agnes Wastoun who, 'came in
and threw down two papers, and then fled out of the Church without speaking'
only convinced them of the mischievousness of the claims.[43] At Logie in 1710,
not only did no heritors appear, but also no heads of families except the elders
did either, 'in regard they were busid about their harvest'.[44] However, in most
cases the minutes record a substantial attendance.

Visitations always started with the ministerial sermon (except in two cases
where the minister was excused on the grounds of ill health). Once this was
approved, the guidance suggested that the members of presbytery should
have in front of them the results of the revision of session registers and their
minutes of previous visitations. The latter was almost never evident, only
being carried out in the presbytery of Glasgow. The position with session
registers was patchier. In 1710 two registers, those of South Leith in Edinburgh presbytery and Logie in Cupar presbytery, had been examined in
advance and recommendations were given on that basis.[45] This was the
desired practice, but in that year five sessions presented their registers for
subsequent revision and four were ordered to have them filled up and
presented later for that purpose. In the six other cases there is no mention of
the registers. Ten years later only two sets of minutes fail to mention the state
of the records. Again, two had been produced for approval in advance, but
the number to be filled up had grown to nine. We will examine the process of
revision of such registers in more detail below, but the operation of this aspect
of the guidance was only partially effective.

This meant that the main basis for the decision of the presbytery about the
state of the parish had to rest on the questioning of minister and elders, and
this was a feature of all the visitations. There was a subtle difference in a few
of the visitations in the order of procedure. In the *Overtures* it was envisaged
that the visitation would start with the minister being removed and the elders
being questioned about his conduct. This was indeed the general practice: in
two cases in 1710 and another two in 1720 the minister was asked a range of

questions first. However, the broad principles of the laid-down process were adhered to in 1710, except in the case of Lundie. Here the concerns about ministerial conduct that sparked the visitation meant that questioning finished after the elders had presented their case. This was an exceptional case; at the other end of the spectrum was South Leith, where the presbytery of Edinburgh followed the guidance almost to the letter, resulting in a six-page report of the visitation. An analysis of the questions asked at the visitations in 1710 indicates that in seven cases the presbytery recorded that they asked the 'usual' or the 'ordinary' questions. In some cases this contained an explicit reference to the 1704 *Overtures*, as when at Lundie they 'asked them the ordinary questions concerning him, as contained in the Larger Overtures for discipline'.[46] In a further five cases this was, as it were, reversed, with the session being asked '[i]f they had anything to Object to against their Minister's Life or Doctrine'.[47] The remaining five cases, however, contained detailed lists of the questions asked, which enables us to compare them to the guidance advice. Appendix 3 shows the questions asked in six presbyteries against those laid down in the 1704 *Overtures*. Edinburgh demonstrated an almost exact match, although even here some questions were combined (so, for example, amalgamating the questions about the content and style of preaching). This combination process could be seen in several other presbyteries, but in most cases the spirit of the 1704 *Overtures* was followed, with the exception of some of the more 'administrative' questions, such as those to do with the reading of Acts of Assembly. The limit case here was that of the presbytery of Kirkcaldy who in their inspection of Portmoak recorded only five detailed questions (as compared to the sixteen asked at South Leith).[48] Here the importance of ministerial conduct was clear, with the first two questions about his conduct and adherence to his local duties being asked in all visitations. For the Kirkcaldy presbytery, what also mattered was his exercise of discipline and his knowledge of his parish gleaned from regular visiting of his flock. Again, this focus on visiting was found in all visitations and indicates what was consistently regarded as important.

We can conclude from the 1710 questions that the monitoring of ministerial performance as envisaged by the framers of both the 1696 and the 1704 *Overtures* was realised in practice. It continued in 1720, although not in such great detail. Only three reports now gave any questions in detail, and even here they were not as extensive as in 1710. Only in the visitation of Kirkmaiden by the presbytery of Stranraer were all the detailed questions, ten in number just as in 1710, recorded together with responses.[49] At Newtyle:

> Severall Questions were proposed by the Moderator to the foresd people concerning his walk and Conversation keeping at home preaching plainly reproving of Sin, Administrating Baptism when the Congregation was Convened & Severall others as they are more largely contained in the Overtures of the Commisssion of the General Assembly anent visitations.[50]

This tendency to rely on general knowledge of the set of questions that might be asked is found in the eleven sets of records, which now record that the 'usual' or 'ordinary' questions were asked, with only exceptions being noted. In the three remaining cases the questions were asked in the 'negative' form, with the extreme example of briefness here being at Kilbryd in the presbytery of Hamilton, which simply noted, 'The Minister, elders, Heritors, and Heads of families Declared that they were mutually satisfied and pleased with one another'.[51] What this suggests is a reduction in the rigidity of visitations.

A similar process can also be seen in the questions posed to the minister about his session. Appendix 4 shows the detailed questions in three presbyteries. The reduced number of detailed lists may indicate the strong focus on ministerial performance in the earlier visitations. Once again, the spirit of the *Overtures* (and so what other visitations that only record the 'ordinary' questions might have meant by this) is clear. The adherence of the Edinburgh presbytery almost to the letter of the 1704 injunctions was clear. What is also interesting, in the case of Cupar where these questions were posed first, is the germ of what was later to be practice: the reliance on the minister to report on the parish. A similar analysis is not possible for 1720, when there was much more reliance on the 'ordinary questions'. An indication of the more relaxed approach was in the visitation of Port of Monteith in the presbytery of Dunblane, where the minister was 'Interrogate anent their faithfulness and Dilgence and Strengthening his hands in the Lord's work'.[52]

While these sessions of questions formed the main basis of the 1704 recommendations, presbyteries were also to inquire about a number of other matters. They were to ask about the spiritual health of the congregation, to confirm the conduct of the schoolmaster and kirk officer, to check the utensils and to ascertain the material aspects of the parish – the fabric of church and manse, the extent of the glebe and the nature of the ministerial stipend. The latter was often given in considerable detail, as a matter of record. Finally, the recommendations suggested that they should inquire about provision for the poor. This was only done in eight of the 1710 visitations, but in all bar three of the visitations ten years later. What this suggests is a gradual shift away from the focus on ministerial performance to a broader concern with the health of the parish. The examination of practice in both 1710 and 1720 does suggest a broad adherence to the spirit of the 1704 guidance. It certainly provides no evidence that Pardovan's book is a reliable guide to practice. His rather jaundiced view of ministerial activity found, perhaps unsurprisingly, no purchase with the presbyteries that undertook visitations. However, concern with ministerial conduct in the earlier years was certainly a feature that we can see when we examine the outcome of these visitations.

The recommendations that followed from visitations were frequently unremarkable. There was considerable focus on the need for repairs to the fabric of churches and manses. Indeed, the need for attention to the building stock of the kirk, dilapidated through years of neglect in the troubled times of the seventeenth century, was manifest in the number of visitations for repair that were conducted in the early eighteenth century. Table 3.2 shows how these far outweighed parochial visitations.

Table 3.2 Repairing visitations, 1710–40

	1710	1720	1730	1740
Angus and Mearns	8	9	2	2
Dumfries	1	6	2	1
Fife	4	4	6	3
Galloway	0	3	4	5
Glasgow and Ayr	4	5	3	2
Lothian and Tweeddale	3	3	2	3
Merse and Teviotdale	5	4	4	2
Perth and Stirling	4	6	6	3
Totals	**29**	**40**	**29**	**21**

Source: Presbytery minutes.

Some of the recommendations came from the review of the session registers, which is considered in more detail below. A consistent recommendation was the injunction to have deacons as distinct from elders on the session. This distinction, and the difficulties in fulfilling it, will be considered when we look at the composition of the session in more detail in the following chapter. However, it is the more spectacular outcomes that suggest the early focus on ministerial conduct.

Ministerial conduct and the demise of the visitation

As we noted, at least four of the visitations were prompted by concerns about ministerial conduct. In two of these cases these concerns were easily dismissed as being spurious and the result of a discontented minority. In the case of Dunsyre, one of the two papers flung on the table by Agnes Wastoun contained a number of queries about the minster; the second was entitled 'The Devouring poor Widows houses under pretence of Long prayers'. Unfortunately, the text of this intriguing document is not given, but the presbytery suspected the hand of the elder and heritor Andrew Brown of Dolphingtoun behind it, 'in regard also the Elders had declared to the presbytery, that Dolpingtoun hath used pains with the people of Dunsyre, both by himself and others to subscribe a paper for defaming Mr Duncan, but without success'. Nevertheless, they gave her leave to bring her evidence to a following meeting of presbytery.[53] When she did not, the case was declared closed. A swifter outcome was delivered at Ruthwell when the presbytery of Lochmaben was asked by the minister to ask directly about the truth of rumours accusing him of drunkenness. The assembled elders and congregation agreed that there was no truth to them, and the minister was vindicated.[54]

This, however, was not the outcome in two other visitations prompted by concerns about ministerial conduct. In Lundie several elders had left the session because of concerns about the minister; those who remained raised enough grievances that the presbytery had to take them away to another meeting. At this they received a letter from the major landowner recognising the faults of the minister but advocating forbearance, plus rather more forceful complaints in a petition from elders and heads of families. This complained about his treatment of some parishioners, his neglect of his duties of visiting his flock, irregularities in the distribution of the poor's money and complaints that 'Mr Ainslie was so much taken up with worldly business, as in building dykes and the like, that it occassioned much neglect of his Ministerial work'.[55] The minister was given the opportunity to respond, which he did at length in a reply running to ten pages. The visitation happened in January; in March the presbytery returned to the parish to hear witnesses. On the basis of this evidence they referred the matter to the synod, who deposed Ainslie from office in April 1710.[56] At Dalton, the presbytery of Lochmaben heard the complaints of parishioners that their minister had a speech impediment that prevented him from being understood: 'he had ane defect in pronunciation especially at baptism & that the parish is displeased therewith'.[57] Because of this dissatisfaction there was no functioning session and the body of people did not attend services. At a following meeting the presbytery decided to send in substitute ministers and to press Carlyle, the incumbent, to demit office as the problem in their view 'arises from his natural infirmity of halting in Speech which can scarcely be supposed to grow better'.[58] This seems a harsh judgement on one who presumably had this attribute when he was licensed to take office, but he was indeed replaced. So visitations could result in ministers being forced to demit office, especially in the early years of the eighteenth century.

The distinct impression is that over time visitations became more concerned with material rather than spiritual concerns. Thus, the last visitation in the presbytery of Hamilton, which came twenty-two years after the previous one, is a rather lacklustre and unconvincing inspection tacked on to a request from the minister for repairs to his manse. That a visitation happened at all at Cambuslang might have been related to the often stormy relations between ministers and a section of the elders, as will be seen later, but in 1735 such dissension is not reflected in the minutes. After the minister declared his satisfaction with his session and gave some brief details of the state of the poor and the church utensils, 'The heretors Elders and People being successively called in all declared Their Satisfaction with their Minister'.[59] Visitations in the later years appear to be responses to specific issues, rather than a thoroughgoing review of all the activities of the church in the parish. Thus, in 1742 a visitation of Kilmaronock in the presbytery of Dumbarton was appointed because of some dissent between the minister and some heritors. This turned out to relate to a broader dispute about the stewardship of the poor's money that had been raised in the previous year:

> Several of the Brethren having Represented to the Presbytery That the Gentlemen Heritors in their Respective Parishes do Alledge that they are Impowered in Consequence of a late Act of the Justices of the Peace of the Quarter Session of Stirling to be Overseers Or as they pretend conjunct Managers of the poors fund with the Ministers and Kirk Sessions And Threaten them with a Prosecution In Case of a Refusal.[60]

The minister of Kilmaronock had refused to allow any inspection, and in fact the so-called visitation focused entirely on this dispute. It was eventually resolved by local negotiation, the outcomes of which were not recorded. The outcome of the next and final visitation was much clearer: complaints about the conduct of the minister of Old Kilpatrick ended up with his deposition. The trigger was his sudden departure from the parish, with the subsequent investigations revealing a catalogue of allegations relating to his marital and sexual affairs. This took the presbytery more than a year to bring to a conclusion: the sentence of deposition in March 1744.[61] The visitation was more an opportunity to gather evidence from the parish than the inquiry envisaged by the framers of the *Overtures*.

The last of such inquiries appears to have been that of Kilwinning in the presbytery of Irvine in 1742. Again, this was triggered by a request for repairs to the kirk and manse, but the tensions that it revealed perhaps indicate why parochial visitations were abandoned, giving some credence to Graham's claim about the opportunity they gave to malcontents to stir up trouble. In the case of Kilwinning the malcontent was the wright James Leitch, who gave a paper detailing a number of alleged infractions by the minister, Mr Ferguson, culminating in the question, 'if he had not Called some of his parishioners confounded Villains or damned confounded Villains and rascals'.[62] Ferguson responded to these charges and argued that their underlying cause was that Leitch had been summoned before the session for failing to pay for the use of the mortcloth at the funeral of his first wife and two children. However, the proceedings suggest that there were other tensions in the parish. One was the objection of some of the smaller heritors, with Leitch among their number, about paying for repairs to the manse and church, arguing:

> as ye Bells and Area of the Church belongs to ye Heritors, that ye money arising from the Seats and ringing of the Bells at funerals must be applied for Reparation of the Church agreeable to Sundry Decisions of the Court of Session.[63]

It would appear that Leitch, who was, Ferguson alleged, 'well known to ye place where he lives & the people he has dealings with to be of a pleasome and revengeful Disposition', was a 'front man' for one of the heritors, Smithstoun, with much of the opposition come from those on his lands.[64] Further, the parish was also home to a number of Seceders, against whom the minister had written in a number of publications. The visitation was carried out in April 1742, but the affair rumbled on for two years. The following year, 1743, saw Leitch appealing to the synod and when this was rejected, proposing a list of 190 witnesses to prove a revised case before the presbytery.[65] Another failed appeal to the synod in 1744 was followed by an appeal to the commission of the General Assembly.[66] When this was in turn rejected in June 1744 the presbytery reaffirmed their previous decision, 'because ye affair has made a great deal of Noise in the Neighbourhood, ... that a short Abstract of this be intimated from all the pulpits in this presby'.[67] This was done, although Leitch did not turn up for his public rebuke in his home church. The affair blew over, but at the cost of considerable debate in the parish and considerable time in the presbytery. Perhaps because it reached national level as an example of how much disruption a determined individual could cause, it contributed to the demise of parochial visitations. At all events, it appears to have been the last carried out under the terms of the *Overtures*.

The experience of Kilwinning and some of the other visitations certainly lends support to Graham's contention that visitations stirred up more trouble than the value they gave. However, an alternative interpretation of their gradual demise could see them as having served their primary purpose. If that purpose is seen as the imposition of orderly Presbyterian government and, especially, the creation of a disciplined ministerial cadre, then it is arguable that the early years of the eighteenth century, when visitations were at their peak, saw a measure of success. This was reinforced by the association of Episcopalianism with the failed Jacobite rising of 1715, which dealt a fatal blow to the main rival to the form of Presbyterian church polity reestablished in 1690.[68] Such an interpretation can be accorded more weight when we see that visitations were not the only means of exercising presbyterial discipline over parishes. The consideration of privy censures and record revision that follows below lends support to this argument. It could be argued that once the first flush of enthusiasm and disciplinary labour was over that less expensive means of monitoring, in terms of the time spent on it by the presbytery, won favour. We have seen in the case of Kells at the opening of this chapter how much time was consumed by what would appear to be routine business. That is to discount the impact of disputed patronage cases, which could drag on for years. To conduct a visitation on the lines envisaged by the *Overtures* would take a full day, to say nothing of the follow-up actions. We have seen that the notion of the regular visitation of every parish in a presbytery was simply wishful thinking and that even the most determined presbytery could not aspire to it. The framers of the guidance simply failed to take into account the sheer press of business, imagining a system without recalcitrant heritors and ministers without human failings.

Monitoring sessions at a distance

However, the *Overtures* envisaged other means of imposing discipline and over time these came to be more important than visitations. One key mechanism was that of the 'privy censure'. This was expected to be held at both presbytery and session, although it was adhered to more rigorously at presbyterial level. Here the 1704 *Overtures* expected the presbytery to meet for prayer and collective examination twice a year. In this process,

> each of the brethren, one after another, are to be removed, and but one at once; and the Moderator is to inquire the judgment of each member, and to take their report of their brother's carriage and behaviour, either in relation to his charge or otherwise, according to the trial at the visitation of the parishes by the Presbytery, and then he is to be called in, encouraged, commended, or reprehended, as they see fit, and he set in his place again.[69]

We can see here that the censure was expected to articulate with regular visitations. However, while the demise of parochial visitations might have upset this articulation, privy censures at the presbytery endured and were to be found occurring on a regular basis in all presbyteries. The form of recording is often brief and bland, with no indication of the nature and form of questioning. This is not always the case: occasionally dissent broke out. So, for example, in April 1740 in the privy censures of the presbytery of Duns, one minister was asked to explain why he had not attended the presbytery for a whole year, thus missing two diets of privy censures. Although they did not accept his excuse, they proceeded to remove him, recording that 'the Opinions of the Several Brethren with respect to him being asked they found nothing Censurable in his Conduct except what related to his Session book and his long absence from the Presbytery'.[70] Most sessions did not give any detail of the questions, but at the back of the presbytery book of Cupar for 1723–30 were noted a list of seventeen questions to be asked of ministers at privy censures.[71] Mapping of these onto the 1704 *Overtures*, as displayed in Appendix 5, indicates a considerable alignment with the questions proposed there, suggesting that this emerged as an alternative to the direct inspection of the parish. Of course, direct questioning about the conduct of the minister was redundant here, but no doubt this was supplied by his peers. Two questions, about possession of the Acts of Assembly and of a schoolmaster, mirrored aspects of the visitation process. Only two questions, those about papists in the parish and the observation of fasts, were novel. However, the formulation of the question about doctrine ('Are you careful to hold fast the form of sound words, and avoid novelties in Doctrine?') indicates a certain consolidation if not sclerosis of practice. That other presbyteries also used privy censures in this manner is suggested by a discussion of the frequency of communion in the presbytery of Dumbarton in March 1740; reasons were given for its celebration only once every two years in the Highland parishes of the district.[72] This evolution of the privy censure beyond a focus on individual conduct and belief marks a response to the impracticality of direct visitations.

Another mechanism that complemented the questioning in the privy censure was the scrutiny of the written record. We have seen the attention paid in the guidance, building on years of prior experience, to the form of recording of decisions. This was intended, in part, to facilitate the review of actions. Thus the 1704 *Overtures* lay down a whole set of practices built around the availability of records for review. At the General Assembly there was a specific committee for revising synod books, as well as the proceedings of the commission that acted between meetings. They were to check that synods had carried out one of their duties in examining presbytery books. Further Acts were passed by the Assembly in 1713 and 1723 specifying what the 'visitors' of synod books should be looking for. This was much concerned with whether other Acts had been put into practice and observed. In 1713 this included the need to check 'if Presbytery books be punctually produced, revised, and attested'.[73] A whole section in the 1704 *Overtures* was devoted to the way in which this duty ought to be carried out by synods. Again, it was to be done by a committee composed of four or five ministers and one or two elders. They were to examine the book since its last review and, if they found anything amiss, to consult the moderator of the presbytery before reporting their findings. They were not just 'to notice what they think amiss in any of their proceedings recorded, and that whether as to matter or form, but likewise to see if everything proper and fit to have been recorded be there exactly set down'. Their findings were then to be discussed with members of the presbytery and the final report to be engrossed in the presbytery's register.[74] A similar mechanism for the regular scrutiny of session registers aside from visitations was not laid down. However, as we have seen, regular visitations proved impossible and even in those that occurred, the production of session registers for review was patchy. The sample of presbytery records examined for visitations revealed very few *completed* revisions of session registers. The emphasis on completion here is important; as will be discussed below, a lack of completed revisions does not mean a lack of effort. However, here we can also bring in the other side of the coin, because session registers themselves bear the marks of revision. Accordingly, the account that follows draws on both the sampled presbytery records and those parish records that were examined.

Presbyterial registers bear ample evidence of inspection by the synod, with attestations that in the early years of the century in particular show a willingness to correct presbyterial conduct that mirrored interventions in parishes. In some cases this was to do with the form of the record, reinforcing some of the injunctions that we have seen before and so acting as a model for parochial inspections. Thus in 1709 the synod of Fife was broadly satisfied with the presbytery book of Kirkcaldy, but ordered them in future to 'cause their Clerk forbear making Contractions or figures in the Registers'.[75] In the following year the presbytery of Dunbar were to explain interlinings, while the same synod of Lothian expressed its exasperation with the register of Haddington in 1734 finding it, 'exceedingly ill written and desired the modr to recommend it to the pby of Haddington to take care for the future that their Register be written more exactly and in a fairer hand'.[76] The sharpest comment on form, also in Lothian, was that made in the register of Linlithgow in 1720, where the synod:

> declared the blotting out anything in a register after it is approven by the Synod wholly ane unwarrantable and justly censurable practice and appointed the moderator to admonish the said presbytery for obliterating three lines in their register.[77]

Such a comment revealed an ongoing tension between the synod and the presbytery, which is perhaps a precursor to the bitter dispute that was to erupt in 1749 over the presentation of a minister at Torpichen. Here the presbytery refused to settle a minister against the significant opposition of the congregation, and suffered censure at the hands of the Assembly as a result.[78] It may be that earlier disagreements, expressed in attestations on the presbytery's records, had shaped long-term attitudes. The synod found four reasons, besides the form of the records, to object to them. These centred on the way that the presbytery had handled a dispute in Queensferry. In particular they ordered the presbytery to 'enquire into the reasons of Mr Kid's absenting himself so long from the Presbytery and to record the reasons given by him'. Kid was one of those who, the following year, objected to the Assembly's condemnation of the contentious *Marrow of Modern Divinity*. Although he was associated with seceding ministers, Kid himself remained in the church.[79] The power of revision of records was used here to carry the weight of orthodox authority, as in the following year the synod refused to accept the reasons recorded by the presbytery and ordered their clerk to attest the register, 'with this advice that they mark and judge of the reasons given by any Brother why he does not dispense the sacrament of the Lords Supper in his own congregation at least once in the year and to record their diligence'.[80] That such attestations were considered to be weighty matters can be seen in the response of the Haddington presbytery to comments in the synod's minutes in 1735, which censured them for not contributing their share to a bursary to support students intended for service in Lithuania. They recorded that they 'are sorry to find their Deficiency represented in such strong terms', given that only three parishes were at fault and that they had always used their best efforts to secure prompt compliance. They therefore considered it a 'hard censure' for their book to be censured, 'for not doing what they judge impracticable by them'.[81] Most attestations of presbytery books do not bear such censures, but it is clear that they were both a significant means of imposing discipline and one taken very seriously. In this way these attestations set the pattern for presbyterial revisions, which could be equally as sharp and demanding.

However, unlike synodial inspections, which worked to an annual timetable and dealt with smaller numbers of records, presbyterial revisions were much more infrequent. It was not that there were no attempts to establish regular cycles of inspection. In December 1710, the session registers of Bonill and Kilmaronock were brought in for revision to the presbytery of Dumbarton, which 'renews the appointment upon the rest of the Brethren who have not yet brought in their Session books, that they bring ym in the next Presbytery'.[82] This suggests a scheme like that envisaged in Edinburgh in the same year, where it was ordered 'that yearly in all times coming The Minister of each parish present their session register to the presbytery at their first meeting in November Yearly that the same may be visited'.[83] However, despite urgings, this was not completely successful, as in 1730 the same presbytery recorded that the 'visitors of Session Books being desired to make their Report, it was found that none of them were ready'.[84] That registers were expected to be made available for inspection on a regular basis is indicated by the decision of the session of Abercorn session in 1721 that 'a leather wallet to be got for carrying of the said Register that it may not be spoiled when it is carried to the Presbytery'.[85] This seems to suggest both something of the expected process and the importance with which written records were regarded. Efforts continued to establish a regular process elsewhere, with the presbytery of Ayr resolving in 1750 that they were 'at next meeting ... to Appoint a Diet for Considering the Separate Registers'.[86] However this initiative, like the others, appeared to have foundered, and the references to session registers being revised present no coherent pattern, either in presbyterial records or in the session registers themselves. Some revisions followed from visitations where, as we have seen, registers were often produced for subsequent revision. In September 1730 the presbytery of Ayr passed a favourable report on the register of Old Cumnock, the parish they had visited in August. This covered the years 1716 to 1727. A report on the Straiton register in the same presbytery covered the years 1727 to 1729.[87] In 1719 the revisors of Bolton registers in Haddington covered the years 1707 to 1718, while a committee to examine the records of Falkirk in 1740 found that there had been no attestation since 1706.[88] While there was clearly a desire to check records, in practice the fulfilment of this desire was patchy.

One example indicating the problems that presbyteries could face was the experience of the presbytery of Cupar in trying to revise the session register of Abdie. In 1713 their registers indicated that legal action had been taken against the minister there to recover money that the heritors had paid for the bread and wine for the communion in years when it was not celebrated. This suggested considerable dereliction of duty on the part of the minister, John Carsan, and they called for the registers to check. In March of the following year these were finally made available but Carsan, not a regular attender at presbytery, begged for time to consider his answers. Two weeks later the clerk reported that he had delivered a copy of the presbytery's comments to him, but that he had a written response, 'that being oblidged to be for sometime from home, he had not got his answers yet in readiness'. In exasperation the presbytery ordered him to give his answers at their next meeting, but the press of business meant that the matter was adjourned. Carsan then failed to turn up despite his excuses being rejected. It was not until March 1715 that the presbytery was able to record its decision that, 'considering the manifold faults, defects and imperfections of the book, they unanimously were of opinion that it should be transcribed, and accordingly appointed him to transcribe the same'. In January of the following year the minutes record a process to be started against Carsan, but then his death put an end to the matter.[89] Perhaps not surprisingly the synod attested this section of the register with the advice that session books should be revised without undue delay.[90] However, one can sympathise with a presbytery faced with a recalcitrant minister, for a similar story of prevarications and delays in producing books could be told in presbyteries such as Dunbar (Prestonkirk, February 1720–June 1721), Duns (Greenlaw, October 1710–April 1712) and Hamilton (Bothwell, 27 March 1750–January 1752).[91]

When the registers *were* revised, presbyteries were critical of the way in which they had been kept. An extreme example of their displeasure can be seen in the report on the register of Kinfauns by the presbytery of Perth in 1710, which found it:

> to be very unfavourably and insufficiently Clerked, there being may words ill spelled, instances whereof were read before the presbyterie, the book not sufficiently margined, the minutes for the most part being too curtly marked and not so extended as the matters contained therein can be understood: the several affairs transacted in the Session thrown together in a confused manner and not distinguished by paragraphs[.]

They were so exasperated at the standard of record keeping that their censure of the session clerk was not only recorded in the minutes but also publicly read before the congregation, 'these affairs having made so much noise in the paroch'.[92] While this was the worst case of deficiencies in the format of minutes that the sampling indicated, there were other examples that saw presbyteries seeking to ensure conformity to the injunctions contained in the

Overtures. So the session at South Leith was to keep a strict order of business and to ensure that their register had margins.[93] This seemingly trivial matter of format was also picked up by the presbytery of Cupar when the session of Dunbog was 'to leave a large Margent and that every particular be marked there'.[94] Here it is clear the purpose was the better ordering of minutes so that items could be clearly identified from the index maintained in the margin. Here, also, and at Logie in the same presbytery and year, we see the clerk being enjoined, 'in time coming to write the Discipline and accompts of the poors money in two Distinct books'.[95] This will be of some relevance in a later chapter. What these examples indicate is that presbyteries were concerned to enforce some uniformity in the keeping of records.

Formalisation of the letter; relaxation of the spirit

Often their injunctions are hidden from view by a formulation like that in Midcalder in 1710: 'all other things of lesser moment, the same was to be verbally represented to the Minister'.[96] This occurs frequently in minutes, from synod down to session, where advice and instruction on the keeping of records was given clearly in verbal form. One chance insight into such matters is given by the survival of a set of working notes, written in small script on scraps of paper, bound into the session register of Dailly in the presbytery of Ayr.[97] Although the result of the visitation in 1733 is not recorded (and the minutes of presbytery are missing for the period) it clearly represents the thinking of those charged with revising session registers. The writer of the notes picked up forty-three separate items of concern, all carefully cross-referenced with the pages of the register. He found fourteen cases where the sederunt (that is, the record of attendance) had not been recorded and a further three where the session did not either open or close with prayer. In other words, these were matters of very detailed recording, as opposed to matters of principle, and one gets the impression of a very pernickety reviser. At one point, for example, it was observed that two elders were ordained without an edict being moved, but when one turns to the minutes it is found that the edict had been served and recorded previously. The same obtains when four examples were picked up where communion had been intimated but without any record that it had been celebrated. In a further eight cases the reviser was concerned that sentences of discipline being satisfied were recorded without a session being constituted, although it would appear that this was often simply a record of the completion of a previously recorded decision. This level of attention to detail suggests something of what lay behind the bland notes about verbal representations. The revision of records, that is, could be a very thoroughgoing process that must have played a part in engendering a particular style of record keeping, which was almost obsessive in its attention to detail.

The presbytery of Ayr was not alone in attention to such matters. The first two recommendations of the revision of the register of Kirkliston in Linlithgow in 1707 were that it should always record that meetings were closed with prayer and that 'the whole Elders names present at every Sederunt be marked and that absents be also marked and their excuses called for at the next meeting of the Session'.[98] The injunctions that nothing be recorded without a properly constituted session is found in the attestation of Midcalder in 1710, as is the injunction 'that their Register always bear the time when the Sacrament of the Lords Supper is celebrated in their paroch'.[99] Although it is a subjective judgement, and one that would require the transcription of a large number of records to test adequately, the inspection of a large number of records does suggest that, in terms of the form of the records, there was steady improvement in attention to such details.

The increasing formality, of course, could accompany a relaxation in the spirit of discipline. There is a distinct sense of relaxation at all levels in the detail of the disciplinary process across the second half of the century. Although the disputes between the Moderates and the Popular Party have often been cast in terms of theological disputes, McIntosh has shown that such disagreements can often be exaggerated. Rather, the concern of the Moderates with the imposition of a form of hierarchical church discipline conflicted with broadly held views of a more lateral form of discipline.[100] What also seems clear is that the rise of the Moderates coincided with a general decline in the exercise of discipline at the national and regional levels.

One index of this is the attestation of synod books by the committee of the Assembly. Table 3.3 shows the number of presbytery books attested by three synods in the second half of the century.

Table 3.3 Attestation of presbytery books in three synods, 1750–90

	1750	1760	1770	1780	1790
Aberdeen	n.a.	2	3	1	2
Glasgow and Ayr	3	1	3	n.a.	n.a.
Lothian and Tweeddale	7	4	2	1	3

Source: Synod minutes.
Note: n.a. = Data not available.

As well as showing the withering of the practice, it is also remarkable to note that the synod books both of Glasgow and Ayr and of Lothian and Tweeddale bore the same attestation in 1750 despite their manifestly different performance in one of their key tasks.[101] As the century progressed the process of attestation at this level took on more of a ritual character. Something of this can be seen if we examine the patterns of meetings and records of presbyteries. In Chapter 2 we saw something of the volume of records.

Taking the exercise, with all its limitations, down to the level of presbytery records shows the pattern indicated in Table 3.4.

Table 3.4 Average length in pages of presbyterial records by decade and quarter-century

	Ayr	Garioch	Haddington	Hamilton	Linlithgow
Decade ending					
1710	12.2	43.1	28.9	26.5	54.1
1720	n.a.	39.8	27.4	17.4	83.2
1730	n.a.	36.5	39.2	18.3	50.7
1740	10.2	31.5	18.3	16.2	35.4
1750	4.9	24.0	15.1	14.5	43.2
1760	6.1	18.0	8.2	9.9	13.2
1770	13.5	15.2	5.6	12.4	10.4
1780	26.5	10.1	14.2	10.1	5.9
1790	34.8	7.6	2.5	22.8	12.1
1800	n.a.	26.3	9.5	15.8	26.2
Quarter-century ending					
1724	n.a.	40.3	28.8	21.3	66.4
1750	7.4	29.4	22.8	15.9	40.2
1774	12.8	15.4	10.4	11.4	10.1
1799	33.1	15.5	5.6	15.6	17.0

Source: Calculated from NRS catalogue CH2 Church of Scotland.
Note: n.a. = Data not available.

Table 3.4 indicates the average number of pages, as recorded on the electronic catalogue of the National Records of Scotland (NRS), for each of the selected presbyteries, by decade and quarter-century. It shows clearly the contraction in presbytery minutes, especially in the two eastern presbyteries. Table 3.5 shows the frequency of meetings for these presbyteries in the second half of the century. (The meetings include ordinations as well as ordinary meetings, hence in some cases being more than one per month.) While they show a slight reduction in the eastern presbyteries, these figures do tend to suggest a reduction in the business conducted at these meetings, confirming the impression that to a large extent many of these meetings had become rather bureaucratic and ritualistic.

It was not, however, that the traditions of systemic discipline had disappeared, rather that they had become both attenuated and a little different in character. While, for example, the synod of Aberdeen only had one presbytery book, that of Fordyce, to consider at its April 1790 sitting, its verdict did not pull its punches. It was, said, the visitors, full of 'many inaccuracies & ill

Table 3.5 Frequency of meetings of selected presbyteries

	1750	1760	1770	1780	1790
Ayr	8	6	9	8	7
Garioch	7	6	8	4	8
Haddington	12	12	15	8	10
Hamilton	10	8	9	n.a.	10
Linlithgow	13	14	10	8	10

Source: Presbytery minutes.
Note: n.a. = Data not available.

spelling. Find several blanks, particularly some papers of importance omitted which ought to have been recorded'. They ordered the presbytery 'to be more attentive to their Registers in times to come & to fill it up frequently and send it to the Synod as being not only the duty of the Presbytery, but as necessary for the wellbeing and faith of their Register'.[102] The expectations of detailed and careful record keeping, that is, had not changed, but the systematic inspection to see that it occurred had. Thanks to a Victorian indexer it is easy to see that revisions of session registers continued, if sporadically, in the presbytery of the Garioch. Its registers were themselves attested by the synod in 1760, 1761, 1763, 1766, 1770, 1775 and 1786, testifying to some degree of scrutiny.[103] It examined a number of session registers during the period: Meldrum, Kintore and Keithhall in 1763, Rayne in 1767, Culsalmond in 1770, Oyne in 1783 and Monymusk in 1787. In most of these cases the revisers were satisfied and the books approved, but in the case of Oyne:

> instead of a Register they had only got confused minutes, & it is recommended to Mr Morison to get a proper book, & see there be entered into it all the transactions of the Session & the state of their funds &c in a regular form.[104]

Monymusk we will visit again, as it is an example of what seems to have emerged after the end of attempts at systematic and consistent inspections: the drawing on church procedure to tackle special cases.

Such tactical scrutiny was not restricted to the Garioch. One example was the detailed inspection of the session registers, and especially the accounts, of Cambuslang by the presbytery of Hamilton in 1749.[105] This was triggered by ongoing tensions in the parish, which will crop up again when we consider accounting for the poor in a subsequent chapter. However, this was not an isolated event, for in 1775 the register of the same parish was attested by a committee of the presbytery who found that, while generally satisfactory, 'they should balance their accounts at least once every year'.[106] This focus on specific parishes also seems to be found in the Linlithgow presbytery. In 1740 a committee had inspected the registers of Falkirk and, while it found nothing wrong with their proceedings, concluded that they had continued to use the poor's money for repairs of the church and manse, despite having been told (as attested in their register) not to do this at a previous visitation. They were instructed to pursue the heritors for reimbursement, but this evidently did not happen. In 1750 a visitation to clarify the status of the minister's glebe and the state of repair of the church had tacked on to it elements familiar from parochial visitations. Shorn of the focus on the conduct of ministers and elders, this centred on the review of the session's registers, where the presbytery's strong disapproval of their failure to recover the money they had spent was recorded.[107] Although not part of a full parochial visitation, this showed how presbyteries could draw selectively upon the traditions of inspection that accompanied it.

This chapter has examined the context in which parochial governance took place. It indicates a considerable gap between the injunctions laid down in the nationally approved guidance and what took place in practice. In particular, it indicates that Pardovan's *Observations* are a poor guide to practice. His fervent injunctions about ministerial conduct are of interest in indicating the particular suspicions of devout laymen about the potential emergence of a priestly caste. His rather fervid concerns about the human frailties of ministers are given a little credence by the problems with ministers that visitations revealed at the beginning of the century. Such visitations may have played a role in the emergence of a rather more disciplined cadre of ministers, although improvements in educational qualifications are likely to have played a considerable part. Such improvements may in turn have led to the relative demise of some of the more intrusive forms of inquiry, as ministers became less willing to subject themselves and their peers to the scrutiny of laypeople, often those with an axe to grind. The problems that this might cause were clearly displayed in the bitter experience of the presbytery of Irvine at Kilwinning, where it took several years to recover from the aftermath of a visitation. At all events, such visitations faded from sight at mid-century. They were replaced to some degree by a rather more concealed form of scrutiny, one that rested on the questioning of ministers by their peers in privy censures. Such questioning could be supported if needed by the selective use of powers to inspect records.

The second half of the eighteenth century saw a distinct decline in the formal systems of governance operating at national and regional level. The inspection and attestation of records continued but developed a somewhat ritualistic quality. However, just because the system became attenuated and failed to live up to the high expectations of the framers of the *Overtures* does not mean that it was a complete failure. Although it is difficult to provide a measure, it does appear that the general standard of record keeping improved over the course of the century. It could be argued that the visitations had tackled some of the major problems that the kirk faced after the settlement of 1690. Functioning sessions had been established across the Lowlands, and the estate of the church considerably improved. Above all, a functioning system of governance at local level had been established and its operation is the subject of the next chapter.

CHAPTER 4

The Kirk Session

O Lord, Thou kens what zeal I bear,
When drinkers drink, an' swearers swear,
An' singing here, an' dancin there,
Wi' great and sma';
For I am keepit by Thy fear
Free frae them a'.

But yet, O Lord! confess I must,
At times I'm fash'd wi' fleshly lust:
An' sometimes, too, in worldly trust,
Vile self gets in;
But Thou remembers we are dust,
Defil'd wi' sin.

O Lord! yestreen, Thou kens, wi' Meg
Thy pardon I sincerely beg;
O may't ne'er be a livin' plague
To my dishonour,
An' I'll ne'er lift a lawless leg
Again upon her.[1]

Robert Burns' satire in 'Holy Willie's Prayer' on the sanctimonious church elder, modelled on Willie Fisher of Mauchline, is a classic puncturing of the pretensions of the religiously self-righteous. It is a trope that endures. In his Lewis trilogy the crime writer Peter May has his hero Fin McCleod denounce the hypocrisy of a Free Church investigation committee as 'a bunch of Holy Willies pour[ing] out bile in the guise of piety'.[2] Images of the church elder in paintings give priority to grave seriousness, making the kirk session a feared body. The connection of the session with the prosecution of sin, especially sin of a sexual nature, has understandably coloured both the popular imagination and the historical record. This has meant that we have relatively little on how such bodies were run in the eighteenth century. This chapter gives some details on the composition and governance practices of the eighteenth-century church at parish level. It starts by considering some key positions on the session – minister, session clerk, elder and deacon – considering in turn their selection and key attributes. It then considers the nature of the business they conducted, with a particular focus on the record-keeping practices that it entailed.

Ministers

The reason for starting with the minister rather than the elders is that meetings of the session could not occur with his acting as moderator. He was, in the words of the 1704 *Overtures*, 'Moderator ex officio, and constant out of necessity'.[3] This could cause some problems when there was a long gap between ministers, which was often occasioned by disputes over suitable candidates. We have seen in the previous chapter how long it took for the various parties in Kells to settle on a minister, which meant that the parish was without a settled minister for over two years. In the interim, given that sessions were responsible for the distribution of poor relief, resort was had to supplies organised by the presbytery. Ministers for neighbouring parishes would be instructed to convene meetings of session to ensure at least a small measure of continuity of parish administration. This need for the minister to chair all meetings could also cause problems with ministers who were absent from their duties. We have seen the value attached to the minister being 'at home in his ministerial work' in the visitation questions. While ministers could be called away to assist other ministers at the sacrament of communion, to cover vacant posts, or to attend church meetings, the real target here was those ministers with competing activities, such as the farming of the minister of Lundie.

However, what one notes from the records as being the major problem in practice was the fact that ministers remained in office until they died. Many who were incapable through infirmity refused to give up office or seek assistance without a struggle – and certainly not without arrangements to preserve their stipend, at least in part, if a helper were appointed. In 1740, for example, Robert Kirkland of Dalton, having served as minister for over twenty-four years sought to demit office, 'being now through age and Infirmity, and because of the Distance of the Manse from the Kirk, unable to continue any longer in it as Minister of the said Paroch'. However, he sought to obtain a small annuity to support him 'during the short time I expect to live'.[4] This could mean that ministers both served extensive periods of office, often in one parish, and were a considerable age when they left office. The *Statistical Account* for the Aberdeenshire parish of Daviot proudly recorded that:

> The late incumbent at Daviot was about 56 years minister. At the time he was 50 years minister of this parish, there were four elder members in the presbytery of Garioch, the eldest of whom was in the 61st year of his ministry, and other two lived till they were 60 years ministers of the Established church. It is strong evidence of the healthy climate of the Garioch, that out of 15 members of presbytery, the 5 oldest upon the roll lived to be all of them nearly, and some of them above 60 years ministers, and from 80 to 90 years old.[5]

As it was ministers who set the tone for the governance of the parish and as they might have been a constant feature of the parish for significant periods, it is worth considering some of the characteristics of their service in a little more detail. This was not a Congregationalist system, although elements of the congregation had some voice in church affairs. It was not that the minister did not have to balance contending forces, as we shall see. However, without the minister those contending forces had limited means of expression within the confines of church polity. The tremendous achievement that is the *Fasti Ecclesiae Scoticanae* enables us to draw out some features of the ministerial cadre. Started by the Reverend Hew Scott, minister of Anstruther West, in 1866, these six volumes (with subsequent updates) give, synod by synod, biographical details of all the ministers who served the church. It contains details such as the date of ordination and, with progressively more detail as records improved with time, education and other matters. This source enables us to conduct a prosopography of the ministerial cadre of the five presbyteries that have been our detailed focus, enabling the calculation of, for example, average lengths of service. Table 4.1 indicates the maximum numbers of years served in a single parish, the average length of service in a parish and the median number of minsters who might serve a parish.

Table 4.1 Length in pages of ministerial service in selected presbyteries

	Max. years	Average years	Median number of ministers
Ayr	69	26.5	4
Garioch	60	20.9	5
Haddington	63	24.1	4
Hamilton	63	25.7	5
Linlithgow	69	26.5	4

Source: *Fasti Ecclesiae Scoticanae.*

These figures suggest that in most parishes several generations might grow to maturity under the aegis of a single minister.

Table 4.2 shows the reasons given for ministers finishing a term of office, confirming the extent to which ministers died in office.

Ministers could, of course, move between parishes by being called and 'transported', subject to presbyterial approval. The Garioch contained two parishes, Keithhall and Kemnay, which both exhibited numbers of ministers serving short terms before moving on, meaning that these parishes had six and seven ministers respectively during the century, one, in Kemnay, serving only two years. However, such high turnover was relatively infrequent except in some particularly unfortunate parishes. The norm was for ministers to serve for long periods. The figures for those who demitted office cover two categories: those who retired of their own volition and those who were

Table 4.2 Reasons for leaving ministerial office

	Died	Demitted	Transported
Ayr	76.8	5.4	17.9
Garioch	60.5	3.7	35.8
Haddington	74.0	11.0	15.1
Hamilton	61.6	6.8	31.5
Linlithgow	81.4	1.4	17.1

Source: Fasti Ecclesiae Scoticanae.

deposed. It was unusual for ministers to be deposed, with the figures for demission being inflated by five (including all those deposed in the Garioch) who were connected with Episcopalianism. So for example the opportunity was taken after the failure of the rising of 1715 to remove from office the ministers of Daviot and Inverurie, whose loyalty to the Hanoverian regime was called into question by their actions. The numbers are also inflated by those who moved to new positions connected with but not in the ministry: one to London and three to academic positions at St Andrews. One demission that blurred the lines and achieved some notoriety was that of John Home, minister of Athelstaneford and author of the controversial play *Douglas*. After its stage production in Edinburgh in 1757 the very association of a minister with the theatre drew sharp condemnation from many ministers. Home demitted office before a libel could be served against him. From the data given in the *Fasti*, only five of the twenty-three ministers were removed because of doubts about their conduct. Two retired because of the infirmities of old age, the minister of New Cumnock being ninety-seven when he demitted office in 1757.

What this longevity of office meant was that opportunities for the ordination of new candidates could be relatively few. Ordination, where the presbytery attended the parish and presented the candidate to the congregation, having previously served an edit and solicited any objections, was the formal induction of the candidate to the ministry (in the case of a probationer), the parish and the presbytery. It was also an opportunity to take stock of the state of the parish. This practice, at least, was consistently exercised in the presbytery of Ayr from ordinations recorded in 1770. At the ordination of James Wright at Maybole in November 1770 the members of presbytery sat down with the session and heritors and ascertained:

> [that] the state of the Session being asked it was answered there were 10 Elders, being asked if there was a Decreet of Locality, it was answered in the affirmative. There is a Schoolmaster whose salary is 300 merks and the Poors funds amount to 1400 merks. As to the Manse and office houses, there is reason to believe they are all in reasonable repair.[6]

Similar results are recorded at ordinations in 1780 and 1790. This practice does not appear in the earlier records of ordinations, either in this presbytery or in the others examined.

Although ministers were expected to have a university education, many, especially before the final quarter of the century, did not formally graduate.[7] The data in the *Fasti* indicate that 70 per cent of ministers in the five presbyteries possessed a degree. Table 4.3 shows the universities that prepared these 291 ministers for their labours.

Table 4.3 Universities for those ministers recorded with degrees

	Glasgow	Edinburgh	St Andrews	King's	Marischal
Presbytery	%	%	%	%	%
Ayr	60.0	28.0	9.3	0.0	2.7
Garioch	1.5	0.0	1.5	38.2	58.8
Haddington	22.0	62.0	8.0	6.0	2.0
Hamilton	73.0	22.2	0.0	3.2	1.6
Linlithgow	45.7	40.0	5.7	0.0	8.6

Source: Fasti Ecclesiae Scoticanae.

These figures indicate the virtual autarky of the hinterlands of Aberdeen, with very low levels of infiltration from south of the Mounth. There is much more interchange between the universities of Edinburgh and Glasgow in the central belt, but there remains a strong affinity between these universities and the presbyteries in their hinterlands. The nature of the education that these ministers experienced evolved in both form and content over the century. At the outset, university education was conducted by regents: men who took a whole class for all their subjects throughout a four-year degree. The shift to more specialised pedagogy, shaped by the experience of many in the Dutch university system, came with the reforms carried out by Carstares at Edinburgh. This was followed by Glasgow soon afterwards, but not at Marischal until 1753 and King's until the very end of the century.[8] The shift meant the introduction of more specialist topics into the curriculum, such as the moral philosophy of first Francis Hutcheson and then Adam Smith at Glasgow. These institutions tended towards a less conservative approach. However, much of the preparation of ministers was devoted to a rather scholastic acquisition of ancient languages and an adherence to a literal view of scriptural authority. The sermons they produced were focused on the exposition of this authority, rather than on moral precepts. The military engineer Burt, writing of his time in Scotland in the 1720s, observed:

> the subjects of their sermons are, for the most part, grace, freewill,

predestination, and other topics hardly ever to be determined; they might as well talk Hebrew to the common people, and I think to anybody else.[9]

Sermons took a passage of Scripture, broke it down into a number of heads and lectured on these at great length.[10] In 1707, reported Edgar, the parishioners of Craigie complained that their minister, 'doth often change his text, and doth not raise many heads'.[11] The conservatism of the early years, that is, rested not only with ministers, but, as we will see, was often a feature of their flocks.

This adherence to the strict authority of Scripture was shared by Pardovan, whose stern words on the subject of church governance were frequently interlaced with biblical authorities. However, part of his concern was that the inspiration of the scriptures for the right governance of the kirk might not find its way into the curriculum. Worried that the rules for proceeding lay scattered in a number of sources, his aim was to bring them together in one compendium, which:

> [he] humbly offered, to be recommended by professors to their students: For, except this subject be studied and understood by ministers and elders, their memories may well be burdened with their duty, but their judgements, till then, shall still remain ignorant and unsatisfied about it.[12]

The degree to which this was done by the universities is not clear, although his book was frequently used as an authority by Edgar, writing in the late nineteenth century.[13] Indeed in 1929 Clark, in his *History of Church Discipline in Scotland*, referred to his work as 'perhaps the greatest authority on early Scottish standards'.[14] While his book went through several editions in the eighteenth century, views on the scriptural basis of church polity began to shift under the weight of the new biblical criticism. Thus the influential George Campbell at Aberdeen prepared his course of lectures on ecclesiastical history for his students in order to express his scepticism about the strict scriptural warrant for any form of church polity, while still adhering to the virtues of the Presbyterian system. In particular, argues Suderman, 'the appropriate function of the church, said Campbell, is the discipline of its own members, particularly its ministers – a discipline which he believed was too relaxed in the Scotland of his day'.[15] So the focus on the overall system of governance evolved from one based on strict scriptural warrant to one based on broader foundations, but the focus on discipline endured.

The Session Clerk

This educational experience, together with the management of the session, was increasingly shared with the session clerk. The clerk was to be, held the *Overtures* of 1696:

a person of a Christian Walk and Conversation, of entire Credit and reputation
for Fidelity, of Prudence, and able to keep the secrets of the Judicatory; of
competent Ability and Dexterity, a good hand of his own writing, his Records
being to be preserved for after-Ages.[16]

Such a person was conventionally found in the form of the parish schoolmaster. With the expansion of university education over the century, many
were divinity students waiting for a ministerial opportunity. Their career
paths can be illustrated by two individual experiences, both in the Garioch,
gleaned from the pages of the *Fasti*. Thomas Tait was born in the parish of
Chapel of Garioch and became its schoolmaster in 1763.[17] In the presbytery
minutes for 1767 we learn that he 'had for several sessions been attending the
Lessons of Divinity at Aberdeen'. Following the receipt of testimonials from
the professors of divinity of 'his good behaviour & proficiency in his Studies',
they agreed to recommend to the synod to put him on trials for being licensed
to preach.[18] It would appear that by then he had left the school, but what he
did in the interval before being ordained to the second charge at Old Machar
in Aberdeen in 1774 is not clear. Perhaps it was connected to his presentation
to that charge by the Earl of Fife, for the same very influential landowner
also presented him to his next living, that of Auchindoir in 1780 in the presbytery of Alford. He served here for four years before being translated to
Meldrum under the patronage this time of the Urquhart family. After
fourteen years, during which he authored the *Statistical Account* of the parish,
he moved once more and for the final time to the parish of Ellon, where he
died in the pulpit in 1810. He had married the daughter of the minister of
Cabrach in 1789. He appeared prosperous enough at his death to leave behind
not only the mahogany furniture of the manse but also the stock of his farm
at Loch Hills.[19] His career thus nicely illustrates something of the nature of
the ministry of the time, as well as the trajectory from schoolmaster to
minister, which many would aspire to. The second is that of Robert Lessel,
born fifteen years after Tait in 1758, son of a crofter in Kintore. Educated at
Marishal College, he worked on the family croft in the vacations. After
receiving his MA in 1779 he took up a number of schoolmaster's posts in
Inverurie, Grange and Chapel of Garioch (in the last of which he definitely
acted as session clerk). Although licensed by the presbytery of Strathbogie
in 1787, he had to teach for twenty years before being ordained to Inverurie
in 1800.[20]

We have seen the criticism the session clerk might be subjected to if the
all-important registers of discipline were not kept in an appropriate fashion.
Lessel was to attend all session meetings and take scroll minutes, which were
to be approved by the session before being entered into the formal record.
For this he received an annual salary paid out of the money collected by the
session. This was entirely the case in the sessions reviewed, although open to
challenge, as we will see in the next chapter. He might also receive fees for

particular services. Thus in Aberlady in 1765 it was noted that 'the Session Clerks fees for proclamations were too little the Session therefore agree that they... each Proclamation fee shall be four shill Sterl to the Session Clerk after this date'.[21] However, the payment of salaries could be at the mercy of the session. Edgar notes for Ayrshire that 'one Session-Clerk after another made off with a volume of minutes in retaliation for non-payment of salary, or with the view of compelling payment'.[22] On occasions, the clerk in his position as schoolmaster, and so a respected member of the community, was also a member of the session as an elder.[23] In some cases he also served as treasurer, and his involvement in financial affairs will be considered in more detail in the following chapter. The centrality of the session clerk in the affairs of the parish is rather buried in conceptions of it as an administrative position, but something of its perceived importance can be seen in a dispute at Humbie (precursor of events that will also crop up in the next chapter). In February 1730 the session received a letter from John Hepburn, Laird of Humbie, requesting that they take on Alexander Cuming as schoolmaster, precentor and session clerk. The session rather prickly responded that it was for them to decide who would be their session clerk, perhaps influenced by an ongoing dispute with Humbie over his failure to repay money lent out of the poor funds. They proceeded to appoint one of the elders, James Cuming, as their clerk. Nothing daunted, Humbie returned with another candidate, Robert Young, who was, he argued, better qualified and with excellent testimonials. Young proceeded to seek the approval of the presbytery, which he received, but ignored the advice of the session to obtain support from the other heritors. Young further blotted his copybook by taking money for proclamations before his appointment had been confirmed. This caused the session to dig their heels in, despite the wishes of the presbytery. Further aspersions on Young's character followed, including the uncovering of his having satisfied discipline for fornication in a previous parish, meaning that he was frozen out altogether.[24] This round went to the session, although this was a parish riven with tensions that would surface later. However, the affair shows how important it could be to have a supportive session clerk.

In some parishes this support could mean that minister and session clerk together managed the parish. In Bothwell, for example, this seems to have been the case.[25] However, events in another session in the same presbytery of Hamilton, that of Cambuslang, indicate just what a minister could be up against. Graham observed that T. H. Buckle argued that the Scottish people were priest-ridden. 'The reverse,' he argued, 'is far nearer the truth, and the ministers may rather be called a "people-ridden clergy"'.[26] Nowhere does this seem to have been more the case than in those areas, like Cambuslang, that could draw upon a Covenanting heritage. The trouble here began in early 1740, when an elder, John Bar, complained to the presbytery that he had been frozen out of the session by other elders, who had refused to carry out their duties until he left the church 'to the great grief of my mind and scorn of many beholders'. The rather confusing response of the other elders when appearing before the presbytery related the offence that Bar had given to the congregation on the broader issue of patronage. 'We cannot join in the exercise of Discipline', they declared, 'because its broken down in the Kirk Session of Cambuslang by not suffering the members to have a free Voice in that Court'. The members of the presbytery were not convinced by this reasoning, rebuking them and ordering them to act as a session including Bar in their number. However, the recalcitrant elders 'Refused to Submit to the Rebuke and Appealled to the Tribunal of Christ'. Two of their number were duly deposed as elders. Their appeal against this sentence invoked numerous passages of Scripture as well as the Solemn League and Covenant. At considerable length they rejected the decision of the presbytery as unscriptural and refused to accept that they were no longer elders. A specimen of their fulminations includes this declaration:

> Therefore we desire through Grace to own all our Covenanted Principles and especially Christ's leadership in his own House we reckon whatever invasions be made by any Judicatory upon His Kingly office must be Void and Null in itself as having no foundation in his word But if it must be so now as it is in [16]59, that judgment is turned away backward and justice standeth afar off, for truth is fallen in the streets and equity cannot enter, yea truth faileth.[27]

They remained deposed. Two years later, after the start of the 'Cambuslang Revival', which will feature in the next chapter, one of their number, Archibald Fife, appeared before the presbytery, supported by the minister and a prominent heritor, to apologise for his previous behaviour.[28] However, the events of Cambuslang give an insight into some of the tensions that a minister had to deal with. To argue, as has been argued above, that the minister and session clerk set the tone for the activities of the session is not to suggest that the elders did not have a strong voice, especially when they could draw on the traditions of radical resistance to authority in the name of a belief that characterised much of the south and west of the country. Accordingly, we turn next to consider the characteristics of the elders (and sometimes deacons) who made up the bulk of sessions.

Elders

In selecting men to be elders, sessions were enjoined to look to for those of 'greatest prudence, gravity, and interest, in the parish'.[29] This was a profoundly patriarchal society, in which the injunction in visitation questions to check whether the minister ruled in his own household was because he was to act as a role model. Men were to be the masters in their own houses, and only those who were could be fit to manage the affairs of the parish. It follows then that only men were considered as suitable candidates for the eldership. They were expected, too, to have a stake ('interest') in the parish, thus explicitly ruling out, in the words of the 1704 *Overtures*, 'menial servants'.[30] As late as 1776 in a seceding congregation a nominee for elder was rejected because, being, 'servant to a merchant', he could not attend weekday sermons.[31] We have seen the focus on the status of putative electors in the disputed call at Kells. Much rested on the blurred boundary between the head of a family and being a menial servant. John Moffat in Liggot, for example, was a widower who lived on his own but it was argued that he retained his status as a head 'till he turn a menial servant'. The key test was freedom to act. John Grierson might be a subtenant to Wiliam Rorison, but he in turned employed servants and 'Mr Rorison Dyets with him when he is there'.[32] These matters were never adjudicated on, but they give an indication of how elders might be selected. It was key that they had a stake in the parish and knowledge of those who they would be watching over. In July 1776 a petition was presented to the session at Dalmeny:

> greatly disatisfied with the nomination of Mr John Eiston writer in Edinburgh and Mr Thomas Hay Surgeon there to be ordained Elders in this Parish in regard they were persons unknown to the Parish in General, neither residing, nor having any natural Interest within the Bounds of the Parish.[33]

Their nominations were rejected. That they had been considered at all was due to the difficulties a new minister had in finding willing candidates. It might have been such examples that triggered an overture to the General Assembly in 1784 that 'no minister should set apart any person to the office of elder in his congregation who has not a fixed residence in the parish, or who is not an heritor in the parish'.[34] Despite being under consideration until 1791, this was never promulgated into an act.[35] That recruitment was a common problem can be gleaned from session minutes.

In order to get a sense of broad patterns of sessional activity both across the country and across time, a sample of two parishes from each of the five presbyteries we have been examining in detail was considered. Here we run up against the limitations of clerks in following the guidance, for although they were enjoined both in that guidance and in visitation reports to mark the full details of the 'sederunt' (i.e. the record of attendance), many did not do so. In some parishes (Dailly is a notable example) the detail given enables us to look at patterns of attendance, but in others only the frequency of meetings is available. Table 4.4 shows the results for a sample at twenty-five year intervals.

The level of detail for meetings is rather better than that for members (which often has to be reconstructed from a multiplicity of entries), but this gives an indication of some broad patterns for our examination. The problem with such cross-sectional snapshots is, of course, that they do not show the

Table 4.4 Meetings and composition of selected sessions

	Number of meetings				Number of members			
	1725	1750	1775	1800	1725	1750	1775	1800
Dailly	21	16	6	5	14	14	10	5
Dundonald	12	10	4	8	n.a.	n.a.	8	6
Kintore	14	7	8	5	n.a.	7	n.a.	n.a.
Rayne	19	12	15	5	n.a.	7	n.a.	n.a.
Bolton	5	4	2	1	n.a.	n.a.	n.a.	n.a.
Gladsmuir	n.a.	1	10	1	n.a.	12	n.a.	6
Cambuslang	6	20	4	n.a.	7	7	6	n.a.
New Monkland	12	30	12	2	14	n.a.	4	6
Abercorn	21	7	3	3	9	3	3	3
Dalmeny	21	13	5	2	10	8	3	n.a.

Source: Session minutes.
Note: n.a. = Data not available.

ebb and flow of membership over time. The richness of the local records is in one sense problematic, in that uncovering the full changes in membership requires considerable detective work. While, for example, the recruitment of new elders is usually explicitly recorded, their demise or departure is generally not. This is the value of detailed local case studies, such as that of Inglis on Dunblane.[36] However, sampling of other parochial records for details of financial transactions (as explored in more detail in the following chapter) also throws up supporting material. For example, in some cases, often at the beginning of new registers, clerks might provide details of the session at a particular point in time. Table 4.5 shows for such parishes the various sizes of session, ordered by date.

This does suggest that a session of some six to eight elders was quite typical. In the case of Kintore, which had declined to four members by the time of the ordination of James Darling in 1738, the new minister moved to add a further two members. His ministry only lasted four years, and in 1745 his successor had secured a further three elders. In 1756 he added another three, but by this time all the original session before Darling's admission were dead. This pattern of sporadic appointments, often at ten–year intervals, can also be seen in some of the parishes where a detailed run of minutes can be examined in some detail. In all three of these Garioch parishes new elders were sought at considerable intervals (Table 4.6).

Often the reason given was the 'paucity of number'. As the clerk of Chapel of Garioch recorded in 1771, 'as Some of their number were turned old and infirm, it would be proper to get two Elders more'.[37] Such reasons were to

Table 4.5 Composition of kirk sessions

Place	Date	Number
Dirleton	1703	16
Keithhall	1710	4
Kintore	1713	8
Midcalder	1714	7
Inverurie	1720	7
Insch	1720	6
Chapel of Garioch	1738	6
Kintore	1738	4
Gladsmuir	1740	10
Rayne	1744	7
Saltoun	1760	4
Dirleton	1765	10

Source: Session minutes.

Table 4.6 New elders in three Garioch parishes

Chapel of Garioch		Inverurie		Keithhall	
1726	2	1726	1	1712	4
1731	3	1734	1	1723	2
1748	2	1743	4	1729	2
1758	3	1752	2	1748	2
1771	2	1770	2	1751	5
1776	3	1785	2	1764	1
1793	3	1796	1	1771	1

Source: Session minutes.

be frequently encountered across the country, but we should not be too critical of ministers letting numbers get dangerously low, for they often struggled to get suitably qualified candidates to agree to serve.

Generally the process appears to be that sessions suggested a number of potential candidates who would then be approached by the minister to both test their suitability and to exhort them to accept. Two men discussed by the session of Keithhall in 1729, 'were of good Report both as to a Sober morall Conversation as also with respect to Intellectual ability'.[38] In Daviot in 1796 the two suggested candidates were 'two well respected and decent men'.[39] However, not all those considered suitable would agree to take on what was an onerous commitment. The minister at Keithhall approached John Molyson and Alexander Young, as well as other candidates, in 1723, but both had 'peromptorily refused'. Six years later Molyson was finally persuaded, but Young, despite another endorsement by the session, continued to hold out. Nearly twenty years later another minister had the same lack of success. All those he tried to persuade in July 1747 declined to accept; only by November 1748 was he able to persuade two new recruits to join.[40] While this reluctance might have been to the perceived burdens of office, both spiritual and material, in other parishes tensions with the minister might have been at work. At Mid-calder, in the presbytery of Linlithgow, for example, the minister struggled to attract and keep a session. In 1730 he had spoken to five candidates, but could only persuade two to accept. By 1734 the session appeared to be down to three members, but attempts to recruit a further two failed. They struggled on, but even one of their existing number was 'separated from the Congregational worship' by 1741. Even worse was the defection of the schoolmaster, who 'could never be Edified by the Minr['s] Doctrine or Example'.[41] In Dalton, Dumfriesshire, where we saw a visitation which revealed profound dissatisfaction with a minister, 'he has had no Elders but that three men at his desire sitts with him in the Session'.[42] This ultimately led to him leaving the parish, but these were rather extreme cases. While there might have been reluctance to serve, in most cases parishes had functioning sessions, although with a marked tendency to diminish in numbers over the century.

Once the session had got agreement to serve, the congregation would be asked to state any objections that they might have at a service before the ordination. At Chapel of Garioch for example, this happened 'after calling at the Church door that if there was no objection against the life and conversation' of the candidates.[43] Objections were unusual but they were recorded. In New Monkland in 1776 two candidates were objected to. Mary Lang complained that John Lang had refused to pay money due to her and had used oaths in the process. The reasons why William Mack objected to William Telfer are a mystery because he refused to appear before an ecclesiastical court (although he was willing to put his reasons before a civil one). In the event, it would appear that neither candidate was ordained.[44] However, such objections were the exception and most candidates proceeded to ordination unopposed. This ceremony, conducted in the face of the congregation, gave them a special status. They were no longer 'lay', but ordained members of the church, responsible for the spiritual health of the congregation. After ordination they attended session where they 'received from the Minister and the Rest of the fellow Elders, the right hand of fellowship, and were welcomed to sit as members of this judicature'.[45]

If elders moved parishes they were usually accepted onto the session of their new parish, often as a welcome addition to thinning numbers. If so, their original ordination did not need to be repeated. Just as with ministers, elders were ordained for life and expected to serve until they died. In cases of illness their service might be suspended, as with Archibald Smith in Saltoun who in 1762 was 'under a distemper rendering him unfit – not to act as elder until lifted by providence of God'.[46] However, there were more serious reasons for being suspended or deposed. The most common offence was linked to drinking, often either at weddings (at Midcalder in 1730) or funerals (at Dailly in 1726). More serious still was fighting, especially on the Sabbath. So James Diack, elder of Chapel of Garioch, and three members of the congregation 'had been guilty of the breach and profanation of the sabbath by beating and blooding of one another in the morning of this day'.[47] The session rebuked Diack and warned him as to his future conduct, recognising that he had been provoked by others allowing their beasts into his crops. What was even worse was when one elder struck another, as when James Lockhart was suspended from the eldership of Dailly for hitting his fellow elder, James McCrindle.[48] Breaking the Sabbath was regarded as an extreme fault in an elder, who ought to have been setting an example to the rest of the congregation. Apologising for leading hay on a Sunday, David Gray in Saltoun offered to demit office, but he was deposed. In the same session, another elder committed the serious offence of fathering a child out of marriage, for which he was not only deposed, but also had to stand before the congregation on three occasions.[49] Elders, notwithstanding Burns' satires, were held to a high standard of conduct. They were expected, in the 1704 *Overtures*, to undergo privy censures twice a year, just like their minister at the presbytery:

> they are one by one after another to be removed, and then the rest of the members are, by the moderator, to be inquired concerning the walk and conversation of the person removed, concerning his diligence and prudence in his station; and whatever any have observed and been informed, worthy the noticing, is freely, and with love and tenderness, to be communicated.[50]

This certainly was recorded in a number of session minutes, with, for example, the record in Dalrymple, Ayrshire, in 1730:

> According to appointment, the Session Employed a part of this day in prayer and then they had all the usual questions put to them, one by one and were put upon the Privy Censures and all well reported of.

The practice was noted again in the same parish in 1740.[51] However, it is not widely noted, and so may be another example where practice departed from the guidance.

Deacons and heritors

We have so far considered the session only as an undifferentiated body, but in the previous chapter we noted a particular emphasis in visitation reports and attestations of session records on the need to have deacons as distinct from elders. The distinction was one that mattered a good deal to Pardovan, who linked it directly to a strict adherence to Scripture,

> Where it follows, that, seeing this office is of divine institution, it is an unwarrantable omission in some congregations, that either they put no difference betwixt elders and deacons, or else they neglect to appoint any to the office of a deacon.[52]

He then gave a detailed breakdown of the duties of the deacon, which were to collect on behalf of the poor, check on their condition, and apply relief as needed. Deacons were to have a vote on such matters in the session, but otherwise sat in a consultative capacity. This commitment to a separation of duties was continued by an Act of Assembly in 1719, as noted in revised instructions for revisors of synod books in 1723.[53] In 1721 the synod of Fife noted on the presbytery register of Kirkcaldy 'that they endeavour to have Deacons settled in all the parishes of their bounds'.[54] The push on this issue was marked in privy censures. In 1720 the presbytery of Cupar recorded:

> The members being enquired if they had ordained Deacons distinct from Elders in their respective parishes, Mr Gillespie signified that he had ordained six deacons in his parish. It was recommended to such as have not done it to do it as soon as possible.[55]

All these exhortations, however, failed to make much impression. The recommendation that sessions secure deacons as distinct from elders was found in twelve visitations, while sessions that explicitly declared that they had such officers numbered seven. It is clear from other evidence that other parishes did have deacons. At Kells, for example, two deacons are listed among the voters.[56] However, in many more it would appear that it was hard enough to get sufficient elders, and so the two roles were combined. In the ten parishes examined, only two, Dailly in Ayrshire and Cambuslang in Lanarkshire, had deacons marked in their sederunts (although there is an isolated mention of a deacon in the other Lanarkshire parish, New Monkland, in 1750). Cambuslang only had one deacon from this evidence, whereas Dailly had six (to complement eight elders) in 1725. This particularly well-recorded and conscientious session continued on with deacons through to 1770. In that year, faced with the need to select new elders, 'as their Number is much diminished by Death and Removal from this parish', they decided unanimously 'to admit as Elders those who had served in this parish as Deacons for many years & who had approved themselves in that Office'.[57] As the numbers on sessions diminished over the years, the distinction between elders and deacons appears to have faded. In some areas, such as the Garioch, it never seems to have been implemented in the first place.

Who served on the sessions? Not surprisingly in a predominantly agrarian economy it was farmers, supplemented by some tradesmen, who dominated sessions. Here is where the limitations of a cross-sectional approach are clearest, for it would take detailed work and complementary records, such as estate papers, to be able to draw out the fine distinctions of farm size and value that would be helpful. One such investigation was essayed by Inglis for an earlier period. His exploration of the composition of the session of Dunblane in Perthsire in the years spanning the restoration of Presbyterianism in the 1690s revealed some interesting contrasts. While the session under episcopacy contained five lawyers, none served after 1690 until 1797. Similarly, no landowner returned to the session for 150 years. They were replaced by artisans and merchants of some standing from the urban part of the parish, and by farmers and tradesmen from the landward area. The farmers were not, he finds, the highest paying tenants.[58] At a much later period, the session of Monymusk in Aberdeenshire contained five elders in 1796, all tenants of the Grant of Monymusk estate. In that year an assessment was made for the army and navy, which indicated that of 122 tenants, the vast majority (eighty, or 66 per cent) held land valued at under £5. In their ranks was the kirk treasurer, Peter Ewan, whose rent at Upper Coullie was £2 15s. Another elder, George Dodd of Dorandle, fell into the 7 per cent of tenants paying between £5 and £10, with the other three being in the 14 per cent paying between £10 and £15. None of the elders was drawn from the ranks of the more substantial farmers on the estate.[59] This was an estate at the forefront of improvement in this region, drawing substantial tenants from further south to bring with them new agricultural practices. In the Lothian parishes there is perhaps a subtle indicator of changing status, drawing on the widespread distinction between landowners, who were *of* their possessions and tenant farmers, who were *in* their holdings. So, for example, in Dailly in 1725 we have the heritor Alexander Kennedy of Drumolland, the smith John McCrearie at Palbroom and the farmer William Hog in High Mains of Barclamachan. An indicator of the shift in the social status of farmers is marked in the Lothian parish of Gladsmuir, a location of large, highly profitable and efficient farms, with the accession to the eldership in 1795 of 'Mr James Mitchell Farmer in Trabrown and Mr Andrew Cuthbertson, farmer in Penston'.[60] The 'Mr' is also a marker of social status; in other records, elders of plebeian social status are always listed by their name with no honorific.

These fine distinctions allow us to look at one aspect of the membership of sessions: the involvement of heritors. The ten parishes examined indicate something of a divergence. In the west, the earlier involvement of heritors seems to fade away, to leave completely plebeian sessions. In Dailly, for example, Alexander Kennedy of Drummelland was an active member of session in 1725, attending thirteen out of twenty-one meetings. However, no other heritor appears in the following years in a session whose attendance is well recorded. The other Ayrshire parish, Dundonald, gives us attendance records from 1775 but no indication of heritor involvement. Cambuslang records the reasonable activity of Mr Duncan in 1750 (ten out of twenty meetings) but that is the only evidence. In New Monkland, which also has good attendance records, there is no evidence of heritor involvement. The Garioch parishes unfortunately do not record sederunts. In the material at the beginning of registers in 1744 the clerk of Rayne proudly noted 'The Honourable Hew Dalrymple Esq one of the Senators of the College of Justice and one of the Commissioners of Justiciary' as the first member of the session, but there is no other evidence of involvement.[61] A similar list for Kintore for 1738 does not indicate members outside the farming community.[62] In 1765 the session of Daviot agreed that 'it would be of great use in all Session's affairs to have an Heritor an Elder', and proceeded to nominate a Mr Elphinstone.[63] In the parishes around Edinburgh, by contrast, the trend appears to have been for greater heritor involvement, to an extent that changed the character of these sessions.

In Abercorn, its church dominated by the laird's loft of the Hopes of nearby Hopetoun House, the session had elite representation throughout the century. In 1725 Dundas of Philipstoun was on the session, to be joined in 1750 by Dr William Dundas. By 1775 their place had been taken by a Mr Sansom and by 1800, possibly by those of a somewhat lower social status. In nearby Dalmeny the two heritors involved were George Dundas of Dundas and Andrew Dunbar of Leuchold, the latter undertaking a good part of the treasurer's duties over several years. Both had good attendance records in 1725, attending seventeen and nineteen meetings out of a possible twenty-one respectively. Their successors in 1750, the Honourable George Dundas of Dundas and Mr John Dundas of Newhalls only managed three meetings each out of thirteen. Unfortunately the attendance list does not allow for such a review of the involvement of the Honourable Charles Hope of Craighall in 1776, and by 1800 the records are not clear.

The same is true for one of the other parishes, Bolton, but Gladsmuir has an interesting tale to tell about the changing dynamics of Lothian parishes. The session had twelve members in 1750, including three of genteel status: Mr George Buchan, Mr William Baillie and Mr William Law. It was the latter of these three, the advocate William Law of Elvingstoun, ordained elder in 1740, who was most involved in the affairs of the parish. He was active in helping the minister to administer the financial affairs of the parish, using his financial expertise to chase bad debts in Edinburgh. In 1759 a new minister, Francis Cowan, was ordained. Matters appeared to continue in a satisfactory vein for several years. In 1763 Law proposed John Pringle, an advocate in Edinburgh and son to Lord Edgefield as an elder, securing a letter from William Robertson, now principal of the university, which commended him as 'a young man of a decent and unexceptionable character'.[64] Six years later Mr John Baillie at Denston and Mr Alex Law, advocate, were admitted as elders, suggesting a rather 'polite' session. However, at some point between then and the start of the next register in 1775 relations between the minister and his principal elder had broken down irretrievably. He was no longer attending either the session or public worship, citing the length of the minister's sermons. The minister sought the support of his session, inquiring:

> whether he had been guilty of any immoralities in practice or Error in doctrine to give him just cause for so doing or even in the matter of long preaching whether his preaching had been of such a great length as to oblige any person in health to go out of the Kirk in the middle of divine Worship as he had done.[65]

Not surprisingly perhaps, the minutes record the session's full support. Cowan's response appears to have been to change the social complexion of the session. In July 1780 a whole new set of elders, six in number, was admitted: Mr Andrew Thompson, wright in Samuelston, William Bone, tenant in Longniddrie, Robert Bone, weaver there, David Bisset taylor there, Walter Horsbrough, taylor in McMarry, and William Forrest, taylor in Samuelston. In October of the same year the minister also sought and won the ordination of John Duncan, Coalier at Hodges, as another elder (a colliery manager or proprietor, one suspects, as he later took on the role of treasurer). This seemed to mark a more activist cast to the session, with three women being subject to further inquiry before they were allowed access to communion, a woman appearing before the congregation at a time when public appearances were much diminished in this area and, in 1785, a declaration of the session in favour of the abolition of patronage.[66] All this time disputes with Law rumbled on, with minutes deploring his intimating meetings, which were properly the province of the minister. In 1788 new elders were appointed, which appeared to confirm the earlier appointments: Mr Hugh Ramsey, schoolmaster and Mr Peter Brown, mason in Samuelston. In the following year Cowan refused to take payment of a fine from a farmer, Mr Bairnsfather, for the sin of fornication with one of his servants.[67] To force one of such social standing to appear for public rebuke before the congregation (albeit he was allowed to appear only once rather than the customary thrice, in the light of his voluntary confession) was not a common practice in this area, where the payment of fines by the more prosperous was more usual.

Cowan died in the October of 1789 and was succeeded by George Hamilton in April 1790. His first session was not constituted until June, with the next meeting recorded being in January of the following year. In 1795, as noted earlier, two farmers now dignified with 'Mr' were ordained to the session, to be followed in 1798 by Mr James Law younger of Elvingston. George Hamilton was the son of the minister of Bolton and was initially intended for the law. He was to be a candidate for the chair of Moral Philosophy at the University of Glasgow in 1797 and Moderator of the General Assembly in 1805.[68] He also achieved a degree of fame for writing, in response to Burns' lament for the passing of the Stuart line on visiting Stirling Castle:

> These few rash lines shall damn thy name,
> And blast thy hopes of future fame.[69]

A clear supporter of the settled order, then, and not one to disturb the general shift in Lothian parishes towards polite sessions, in which the prime concerns were with poor relief and parochial administration, rather than spiritual health. In another parish, Garvald, the session was initially composed of the usual farmers and tradesmen. In 1754 Robert Dods, tenant in Garvald and John Miller, weaver in Danskin, were ordained 'Elders and Deacons', to be followed in 1764 by Patrick Lamb, wright and Alexander Bartram, school-master. In 1773, however, there was a distinct jump in social status with the next two candidates: Charles Hay of Hopes and Hew Dalrymple of Nunran. This was confirmed in 1789 with the record that the 'most noble George Marquis of Tweeddale, John Hay of Hopes, Esq, Captain John Douglas & Richard Sumner Esq (Provost of Haddington) be elected and ordained Elders of this Parish & members of this Kirk Session'.[70]

Life of the Session

This threefold distinction, between a plebeian and rather rebellious (if conservative) southwest, a disciplined and obedient northeast and a polite southeast, can be traced if we look at the pattern of meetings and then the recording of those meetings. Table 4.7 shows the pattern of meetings extracted from ten parishes at twenty-five year intervals.

Table 4.7 Meeting frequency of selected sessions

	Number of meetings			
	1725	1750	1775	1800
Dailly	21	16	6	5
Dundonald	12	10	4	8
Kintore	14	7	8	5
Rayne	19	12	15	5
Bolton	5	4	2	1
Gladsmuir	n.a.	1	10	1
Cambuslang	6	20	4	n.a.
New Monkland	12	30	12	2
Abercorn	21	7	3	3
Dalmeny	21	13	5	2

Source: Session minutes.
Note: n.a. = Data not available.

This suggests that at the opening of the century most sessions managed to meet at least monthly, with three managing nearly twice-monthly meetings. Interestingly one, Dailly, was in Ayrshire, with another two being in the

presbytery of Linlithgow, home presbytery of Steuart of Pardovan. Although
we do not have the records for Gladsmuir, the two parishes in the presbytery
of Haddington already show a low number of meetings. This continues, and
after mid-century the two Linlithgow parishes also show a low number of
meetings. The activism of Francis Cowan in Gladsmuir that we have already
observed accounts for the spike in 1775. What the table also indicates is a
general decline in the frequency of meetings. The detail supplied by the clerk
of Dailly allows us to trace this decline in a little more detail in one parish.[71]

The twenty-one meetings in 1721 took place on Wednesdays and were
attended by most of the fourteen elders and deacons. The exception was in
September when, no doubt due to the harvest, attendances at three meetings
were by five, six and five members respectively. Eleven of the meetings
recorded full attendance. Two elders and one deacon had nearly perfect attendance records, missing only one meeting each. As noted above, the heritor
on the session (judging by title; other members may have been heritors but
this is not accessible from the current evidence) attended a majority of
meetings. Twenty-five years later there were fewer meetings (sixteen), but
they were still more than just monthly. Now only two meetings attracted a
full attendance, with five meetings at the beginning of the year slipping below
half attendance. Two elders, however, managed perfect attendance. Both
appear to have continued in office from 1725, with one possibly being
upgraded from deacon to elder. Another two elders seem to have been carried
forward (although the replacement of first names with initials at this stage of
the records makes this tentative rather than definite). Two members continued
in office in 1775 (and one notes similar surnames suggesting a degree of
family tradition), but now there were only six meetings. Attendance was still
healthy, though, with five elders having perfect attendance. By 1798 (the
closest year to 1800 for which records are available) the session has shrunk to
five elders who meet only five times. Indeed, the session had got down to
three members, with two more fortuitously moving into the parish during
the year to bolster numbers. This was an active session and its experience
suggests a general process of contraction of numbers, something that can be
seen in the broader set of records that survive. Before considering these
however, it is worth briefly considering the location of session meetings, as
this will be germane to later contrasts with the English experience.

For the framers of the 1696 Overtures the location of meetings was
important. 'All Kirk Judicatories,' they stipulated, 'are (in ordinary) to meet
in some Church or convenient Room belong thereunto'.[72] This requirement
was dropped in later versions, but adhered to in practice. This could not
always have been a comfortable experience, given what we have learned about
the poor condition of the general run of Scotland's churches in the early part
of the century. In a poor country anyway, and one racked by wars and famines
during the seventeenth century, not much was available for building work.

One visitor was dismayed by what he found in one of the surviving pre-Reformation churches, that of Linlithgow in the 1720s: 'that great part of the floor was broken up, and that the pews were immoderately dusty, the precentor, or clerk, who attended, us took occasion to say, he did not apprehend that cleanliness was essential to devotion'.[73] As part of the rebuilding that occurred during the eighteenth century, provision was often made for a 'session house'. In Dirleton, for example, the session met in their new session house in 1769 to clear their accounts. Among the items were building costs, including the provision of a grate so that at least they might have some warmth.[74] This was a matter of some importance. During one January meeting in the extended dispute between heritor and session in Monymusk, Sir Archibald Grant suggested that they move the meeting to the schoolhouse 'where they may have a little fire, as it is impossible to examine the Accts he has to produce in a cold Church at this time of the year'.[75] One exception that was generally practised, although evidently not in Monymusk, was that meetings to settle the accounts, to which heritors were also invited, were usually convened in the manse.

Wherever they were held, meetings were to be recorded. We have seen that visitations, especially in the early years of the century, paid particular attention to the quality of record keeping. Not only was this because such records were part of the inspection routine, but also it was because they were regarded as legal documents, recording the session's activities as a court. While the 1704 *Overtures* may never have been promulgated as an official document, sections of it were officially adopted as the *Form of Process* in 1707. This laid down, in considerable detail, the processes to be followed for calling and examining witnesses, and accounts for the great detail that is often found in registers. Numerous witness statements are recorded, especially in those cases of sexual misconduct that then form the basis for many subsequent accounts. However, in one churchman's later view, 'there is no doubt, however, that after the adoption of the *Form of Process*, its legalistic nature made discipline more and more difficult'.[76] We have noted how the dissident Leitch in Kilwinning strained the process of church justice by calling an extraordinary number of witnesses, perhaps thereby contributing to the lapsing of visitations. While church discipline does continue to be applied after mid-century and some exceptional events occasion extensive recording (as with the events in Monymusk that we will consider later) in general there was a marked reduction in the volume of record keeping. This was most noticeable in the Lothian parishes, as Table 4.8 indicates.

This analysis covers fifty-five parishes and, drawing on the electronic catalogue of their records in the NRS, records the average number of pages per year in their session registers grouped in both decades and quarter-centuries. The longer period makes the trend towards shorter records clearer, but also indicates some regional variation. Obviously, such an analysis has

Table 4.8 Length in pages of session records

	Ayr	Garioch	Haddington	Hamilton	Linlithgow
Decade ending					
1710	11.7	11.1	9.2	4.2	13.9
1720	8.2	8.7	15.5	3.0	10.7
1730	5.7	10.8	16.0	2.6	10.1
1740	9.2	10.5	9.7	3.3	9.8
1750	6.0	10.4	9.3	4.0	8.5
1760	6.0	9.6	4.5	9.8	10.1
1770	5.6	9.3	4.5	3.4	5.9
1780	9.4	7.4	3.6	5.9	5.1
1790	12.8	7.1	6.6	8.5	5.1
1800	9.4	6.0	2.7	7.4	3.9
Quarter-century ending					
1724	10.6	10.1	12.4	3.3	11.7
1750	8.7	10.4	10.9	3.7	10.0
1774	6.6	9.2	4.3	6.0	7.2
1799	12.2	6.3	4.2	7.5	4.7

Source: NRS catalogue CH2 Church of Scotland.

clear limitations; a full analysis would use the number of words, rather than page length, which can be affected by the size of pages and the handwriting of the clerk, all impossible to control for. However, such an exercise is impossible on this scale until all the records are electronically transcribed, which will be a monumental task. Bearing in mind these limitations, this rather crude exercise supports the impressions given from examining the minutes. We have already noted above the way in which the Gladsmuir register subsides from detailed recording under the regime of Francis Cowan to one or two brief entries a year under his successor. This is particularly noticeable in the Lothian parishes of Haddington and Linlithgow where this analysis, if anything (because it counts in whole rather than fractional pages) tends to exaggerate the size of records. What an analysis like this cannot indicate are the subtle differences in recording practice across districts. In the Garioch parishes, for example, the text that the minister preached on every Sabbath is recorded right through the century, a practice that is not adhered to elsewhere (disappearing in the Lothian parish of Saltoun in 1736, for example). In the Garioch, as we will see in the following chapter, the records of discipline were frequently integrated with the financial records, such that they formed what is essentially an accounting record of both finance and conduct. What the records also don't always give in detail, but point to,

are the routines that lay behind public rituals. While the focus of historians
has been on the discipline of the kirk, an examination of one central ritual,
that of communion, can give us an insight into the organising routines that
lay at the heart of church governance.

Making communion happen

> Here, some are thinkin on their sins,
> An' some upo' their claes;
> Ane curses feet that fyl'd his shins,
> Anither sighs an' prays:
> On this hand sits a chosen swatch,
> Wi' screwed-up, grace-proud faces;
> On that a set o' chaps, at watch,
> Thrang winkin on the lasses
> To chairs that day.[77]

This short extract from one of Burns' most famous poems, 'Holy Fair', illustrates the very mixed motives of piety and entertainment that motivated the
crowds who attended communion events. Burns' poem, which is drawn from
a communion at Mauchline, was published in 1786. In 1784, Edgar tells us,
1,400 persons were recorded as taking communion in the parish.[78] The
communion season was clearly important for a variety of reasons, but our
focus is on what it tells us about organising practices. For such large events,
as we will see, involved considerable organisational effort – effort that is
pointed to in the records.

Reformed Protestantism reduced the sacraments of the church to just two:
baptism and communion. While Protestantism, and especially Presbyterianism, has been seen as a religion of the Word, rather than of ritual, work
such as that on communion by Leigh Eric Schmidt has shown how important
ritual was.[79] He shows the origins of American revivalism in the Scottish
communion season, which attracted the name 'Holy Fair' on account of its
prominence in the church year. Although the early reformers, such as Knox,
advocated frequent communion, this was at odds with the requirement to
ensure that only those worthy were allowed to take communion. This notion
of a 'closed communion' was not achieved in other Reformed polities, but it
was the central feature of Scottish Presbyterianism. It meant that communion
in practice was taken only once a year, throwing an enormous weight on the
occasion. Indeed the emphasis that church practices had placed on the annual
communion event in the mind of believers then acted as a counter to attempts
to reform the practice so that it could be exercised more frequently. In 1750
the presbytery of Ayr endorsed the aim of more frequent celebration of
communion, but despaired of its practicality. The barrier was the number of
sermons preached, to which people were firmly attached. In this most

conservative of areas, as far as religious practices were concerned, the problem was 'the prejudices of the people who seem to look upon such numbers of sermons as in some Degree essential to the Celebration'.[80] Accordingly, Burns tells us of the performances of five preachers, such as:

> But now the Lord's ain trumpet touts,
> Till a' the hills are rairin,
> And echoes back return the shouts;
> Black Russell is na sparin:
> His piercin words, like Highlan' swords,
> Divide the joints an' marrow;
> His talk o' Hell, whare devils dwell,
> Our vera 'sauls does harrow'
> Wi' fright that day![81]

While the focus of the religiously committed might be on the exposition of theological precepts, as recorded in their diaries, for others it was the performance that mattered.

Such important events required considerable organisation. They were not simply the day on which communion was taken, but that focal event was part of a 'season', which spanned several days. This is nicely indicated in the following from Rayne in 1750:

> after Divine Service intimate that, in regard Sabbath next was the Day fixt for the Celebration of the Sacrament of the Lords Supper here, Thursday next was by appointment of the session to be observed as a day of solemn fasting humiliation & prayer in this Congregation & Saturday next as a day of preparation for the solemn ordinance in view & that public worship would begin on those days about the ordinary time. The people in the west side of the paroch were appointed to attend the session on Thursday & the people in the rest of the parish on Saturday after divine service for receiving tokens.[82]

This indicates something of what needed to be organised. On the fast day the minister of Bourtie preached, followed by the minister of Culsalmond on the preparation day. On the day of the sacrament itself the minister was joined at the tables by the ministers of Culsalmond and Monymusk. At this occasion long tables were set up, either just in the body of the church or, in larger congregations, in the churchyard as well. Access to these tables was guarded by the elders, who collected the tokens mentioned earlier that were the key to access. Seated at the table, the communicants received the bread and drank from the cup, which having been blessed by the minister was passed from hand to hand. The process was then completed with a further sermon on the Monday as a day of thanksgiving, in the case of Rayne being preached by the minister of Kennethmount.[83]

This short description points to a number of organising tasks of which the records, in different levels of detail from place to place, give us indications. Assembling from these fragments we can construct a picture of the routines that needed to be performed. These routines needed to start well before the communion season itself. Efforts at coordination were needed at two levels. At the level of the presbytery it was desirable that communions in different parishes were staggered to avoid clashes not only for the communicants but also for the ministers. As has been seen, several would need to be involved to make communion successful and this necessitated coordination. A number of presbyteries sought to establish timetables that would avoid such clashes. That at Linlithgow, for example, resolved in 1713 that those churches close to a town should have their communion in the spring or at harvest, thus leaving the summer for more rural parishes. Within these parameters, 'it may be proper for ministers to concert the matter among themselves in such a way as those paroches near to one another may have the Sacrament at a due distance one from another'.[84] The second was that of negotiation at the parochial level, where the local knowledge of the session would be called upon. The minister of Garvald was somewhat late in inquiring about a date for communion in October 1725 but so, clearly, was the harvest. His elders advised him somewhat gloomily, 'that the harvest would be exceeding late by reason of the badness of the weather & that it would not be intirely over for a month to come when the days would be too short'.[85] It was decided to abandon all thoughts of communion for the year. The minister of Kintore was a little more attuned to agricultural matters: in late August 1730 the minutes noted, 'if it pleased God to continue good harvest weather it might be conveniently celebrate once in that month' (October).[86] It was not just the cereal harvest that needed to be taken into account: in Gladsmuir in 1783 the minister sought his elders' advice about a date in May 'but that he wished not to interfere with the Hay harvest'.[87]

Once a date was agreed the session needed to agree on who was suitable to receive communion. This had both a spiritual and a communal dimension. The minister was to examine in his visitation of families suitability for communion based on the knowledge of his parishioners of the basics of the catechism. The elders could advise on whether there were any conflicts rumbling on between parishioners. In Dalrymple in 1730, 'those of the Session who met at over Sheldon, according to a late appointment to speak with some people of the Kersland, who were said to have some Differences among them,' reported that these appeared to have been patched up. However, one of these parishioners who appeared the following day to collect his token, 'was charged by the Session with having sworn by the Name of God that his Sister Daughter should not sit in a certain seat in the Kirk'.[88] He confessed his remorse for his offence and was granted a token after being admonished to mend his ways. While Henderson wrote that 'the Communion Roll as we know it is a nineteenth century product', numerous examples can be given of ministers shortening the process of approval by reference to lists of suitable parishioners that they had drawn up.[89] While these rolls might not have survived, unlike later nineteenth-century examples that are recorded on pre-printed pro formas, session minutes confirm their existence. In Haddington in 1711 the minister 'produced the Rolls of all such in his Catchising Roll as he judged to be knowing'. The list was gone through for evidence of any unsuitability and 'those against whom these objections were made and sustained, were expunged'.[90] At Saltoun this process of examining the roll meant that session 'stayed in the Church from 11 to one o'clock'.[91] In a variant on this practice, lists could be kept by elders, as at Gladsmuir in 1740 where 'the several Elders produced their Lists which being read & cognosed upon, they appointed the tokens to be distributed accordingly'.[92] This process of compiling and checking lists of parishioners was one of the examples of detailed record keeping that supported the activities of the session, but leaves only traces in the archive.

Another practice that left a more physical trace, one that remains collectable to the present day, was that of giving tokens to those who were accepted as communicants. The session registers of Perth in 1580 note the allocation of roles at communion, including those who were to collect tokens.[93] Pardovan takes their form for granted, noting, as a matter of course, 'each person, before communicating, doth deliver the parish lead ticket, when sought for, to one of the elders or deacons officiating at the table'.[94] They were so central to the practices of the church that when the kirk at Kirkmaiden was visited by the presbytery of Stranraer in 1720 they found that despite their church being in poor order and having 'no communion Tables, cloathes or cups', it could be noted, '[they] have tokens'.[95] Sessions used local smiths to forge them a supply of tokens, often accompanied by a stamp that would enable them to emboss the token with the year of communion. Tokens would be distributed, either by parishioners coming to collect them at special meetings of session (as in Rayne) or by elders receiving allocations for distribution in proportion to their quarters (as in Haddington in 1782). The cycle would be complete when tokens were counted afterwards to determine how many had taken communion. By this means the session at Haddington in 1787 was able to determine that, having distributed 1,200 tokens, 1,017 had been used to gain access to the tables.[96] The minister at Gladsmuir in 1703 took this still further; he resolved, he told his session:

> to preserve carefully the lists of such persons as receive tokens to the Sacrament, & mark on what form they receive them, to the end their progress in knowledge & practice may be known to the Session from time to time.[97]

So significant was the token that the minister of Dirleton, James Clark, authored a pamphlet in 1702 entitled *The Communicant's Best Token; or, a Practical Treatise of Personal Covenanting with God*.[98]

Once having distributed the tokens to those deemed suitable and having determined who was to collect them in on the day, the session had to proceed to other preparations. Some minutes record in considerable detail who was to perform roles such as bearing the bread and wine to the tables. The minutes at Haddington suggest that there was a jealously guarded hierarchy to these tasks. The session there in 1782 first established a rotation for taking collections and then 'took under consideration bringing forward and Distributing the Elements and they appoint for the future, Seniority to be the Rule'.[99] There were also practical matters to be attended to, such as setting up the long tables at which communicants sat to receive the sacrament and erecting the 'tents', wooden preaching platforms from which sermons would be delivered. At Meldrum in 1730 the session 'agreed upon the making of such alterations in the Kirk as were needfull in order to Accommodate the Communicants & to place the Communion Tables conveniently'.[100] At Dalrymple in 1732 the accounts record payments to a mason 'for making kirk tables and mending the tent', and to James McSkimming for the provision of timber for him.[101] After the event, sessions would also have to tackle the consequences of the communion season, which did not only involve counting the collections (which would be expected to be much bigger than normal). Where events were too big for the church and churchyard, crowds might spill onto adjoining farmland; this was a prime cause of contention in the events at Cambuslang, which will be a focus of the next chapter. At Slammanan, in the presbytery of Linlithgow, the session noted after communion in 1730, 'considering yt Patrick Gray had a considerable losse of his grass upon qch the tent stood on the Sabbath day & some of his corn trod by the people yrfor they did allow him two pound Scots'.[102]

Altogether, the communion season involved a set of organising routines that mobilised the whole session. Indeed, the need for assistance at the sacrament could be a reason for seeking new elders, as when the minister of Dalmeny announced in 1776 that there was not 'a sufficient number in the Parish to assist at administering the sacrament'.[103] Supplementing the registers that recorded events such as the communion season and the administration of discipline were other artefacts. Some, such as communion rolls, do not survive, although they were the precursors of the detailed records that emerged in the nineteenth century. Others were physical artefacts like the communion tokens, which were an essential part of the communion season, being both a practical form of accounting and a symbolic resource redolent of respectability and belonging to a particular community. In this chapter we have seen how detailed practices of organising, predicated on careful record keeping, occurred across the church. There were clear regional variations in such practices and considerable departures from the visions of the early century authors of guidance. However, across Lowland Scotland in every parish, albeit to varying degrees, there was involvement in practices of detailed record keeping and organising. That involvement and the detail of that record keeping did appear to diminish as the century progressed, but the idea of the church as possessing a systemic form of accountability and governance persisted. It also found expression in the way in which it dealt with financial transactions, which is the theme of the next chapter.

CHAPTER 5

Handling Finances

The Church of Scotland's primary role in the relief of the poor in the eighteenth century has meant that its practices for recording financial transactions have come into the view of historians concerned with how poverty was handled. In particular, two legal cases involving the church, those of Humbie (1751) and Cambuslang (1752), feature in the debate over the nature of Scottish poor relief in the period. The visibility of these cases is, in part, because of their inscription in books recording court decisions. Briefly, the Cambuslang decision turned on what expenses could be met from the funds collected for the benefit of the poor. Repairs to property occasioned by the enormous crowds who had attended the communion season in the parish as part of the 'Cambuslang Revival' were held to be improper, and doubt was cast on the payment of fees such as those for the session clerk.[1] At Humbie, the decision was that heritors should be fully involved in the administration of funds raised for the poor. We will return to these cases in more detail later, but for now the important point is the way the cases have been used to draw conclusions about record keeping. For Mitchison the Humbie case was, in her original formulation, a turning point. Because of the decision that heritors should be fully involved, '[f]rom now on poor-law affairs were to be run more formally, kept in separate books from the general session register, and vetted in legalistic spirit by the heritors'.[2] In a response, Cage argued that the Humbie case needed to be seen in the context of legal assessments (that is, the setting of a rate on landowners and others for poor relief) and that too much emphasis should not be placed on it.[3] Although her initial response did not tackle the implications of this, in subsequent work, where she argues for two implications of Humbie, Mitchison was to modify her views. One implication was that 'landowners were deliberately using their dominant position in the structure of justice to reduce the claim of the Church to autonomy', something which we will see further in this chapter.[4] The second was that, having examined a wider set of records, she now modified her position on record keeping, arguing now that it 'became desirable for parishes to keep financial and discipline affairs in different books, a policy also encouraged by presbyteries, though with limited success'.[5] That limited success is indeed one of the themes of this chapter. However, it will also argue that the terms of the debate are a little misleading. Separate books of account, it will be argued, predated the Humbie decision by some time and need to be seen in the context of a much earlier focus on accountability.

Developing the money register

The founding documents of the church laid particular stress on financial matters, especially the relief of the poor, for both theological and political reasons. As salvation was through faith rather than works, leaving the relief of poverty to individual action motivated by the desire to build up credit for the soul's future was not an option. The political reason was the situation in Scotland, where Reformation had been achieved through an uneasy coalition between nobles and clergy. The preservation of the old church's benefices from the avarice of the nobles was on the minds of the reformers. In that they proved to be unsuccessful, but it meant that careful attention to how financial transactions would be handled was laid out in the *First Book of Discipline*. They could draw on some limited passages in Calvin, who argued that the patrimony of the church was predominantly for the relief of the poor, rather than on adorning churches:

> for they received the daily offerings of the faithful, and the annual revenues of the Church, that they might apply them to their true uses; in other words, partly in maintaining ministers, and partly in supporting the poor; at the sight of the bishop, however, to whom they every year gave an account of their stewardship.[6]

This stewardship needed specific roles and their associated practices. So it was laid down for the infant Church of Scotland that 'we require deacons and treasurers to receive the rents rather than the ministers themselves; because not only the ministers, but also the poor and schools must be sustained from the tiends'.[7] These deacons or treasurers were to be appointed annually and were to be under the control of the session: they 'may distribute no part of that which is collected, but by commandment of the ministers and elders'. In order to ensure that this happened

> [they were] bound and compelled to make accounts to the ministers and elders of that which they have received, as oft as the policy shall appoint; and the elders when they are changed, which must be every year, must clear their accounts'.[8]

All the money was to be accounted for and handed on to their successors, together with supporting documents. In the *First Book of Discipline* the office of superintendent was envisaged and the results of such annual accounting were to be forwarded to the office-holder, so that there might be an overview of the financial health of the whole church. By such measures its framers hoped to avoid the siphoning off of church funds for secular purposes. What is of particular note here is the attempt to describe and implement a comprehensive system of checks and balances, one whose spirit endured in later years regardless of the degree of its practical success.

The impact of these structures can be seen in the earliest surviving records. In March 1583 the presbytery of Stirling ordered that every sessional register should include 'almws collectit to the pure with the distributione thairof'.[9] The session of Perth in August 1585 'ordainis Andro Stoup to be collector of the puris almos and to gif his compt everie Monday befoir the session'.[10] Andrew was recorded as presenting his accounts a further three times, but then this practice of regular accounting ceased with the appointment of a new treasurer. In July 1590 a committee was appointed to audit the accounts of John Jakes. In the same month the minutes mentioned 'the box being opint', the first mention of this key artefact in the context of accounting.[11] The elements of an accounting system being put into place were present in fragmentary form, although their precise nature was open to development. From an early stage, that is, the church at both national and local level paid attention to the recording of financial transactions.[12] However, the development of such practices became submerged by the turbulent events of the seventeenth century. One suspects, as illustrated further below, that these practices came to be developed during that century, especially in the areas around Edinburgh, to such an extent that they became taken for granted and so faded into the background. This might seem to explain the almost complete lack of attention to such practices in the spate of guidance documents that were produced at the end of the century.

We have noted that the anonymous framers of the 1696 *Overtures* gave considerable detail about the format of the registers of discipline to be kept at all levels of the church, but in no place did they specify how financial transactions should be recorded. There was no consideration of how a treasurer was to be selected, the accounts presented or auditing might be carried out. There was nothing about the keeping of separate books of account. Indeed, the only mention that related to the whole system of financial accountability was that of the need to produce the poor's box at parochial visitations. The 1704 revised *Overtures* also repeated the considerable amount of detail about the format of records without specifying accounting details. However, they did add the laconic note, in the context of biannual privy censures in sessions, that 'here also the kirk-treasurer's accounts may be taken in'.[13] This almost incidental note, coming at the end of a long section, is all, aside from the repetition about the poor's box, that the 1704 *Overtures* contained to guide sessions in this fundamental aspect of their duties. Pardovan gave little more. We have noted his stance on the importance of deacons but, while he supplied a list of their duties, there was no discussion of what practices might facilitate and check the performance of those duties. All he hinted at was that 'matters of civil right, such as discharging of the almoner's intromissions, securing of money, or ordering of diligence for recovering the same' should be topics for meetings held during the week, as such matters should not be discussed on the Sabbath.[14] Here it is necessary to delve into the surviving records in order to reconstruct practices that were certainly followed.

A useful starting point is the catalogue of the surviving records.[15] Because this is in electronic form, and because the collection is so comprehensive, it is possible to analyse the catalogue itself to discern some broad patterns. There are, of course, some severe limitations to such a process. The coverage of the collection is partial when it comes to Highland presbyteries, reflecting the slow progress of the church in establishing its hegemony there. While the analysis presented below examines the existence of separate books of account, we have to understand that in many cases, especially for the earlier records, the boundaries between books of discipline and books of account are fluid and blurred. In some cases what survives are artificial collections of fragments that may bear little resemblance to the original form of the records. In others, notably in the northeast, as we will see, there is a hybrid form, which looks at first blush like an accounting register but in fact integrates records of discipline.

However, given these limitations, an analysis of the catalogue does reveal some interesting broad patterns. The first observation of interest is that the oldest surviving separate book of account is for the session of St Cuthbert's in Edinburgh. Dating from May 1608, this fragmentary register recorded collections under the label 'almes' for each Sabbath collection in a format that gave the date and amount, but in an unstructured form (that is, lacking the columnar format in later records). On 17 November there was an entry recording the receipt of 10d '@rent' (the label used for 'interest' throughout this and subsequent accounts) as being an amount due at Martinmass. The book was a record first of collections (the 'charge') and then in the second half the expenditure (the 'discharge'). These figures were not totalled, but the transactions were used to confirm the conformity of the transactions to the session's wishes in December 1608.

The use at St Cuthbert's of separate records for its financial transactions was followed by Edinburgh Canongate in 1637, then by Cramond and Dundee in 1638 and 1640. An examination of the catalogue indicates some broad patterns, suggesting that the emergence of separate money registers was a feature chiefly of eastern areas. Given 870 parishes in the church as a whole at the end of the eighteenth century, the adoption of separate accounts in 232 of them represents just over a quarter of all parishes. Detailed examination of the records for parishes in the presbyteries that we have been looking at in detail enables us to infer the existence of separate accounts from the format of the register of discipline, even if the money register itself has not survived. Thus the minutes of Bolton contained the figures in the right hand margin of the minutes until 1744.[16] Then a new book was started, which had the minutes at the beginning of the volume and separate accounts at the rear. In this case the accounts ran with the minutes until the end of the century. In other parishes the transition was much more abrupt. In Dirleton, for example, the left hand page in February 1752 had figures recorded, but then these simply disappeared.[17] What this means is that we can sometimes date the transition to a separate money register accurately, but in other cases we have to infer it. The inspection of the eighty parishes for which records survive gives thirty-six with separate accounts by the end of the eighteenth century, based on catalogue entries. However, closer examination of the records themselves indicated that twelve of these parishes had earlier accounts than those recorded in the catalogue, as inferred from the content of minutes. Five of these parishes were in the Ayr presbytery. Another fifteen parishes had no separate surviving accounts but their existence could be inferred. Six of these parishes were in Linlithgow presbytery, six in Hamilton. If the pattern of inferred accounts from the presbytery analysis were to hold good across the country then this might imply that a further 119 parishes might have had separate accounts. This assumption would indicate that perhaps 40 per cent of parishes had separate records. Of course, we have seen that these inferred accounts were to be found particularly in central and eastern presbyteries, which is, as we will see, just where separate accounts were more prevalent. So the figure of 40 per cent might be regarded as a maximum. This suggests a number of things. It suggests that Mitchison's observation about the limited success in separating out books of accounts from the registers is right. It further suggests that the emergence of separate accounts is a process that began early in the seventeenth century and, as we will see, was a feature of the eastern Lowlands. It therefore considerably predates the Humbie decision, although the biggest single increase in separate registers comes in the quarter-century after that decision.

Table 5.1 shows the top ten presbyteries with separate accounts by the end of the eighteenth century.

Table 5.1 Leading presbyteries with separate money registers

Presbytery	Number of parishes with separate money registers	Total parishes in presbytery	% with separate money in register
Stirling	9	11	81.82
Linlithgow	13	19	68.42
Kelso	6	9	66.67
Fordoun	8	13	61.54
Haddington	8	14	57.14
Dalkeith	9	16	56.25
Edinburgh	11	22	50.00
St Andrews	10	20	50.00
Perth	7	15	46.67
Auchterarder	6	13	46.15

Source: Mutch, 'Data mining'.

The east–central bias is clear. (It should be noted that, if we were to take inferred accounts into consideration, Linlithgow would be at 100 per cent.)

It was these areas that saw the development of assessments for poor relief. Haddington, of course, was the home presbytery of the parish of Humbie, which triggered the court case that Mitchison explored. However, stents for poor relief could also be found in west coast parishes. Unfortunately the Cambuslang records are missing for the period in which it also figured in a court case that turned on accounting for poor relief. This distribution does suggest where the move to separate accounts originated, which might well be reflected in the assumptions that lay behind the production of the 'procedure manuals', remembering that Pardovan had been a ruling elder in Linlithgow at both parochial and presbyterial levels.

Aggregating the figures by synod makes the spatial distribution easier to see, with the three east–central synods having the highest concentration. In Table 5.2 the percentage of parishes with money records is recorded in respect both of parishes with more than one set of records, and of all parishes. The comprehensive survival of records for the 'heartland' synods is seen clearly, as is the greater proportion of separate accounts. Even in the Lothians, however, the figure did not exceed 50 per cent of parishes. (This table also indicates the weak survival of records for the Western Highlands and Islands.)

Table 5.2 Separate money registers by synod

Synod	Registers	Of recorded parishes		Of total parishes	
	n	*n*	%	*n*	%
Lothian and Tweeddale	49	104	47.12	104	47.12
Perth and Stirling	29	63	46.03	63	46.03
Fife	26	69	37.68	69	37.68
Dumfries	12	40	30.00	48	25.00
Orkney	4	14	28.57	14	28.57
Glasgow and Ayr	36	134	26.87	134	26.87
Merse and Teviotdale	18	67	26.87	67	26.87
Angus and Mearns	17	65	26.15	76	22.37
Shetland	1	4	25.00	4	25.00
Aberdeen	20	89	22.47	89	22.47
Argyll	3	14	21.43	34	8.82
Moray	7	33	21.21	48	14.58
Galloway	7	36	19.44	36	19.44
Caithness and Sutherland	1	9	11.11	22	4.55
Ross	2	18	11.11	24	8.33
Glenelg	0	0	0.00	42	0.00
Totals	232	759	30.57	874	26.54

Source: Mutch, 'Data mining'.

Table 5.3 shows the temporal progression of this process. It is sorted by the earliest adopters, showing how central the Lothians were to this process. After early beginnings in Edinburgh, there was a strong concentration of adoption around Dalkeith in the later seventeenth century. The early adopters in Angus and the Mearns did not appear to lead to any sustained adoption and may reflect particular contingent factors. In Dundee this might be related to an urban mercantile elite, but the same would not be true for Bervie. In the early eighteenth century the impetus was taken up in Fife and moved to the west in the shape of Glasgow and Ayr. The second half of the century saw the trend accelerate here, which may indeed reflect the decisions at Humbie and Cambuslang.

Table 5.3 The progress of separate money registers

Synod	1600–49	1650–99	1700–49	1750–99	Cumulative		
					To 1699	To 1750	To 1799
Lothian and Tweeddale	5	17	15	12	22	37	49
Angus and Mearns	2	0	3	12	2	5	17
Glasgow and Ayr	0	4	12	21	4	16	37
Perth and Stirling	0	4	6	19	4	10	29
Fife	0	2	12	12	2	14	26
Merse and Teviotdale	0	1	9	8	1	10	18
Aberdeen	0	1	3	16	1	4	20
Dumfries	0	1	1	10	1	2	12
Galloway	0	0	4	3	0	4	7
Moray	0	0	2	5	0	2	7
Orkney	0	0	1	3	0	1	4
Ross	0	0	1	1	0	1	2
Argyll	0	0	0	2	0	0	2
Caithness and Sutherland	0	0	0	1	0	0	1
Shetland	0	0	0	1	0	0	1
Glenelg	0	0	0	0	0	0	0

Source: Mutch, 'Data mining'.

Unfortunately, the accounting records for the parish of Linlithgow itself do not survive, but an examination of two parishes where a complete run exists for the eighteenth century is instructive. In both Abercorn and Kirkliston transaction records were maintained to support regular processes of the review of accounts.[18] In Kirkliston, accounts were reviewed on a quarterly basis right through the century: the most complete form of record keeping and reconciliation to be found of the parishes examined for the selected presbyteries. In neighbouring Abercorn (which bordered the lands of Pardovan) a regular process of half-year accounting based on very clear ledgers took place from 1703 until it was disrupted by both the events of 1745–6 and the departure of a minister. It could be that this represented the continuation of taken-for-granted practices in the presbytery that commenced with Falkirk in 1660 and saw another six parishes adopt separate money registers between 1688 and 1692. In turn, the creators of the guidance might have assumed that this standard would be expected by other readers of their work and so they did not need to include it explicitly.

Record format

Establishing that separate accounting records were by no means simply a response to the Humbie decision confirms the centrality of accounting to Scottish church governance, but tells us nothing about the format of these records. In order to appreciate the format, we need to move from general patterns to the investigation of the records themselves. This investigation indicates a range of ways of recording financial transactions. Financial records can be used for a variety of purposes, each of which shapes the format that is used. For the records to confirm that transactions line up with decisions taken by the session, each transaction should be recorded separately with a mean-ingful description. In order to use this information for decision making, we would want these transactions to be made in a form that would enable the financial position to be easily determined. Finally, to ensure that the steward-ship of the session's money had been faithfully carried out, we would want to be able to strike a balance and compare it to the resources, chiefly cash in the box, held at the date of the balance.[19] We can see from the surviving records that different parts of the church moved at different paces towards fulfilling these criteria.

At its most basic, financial information was integrated into the minutes of the session. As an example, here is the first entry for the session of Kemnay in 1750:

> The Minr of Monymusk preached Proverbs 13th Chap Verse 32nd. This day there was collected o=11sh=6d and Left in Geo Reid hand £3. There was Given out of the former Collection in Geo Reids hand for Shoes to Agnes Gray in Lachintilly o£=12s=od Given John Thomson a blind man Beging: So that what remains in his hand of the Collections Since Decr 17th is only 2£=6s=od[.][20]

This was the complete entry and it shows that even at a late date (bearing in mind that this was as the Humbie judgement was being reached) some sessions were using a completely textual form of recording, which might contain the necessary detail but in a format that would require considerable work to summarise, let alone analyse. As the incoming treasurer of Humbie observed on his reorganisation of the books of that parish in 1729, 'he hath gathered all the particular items of their depursements together it being tideous to search them out and add them together in case the Session shall enquire thereanent'. A development from this was to make the figures stand out more clearly, if still part of the minute. Thus the first entry for January 1750 in the register of Insch read:

> Minr Lect John: 19th from v 30th to ye end Coll. 10s 6d.

This form of presentation evolved to the placing of the relevant detail in the margin, as in this, the first entry in 1750 in Chapel of Garioch:

| The Minr preach: text Acts 16.14 Coll: Thirteen Sh: two D | o: 13: 2[21] |
| The Minr intimate that he was now to begin dyets of Examination & Visitation of Families & appointed five days for that purpose this week. | |

Here both collections and disbursements were recorded in the same column, making it difficult to distinguish between the two. What emerges, earlier in some parishes than in others, was the practice of ruling in two columns, generally headed 'Charge' and 'Discharge'. In Inverurie, for example, as early as 1716 the minutes had separate columns on each page for charge and discharge, with a running total being struck at the foot of each page. The next development was the separation out of this data, either into pages at the back of the minute book or into a separate 'money register', which often came to contain full details of all transactions. The examples given have all been derived from the presbytery of Garioch, which exhibited a greater variety of formats at a later date than those to be found elsewhere. These are useful for illustrating the development of transaction records. Understanding these distinctions allows us to code records from 1, representing the textual embeddness of Kemnay, to 11, where a separate register was maintained.[22] Using this coding scheme across the five presbyteries selected for detailed examination gives the summary in Table 5.4.

Table 5.4 Transaction detail in accounting records by presbytery

	Ayr	Garioch	Haddington	Hamilton	Linlithgow
1725	10	7	11	10	11
1750	11	9	11	10	11
1775	11	10	11	n.a.	11
1799	11	9	11	11	11

Source: Calculated from session accounts.

Note: n.a. = Data not available.

This table, which gives the modal value for each presbytery in quarter-centuries, indicates the conservatism of the Aberdeenshire presbytery but also a general move towards separate money registers, confirming the trend gleaned from the broader analysis. However, while this confirms that the practice in the eighteenth-century Church of Scotland at local level, as represented by these parishes (between thirty-five and forty-two parishes for each year examined, conditioned by record survival) was to keep detailed records of financial transactions, this tells us nothing about the format of these transactions.

It is difficult to code the full variety of these records, but a number of key dimensions were examined. From inspection, a 'classic' pattern was that where for each year discharge and charge were presented on facing pages.[23] On each page there was a column for the date, a description of the transaction and a column showing the value. In this 'classic' pattern, illustrated in Figure 5.1, transactions were recorded across the full year and continued until the formal balance was struck, often at the end of the year.

Charge					Discharge				
Date	Description	£	s	d	Date	Description	£	s	d

Figure 5.1 Double-page accounting layout

A refinement of this that emerged over the century was a more periodic balancing, initially quarterly but in some parishes monthly. Here, transactions for the period were displayed against each other and, if this did not take up the full page, blank space was left. By contrast, in some parishes, especially in the earlier periods, methods of recording were used that were more conserving of paper, with a double column format on each page being employed. This clearly produced a more cramped layout, with less room available for descriptive text (Figure 5.2).

Charge					Discharge				
Date	Description	£	s	d	Date	Description	£	s	d

Figure 5.2 Two columns on a page accounting layout

In order to see what patterns were more common from these observations, accounts were coded according to whether they adopted a one- or two-column-per-page format, whether transactions simply ran on or were segregated by period and whether charge and discharge faced each other or where intermixed. Of the 115 observations made, seventy-five, or 65 per cent, were of the single-column page variety and this was particularly the case towards the end of the century, where the percentage climbed to 68 per cent. It was noticeable that the two-column format was concentrated in the presbyteries of Ayr and Hamilton, the two accounting for 85 per cent of the instances. This is suggestive of practice being shaped by the sharing of ideas within administrative units, although no evidence of formal guidance has been found. Examination of the order of entries suggests that the majority ran continuously for a year, although there was a trend towards more periodical presentations by the end of the century. Most account books, as well, followed the format of having charge/discharge on facing pages (71 per cent). In twenty-four sessions (20 per cent) the transactions were presented after each other; that is, charges were presented first in a continuous stream, followed by discharges. In the rest of the cases transactions were mixed together, a format found when each page had columns for date and description, but two sets of columns for charge and discharge (Figure 5.3).

Year								
Date	Description of charge item	£	s	d				
Date	Description of discharge item				£	s	d	
Date	Description of charge item	£	s	d				

Figure 5.3 Mixed transactions on a page

What this indicates is that there was a 'classic' form of transaction recording, which was indeed the biggest single category, but that there was no uniformity of practice. That is, while all the parishes examined outside of some in the early years of the century in the Garioch kept detailed books, there was no standard format. The format adopted varied according to local practice and it is not clear why this should be the case. It suggests that, in the absence of formal national guidance, practice was shaped at the level of the presbytery. Visitations of parishes by presbyteries certainly contained injunctions about the recording of transactions and sometimes injunctions about how this was to be done. So, for example, among the nine recommendations following the visitation of Kirkliston in 1707 was that 'they revise their Treasurers Accompts, Charges and Discharges and Balances the same exactly and that they record the same in their Register'.[24] In 1710 the presbytery of Cupar recommended to the minister of Dunbog, whose registers they had just revised:

> to have but one column on every page, and to leave a large Margent and that every particular be marked there; As also that the collections be not mixed with the Discipline but in distinct places of the book, or in different books.[25]

In similar vein the same presbytery recommended at its parochial visitation of Logie that 'in time coming to write the Discipline and accompts of the poors money in two Distinct books'.[26] As noted above, this was precisely the time at which the shift to separate books took off in Fife. However, there was nothing here about how these separate records should be kept. In Cambuslang in 1775 the presbytery found that that transactions seemed to be accurate, but that 'they should balance their accounts at least once every year'.[27] However, it is unusual to get observations like that in Old Meldrum in 1767:

> [the] Session could not but highly approve of their Clerks exactness yet recommended to him to keep Collections and Distributions on One and the same page, distinguishing the Columns at Top of the page by the Titles of Collections and Distributions.[28]

If we combine the dimensions examined, then the biggest single category was indeed that represented by the classic pattern that provided the template for Figure 5.1, but this only represented 40 per cent of those parishes with detailed accounts (and 33 per cent of the 141 parishes examined if we include the 'textual' records noted above). The next two groups were those with a similar format but with either more periodical presentations or continuous transactions (13 and 12 per cent respectively).

Using the records

Having established that detailed bookkeeping was a feature of local practice, but that this bookkeeping was not of a standardised form, what was the effect of this detailed recording? The continuous corporate form of the kirk session, coupled with detailed record keeping, meant that accounts could be used to adjust and monitor spending, which ought to manifest itself in positive balances at periodic reconciliations.[29] The balances were recorded for all the records available in the presbyteries and for the years examined in Table 5.4. The result was that of 122 balances only three (that is, 2 per cent) were negative. However, this is only a snapshot, which might be misleading. Accordingly, two parishes were selected from each presbytery, based on those with the most extensive run of accounts, and balances were examined throughout the century.[30] This gave a total of 1,052 balances examined, of which thirty-eight, or just over 4 per cent, were negative. (A further twenty-six recorded a zero balance, 3 per cent of the total.) It is possible through this analysis to find pockets where the keeping of detailed books failed to prevent runs of negative balances. Most noticeable was Kirkliston in the 1790s, where the elegance of its accounts could not help in tackling a structural imbalance between the demand for relief and the funds available. It is interesting to note that this was a parish where a wealthy treasurer stepped in to fund the deficits. However, this analysis does suggest that financial control was aided by bookkeeping practices. The significance of this will become clearer when we contrast it with the situation in England in Chapter 7.

The balances recorded in this exercise were only those where a formal note was made of reconciliation between the minutes that authorised expenditure, the financial records that contained the transactions and the money held in the poor's box (of which more below). These reconciliations are usually noted in considerable detail, often in rather ponderous language, as in the following from Rayne in July 1750:

> And then proceeding to revise the treasurers account & having diligently collated and compared them with the accounts kept by their clerk and finding them to agree in omnibus found that the hail money intromitted with by him from the Day of last clearance (vide page 61 & 62) amounts to the sum of Ninety six pounds ten shillings & Eight pennies Scots money That he had at sundry times from the date foresaid with the knowledge of the session & by their orders & with their special approbation including the articles in his Discharge of this Date deburst all & whole the sum of sixty three pounds three shillings & four pennies Scots money, from whence it appeared that the sum remaining in his hands & now to be accounted for by him is thirty three pounds seven shillings & four pennies Scots.[31]

As we have noted above, in some parishes such reconciliations took place quarterly. However, this proved to be unusual in the sample and, in fact, to be limited to Kirkliston parish (throughout the century) and Inverurie (later in the century). The biggest number was annual balancing at 456 of the 1,052 balances, or 43 per cent. In 21 per cent of cases reconciliation was performed half-yearly. These figures deserve further analysis, especially to examine longitudinal shifts, where the evidence indicates a move to both more frequent and more regular balancing as the century wore on, something supported by the move to more periodic presentation of accounts as noted above. In Gladsmuir, in 1760, for example, 'the Session further resolve to have two annual meetings for considering the State of the poor and their funds and that the said Meetings shall be held at the Kirk the first Monday after Whitsunday & Martinmass Yearly'.[32]

As well as these moves towards more regular balancing, there are hints of a more analytical approach to recording. In some parishes this is imposed on the recording of transactions where, for example, an initial classification of income into collections, interest on money lent and other sources of income shapes how transactions are presented. In some cases this has led to a more detailed analysis of finances. In the parish of Bolton, for example, a hearse was purchased in 1723. This was then lent out for a flat rate for the first mile, with a mileage charge for each mile thereafter (and higher charges for extra-parochial use). In 1744 the reconciliations started to analyse income, so that £14 6s od had been raised by the hearse. From 1762 there was an analysis of income and expenditure on the hearse, from which we can ascertain that by

1783, when a new hearse was purchased, income from its use had amounted to £1,141.15.0 against maintenance expenditure of £271.11.0.[33] The same accounts also contained 'T' accounts of the state of various loans that the session had made. This did seem to be a particularly entrepreneurial parish, however, and there are only limited traces of the use of transaction recording to analyse financial positions elsewhere. This is about bookkeeping rather than sophisticated accounting, but the evidence suggests how widespread the practice of the careful recording of financial transactions was.

One consequence of this careful recording is that we are able (especially later in the century when separate accounts, either physically in different registers or in discrete parts of the register of discipline, were more prevalent) to get a sense of the broad patterns of income and expenditure. This then sets the duties of the treasurer in context, giving an appreciation of what they needed to achieve. For 1790 twenty-four sets of accounts across our five presbyteries were analysed to show patterns of transactions across a number of broad categories.[34] Table 5.5 shows average income and expenditure for each of the five presbyteries. While it shows some interesting variations, which will be touched on in the discussion that follows, it does show some broad similarities.

Table 5.5 Income and expenditure, pounds sterling, 1790

	Ayr	Garioch	Haddington	Hamilton	Linlithgow
Income					
Collection	17.42	11.88	12.52	21.75	17.83
Interest	9.27	3.42	14.91	11.04	19.01
Seat rents	0.20	2.03	0.50	0.00	0.26
Discipline	1.14	1.36	0.16	0.80	0.70
Mortcloth	0.61	0.43	3.35	7.91	5.59
Miscellaneous	0.61	0.96	2.48	2.10	3.05
Donation	0.00	0.00	2.42	7.25	4.45
Assessment	0.00	0.00	6.26	0.00	0.00
Totals	29.25	20.08	42.60	50.85	50.89
Expenditure					
Poor	27.21	12.96	37.60	46.75	43.47
Fee	1.83	4.05	3.51	3.13	3.50
Fabric	0.02	0.44	0.35	0.00	0.25
Miscellaneous	0.31	1.17	2.93	0.02	0.33
Totals	29.37	18.62	44.39	49.90	47.55

Source: Calculated from session accounts.

These figures are for spending in the year, and so do not show movements in funds that would support the deficits in two of the presbyteries. However,

Table 5.6 Percentage income and expenditure by categories, 1790

	Ayr	Garioch	Haddington	Hamilton	Linlithgow	Total
Income						
Collection	59.58	59.16	29.39	42.79	44.16	44.74
Interest	31.69	17.02	35.00	21.71	21.06	25.58
Pews	0.68	10.10	1.16	0.00	0.64	2.22
Discipline	3.88	6.79	0.38	1.57	1.74	2.50
Mortcloth	2.10	2.16	7.86	15.55	13.84	9.12
Miscellaneous	2.07	4.77	5.83	4.12	7.55	5.04
Donation	0.00	0.00	5.68	14.25	11.02	7.05
Assessment	0.00	0.00	14.69	0.00	0.00	3.75
Expenditure						
Poor	92.68	69.60	84.70	93.69	91.42	87.06
Fee	6.22	21.74	7.90	6.27	7.36	9.27
Fabric	0.05	2.38	0.79	0.00	0.53	0.69
Miscellaneous	1.05	6.28	6.61	0.04	0.69	2.97

Source: Calculated from session accounts.

given this, the income and expenditure were broadly aligned. Average income in the Garioch fell far below that of the more improved and richer areas to the south. If we look at percentages under each broad heading then the similarities become clearer.

As we would expect, the vast bulk of the spending was on the poor, although the poverty of the Garioch parishes meant that their spending on fees, which were a relatively fixed item, was a much higher proportion of their expenditure. It is interesting to note that income from seat rental was a significant figure here, whereas it was insignificant elsewhere. In these other presbyteries the ability to accumulate money and lend it out generated a significant proportion of income from interest. The presence of relatively wealthy nobility in some parishes meant they could also count on substantial charitable donations. In 1777, for example, the kirk session of Saltoun recorded that it was 'penetrated with a sense of the Divine Goodness, in exciting so many of the Branches of the Family of Salton to contribute to the supply of the wants of the Poor of this Parish'.[35] What is a little misleading about a snapshot like this is that it underplays the impact of assessments, which might only be called for at irregular intervals. However, all these factors form the backdrop to a closer examination of the duties of the treasurer, and some of these figures will be explored more in that examination.

Getting the money in

Hanham, in her detailed study of the Lothian parish of Cramond, notes that from 1651 the treasurer was always chosen from the ranks of the heritors on the session.[36] It was not until 1774 that Robert Spotswood, a surgeon, became the first non-heritor to fulfil the office, one that he occupied for twenty years. Some echoes of this practice can be found in other Lothian parishes. Andrew Dunbar of Leuchold was session treasurer for Dalmeny in 1710, when it was noted that 'he was very exact in his accompts'.[37] However, this was not the case in many sessions. Consideration of the role of the treasurer requires us to consider some of their duties as well as the social context in which they operated. The pattern obtaining in the polite sessions of the Lothians, where assessments for poor relief were frequent and heritors closely involved in their operation, was not necessarily one to be found elsewhere. Unfortunately, the surviving records do not always identify explicitly who occupied the role of the treasurer, taking it for granted that those who were concerned locally about the activities of the treasurer would know his identity. It is, therefore, difficult to make generalisations about who undertook the role and for how long, although we can piece together some broad patterns from the hints contained in the records.

One key task was the collection of money. The prime source of income was the collections at weekly services and the 'elder at the plate' was a stock figure. Collections were made outside the church, not during the service, and this in itself was a challenge in the Scottish weather. At Gladsmuir in 1739:

> the two timber boxes wherein the Elders were wont to shelter themselves from the weather in attending the common Collections at the Church being worn out & intirely broken & find it impracticable to make these Collections without some covert, especially in Rainy weather & the winter season, they agreed unanimously that it would be by far more profitable to build little houses or Huts of stone covered with blue slate upon one side of each of the two porches.[38]

Once collected, the amounts were counted and deposited in the poor box. Graham asserts that in some parishes this 'was placed at the church door instead of a plate. There were two slits – one narrow, for silver; the other wider, for copper'.[39] However, there is no evidence of this practice in the records examined (and Graham himself gives no source). His account rather suggests that the contents of the box would be a surprise when it was opened, but the records suggest a process of careful recording before deposits were made. There are several references to the clerk keeping a 'by book' or 'cheque account'. So, at Abercorn after their financial affairs had got into a muddle, the session resolved in 1751 that:

> a small Book or paper containing an Account both of Charge & Discharge to be kept in the said Box, & every article to be immediately entered both into that & the principal Book of Accounts, when money is either received or given out.[40]

At Cambuslang, one of the arguments used against the session in the dispute over its management of the poor's money was that they did not immediately count the collections made at communion. In pointing out that this was to demand the impossible, especially given the crowds involved, the session's response gives rare details of the practices that were no doubt repeated in other sessions across the country:

> The Elders after divine worship, counted what they themselves or their substitutes had collected, & put it into the Session-Box, with a Note on a bit paper, Signifying that such a Sum was collected on such a day and then to lock the Box, on which were two locks & two keys, to take the Keys home with them: or if they had not time to count it that evening, to put money collected wrapt up in a Napkin in the Box, and to lock it and carrying away the Keys, and to count it tomorrow or at first leisure and then to put it & a Note with in in the Box.[41]

Once having counted the collection, it then needed to be recorded and here again the Cambuslang case points to some of the problems faced by sessions. Collecting the money was one thing; having the skills to count and record it could be problematic when elders, 'were all persons in low life[,] illiterate Country-men who had not been trained up to writing or Accounts with any tollerable Exactness'.[42] As we will see, this placed the spotlight on the role of the session clerk.

In some parishes, particularly in the Lothians, these collections were not the only source of income. In 1700 the session of Aberlady met with the heritors to consider how much money they needed for the support of their poor. They decided on two elders to be 'collectors and uplifters of the said soum', to arrange for its distribution and to account for it either monthly or quarterly.[43] The collection of assessments in these areas involved the updating of the stent roll, based on valuations of land held or rentals payable, and the collection of the subsequent rate. This was not an enviable task and minutes often record the collection of assessments in several tranches. In Gladsmuir in 1790, the parish that contributed most to the figure for assessment in the Haddington presbytery, the £27 sterling collected was recorded in thirteen transactions spread across the whole year.[44] The collection of interest on bonds could also be a delicate process. In 1778, for example, there was ten years interest outstanding on General Horn's bill of £72 sterling to the Chapel of Garioch session, the minutes noting:

> And General Horn requires that for the future that in order to prevent the Interest of this bond from accumulating, or the poor people lie out of their money, the treasurer call upon him in proper time annually to uplift the same.[45]

Sometimes the minister would be sent to negotiate with more recalcitrant heritors, bringing to the fore tensions that exploded in Humbie and Cambuslang, of which more below.

Treasurers were also responsible for the distribution of money. Most sessions maintained a list of regular pensioners whom they paid either monthly or quarterly. They also paid out 'occasional' distributions in the case of immediate want. The figures for the poor above also contain money paid for the school fees of those too poor to pay them themselves and, in some cases, sums of money to enable the destitute to take up a trade or business. In 1780, for example, the session of Aberlady agreed to give the blacksmith Alexander Richardson 'now in Extreme Poverty' ten shillings to 'buy an Anvil Bellows and other tools necessary in the way of his Trade to enable him thereby to earn his maintenance without being troublesome to the publick'.[46] All these matters were recorded, with varying degrees of detail to be sure, in records that became clearer and more structured as the century progressed. In addition to the recording of transactions, treasurers would also be custodians of the poor box, hints of which have already been encountered. What is frustrating here is that, while the poor box was clearly a central artefact in the accountability practices exercised in the eighteenth-century church, no examples appear to have survived (or at least none in public collections). The guidance documents that we have examined and the records of visitations assume its existence, but also assume that readers will be familiar with its attributes. There is nothing about the nature of the box, how it was to be secured and who was to hold it. For insights into all these features, we have to turn to the clues, often provided in passing, supplied by the local records.

The poor box

A first observation is that there was often not one box, but two. In Dirleton in 1726 'the keys of both the larger and lesser boxes belonging to the Session were in their presence delivered to Geo Worth and Wm Yule the present treasurers'.[47] In others, reference was made to separate elements of the same artefact. So, in Monymusk in 1728:

> the Session therefore knowing that there was not so much in the outer box as would serve, they ordered their Treasurer to meet with the Minister & Clerk this week and [work] out what was in the Inner box & give him.[48]

This points to a differentiation of function, as explored in more detail below. Orders for new boxes suggest that they were made by local tradesmen and that there was not a market for kirk boxes. In 1722, for example, the session of Haddington resolved 'to cause make a Box of Wainscot with Iron bars and with three different locks and keys to keep the papers and money belonging to the poor'.[49]

One functional split was between the little box as a repository for collections and the larger box as the home for the capital stock of the session. So in Garvald in 1727 it was resolved that 'the balance may be putt into the little box att ye end of each month and likewise resolved that these accounts shall be cleared twice a year and what balance is found putt into ye larger poor's box'.[50] Clearly, losing such records could pose real problems for sessions. In Chapel of Garioch in 1730 the clerk was obliged to confess that, 'upon Tuesday night last the Session Box [which was in his custody] was burnt through the negligence of his servant and all the papers which were therein destroyed'.[51] This meant that letters had to be written to those holding the session's money to get new papers drawn up. At Aberlady in 1737 the session discovered to their dismay that, 'the Box in the Session House in which was all the money collected since last Clearing October 15th 1736 Except the Necessary Debursements broken up and all the Money Stolen'.[52] Despite their best efforts, they were unable to discover who had purloined the £135 16s 9d Scots money that it contained. In Bolton the treasurer Patrick Begbie owed money to the session and had failed to settle his accounts with them. However, this did nothing towards enabling the session to access the money held in the box, as Patrick failed to surrender the keys he held. As he still owed the session the money held in his bond of 1703, Begbie might have been using his possession of the keys as a bargaining chip. In exasperation at the failure of legal efforts to obtain redress, the session in 1718 recorded that 'by the Sherriffs order the two boxes belonging to this Session were broken up the said Patrick Begbie having refused to deliver up the keys and that money in both boxes was counted by Baillie Douglas'.[53] This example raises further questions about where the box was held and who had access to its contents. As we have noted above, not all records contain details of where the box was held. In the case of Aberlady above, it is because a crime occurred that we know that the poor box was held in the session house, a room attached to the church in which the session could meet. Not all sessions possessed such a room (although they became more widespread as the century wore on), nor was it necessarily considered to be the most appropriate place. Security was one consideration, but availability was another. In Insch, the rule was that 'the Box must stand in the Kirk officer's house', for unstated reasons, but when in Garvald the box was held by the session clerk this was 'his house being near to the Church'.[54]

The box, therefore, stood at the intersection of a number of actors who all played a part in regulating the financial affairs of the parish. As we have seen, boxes were secured by multiple locks: in the case of Haddington, three, but more usually two. In some unusual cases both of these keys were held by the same person (in Garvald in 1754 by the minister; in Gladsmuir in 1746 by the treasurer[55]), but it was the usual practice to place keys in the hands of different people. So, in 1757 when Charles Watt began what was to be a forty-two year term of office as treasurer in Chapel of Garioch, 'One of the Keys of the Box was delivered to him and the other to the Min[iste]r'.[56] At Kemnay in 1720 the new treasurer 'got one of the keys of the box & the Clerk keeps the other'.[57] It is not clear whether these were duplicate keys for the same lock or keys to separate locks, both of which had to be used to open the box. Logic tends to suggest the latter arrangement, as this would be consistent with the care generally exercised to secure the resources of the session.

The treasurer

As we have noted, the minister was always the moderator (or chair) of the session and meetings could not happen without his presence (or, when the parish was vacant, that of a minister appointed by the presbytery). While his formal role was to sign off accounts when they were revised, because of concern with status he was often involved in negotiating loans or seeking interest from major landowners. However, most of the practical business was conducted by the treasurer and the session clerk. The treasurer was selected from the ranks of the elders, and practice with regards to his term of office varied. This is not always clear from surviving records, but where the details are recorded there were some parishes where treasurers served only a six-month or, more typically, an annual term. In Dalrymple, for example, there were treasurers serving only an annual term up to 1731, but then James Allison served for sixteen years.[58] It does appear as the century wore on that the post of treasurer was more likely to become a semi-permanent one. In Saltoun the session were almost obsequious in their annual recording of thanks to their treasurer, Archibald Horn, noting in 1779:

> They are very sensible of the accuracy of their Accts & present their best thanks to their Treasurer for his care & diligence & unanimously request the favour of him to continue to execute the office of Treasurer for the year ensuing, to which he had the goodness to consent.[59]

This tactic clearly continued to be successful, the session recording their thanks to Horn in 1793 for his 'uncommon attention to the affairs of the Poor and to request that, as soon as his health permitted, he would be so obliging as to resume the management as formerly'.[60] Unfortunately Horn died in office, but that seems typical of a large number of treasurers. Being a treasurer was an onerous duty, and it could be difficult to get elders to take on the task. In Garvald in 1727, Patrick Bertram 'having declined the office of Church Treasurer & desiring to be excused', the session could not find a volunteer to take his place. They decided that the elders who collected for a month in turn should keep their own record of collections and distributions, to be matched up with one maintained by the session clerk, already therefore inferring a level of numeracy and literacy. In Gladsmuir in 1786 the session unanimously selected John Duncan 'Coalier' to be their treasurer, 'as being both qualified for the work and best able to undergo the fatigue & labour thereof:– as being a young man'. This nicely illustrates both the personal attributes and the skills

needed to act as treasurer, skills that Duncan might have honed in his occu-
pational roles. There does seem to have been a shift over the century from
collectors to treasurers: with the spread of literacy, treasurers took on more of
the duties of recording transactions, acting in concert with the session clerk.

In some parishes, because of the combined difficulties in getting volun-
teers and the lack of literacy, the session clerk took on the duties of treasurer
as well. This became formalised in at least three of the parishes inspected,
where in Humbie, Dailly and Dundonald, at least for some part of the
century, the session clerk was also the treasurer. This arrangement lasted
longest in Dundonald, where John Baillie was both clerk and treasurer from
1764 until at least 1780. In 1779 he reported to the session that, 'he thought
necessary that as he is Clerk and Treasurer both, he should have a Comp-
troller to keep a separate account', a wish that was granted. To this combination of roles might be attributed the occasional mention of a fee to the
treasurer, something that was not an approved practice unless the offices were
combined in this way. Thus in Abercorn in 1775 there was payment of fifteen
shillings for the treasurer's 'salary' and in Cumnock in 1799 'To treasurers
fee 10s'. These were rather unusual and isolated entries, and their dates might
suggest the emergence of a more specialised role, one undertaken by a man
like Archibald Horn. Manager of the local bleachfield in Saltoun for the
British Linen Company until 1773, he served as treasurer for at least ten years.

Disputes over accountability

Despite the variability caused by local contexts and traditions, there is a clear
thread of accountability for financial transactions throughout these records.
It became more structured and clearer as the eighteenth century wore on,
but is not the product of the Humbie decision, having far older origins. This
thread of accountability comes despite the lack of attention paid to it in the
guidance books produced at the beginning of the century. The framers of
such guidance, like the minute takers in many sessions, may simply have
assumed the practices that we have been able to reconstruct from fragmentary
traces in the records. These practices meant that in most parishes in the
Lowlands it is possible to reconstruct, to a greater or lesser degree of detail,
patterns of income and expenditure. These have their origins in the deep
attachment of the Scottish church to the care of the poor as a spiritual, not
an administrative, matter, one of the signs of a church in which 'all things be
done decently and in order'.[61] The formalisation of the recording of the transactions entered into in order to fulfil this duty were likely to have come about
partly through the parochial visitations, which enjoined particular types of
record keeping but not their detailed format, and partly through discussions
at presbyteries, accounting for the distinctive patterns to be found within

presbyteries (such as the two-column format widely used in the presbytery of Hamilton, but rarely elsewhere). As the century progressed the steady enhancement of the educational qualifications of parish schoolteachers acting as session clerks and the spread of literacy, especially among the 'middling sorts' who formed the bulk of the eldership, assisted this formalisation of the records. This then forms the context for a return to the cases of Humbie and Cambuslang.

Tensions between heritors and church bodies were a two-way affair. As part of the Reformation settlement, heritors gained control of the tiends that had supported the church, incorporating them as part of rentals. In return, they were responsible for the provision and repair of the kirk, manse and school, as well as the minister's stipend and glebe. We have already noted the difficulties of getting agreement between heritors for the funding of repairs. Visitation reports are replete with complaints about heritors avoiding their obligations. At the same time, in the opposite direction, it was in the interests of heritors that church funds for the relief of the poor were maximised and used in optimal fashion, in order that the burden might not be thrown on them. This led to demands for the inspection of accounts. But behind this functional explanation was also a growing desire on the part of heritors to exercise their authority. Such desires can be found in areas other than Cambuslang and Humbie. Accordingly, the next section examines both of these tensions in turn.

In Table 5.5 we saw that small sums were spent on the fabric of the church: for example 2s 6d on glazing the church widows in Gladsmuir.[62] Properly speaking, all such expenditure was the responsibility of the heritors and reimbursement should have been sought, but in some cases this was blatantly ignored. In Garvald in February 1782, John Hay of Hopes represented to the session (of which his father was an elder):

> that as there had been great Complaints of the Coldness of the Church, Since the late repairs, and the Alteration of the Door, which both prevented the Regular Attendance of Many in the Parish in the Winter season and very hurtful for the Elders to stand and receive the Collections; for to remedy which, His Father and He had ordered the Porch at the Church Door to be Built.[63]

He requested, and received, payment out of the interest due from a donation his grandfather had made, which had accumulated for seven years. This was clearly a use of money intended for other purposes against the heritor's responsibilities and would have been roundly condemned in other presbyteries. Indeed, even in another parish, Saltoun, in the same presbytery, the session observed in 1793 that the poors fund had been used for the 'temporary discharge of the Heritors Acct'.[64] Declaring that this was an improper use, they resolved not to do so in the future. Parochial visitations frequently observe that sessions were improperly applying the money collected for matters that ought to be the province of the heritors. At their visitation of

Kilmarnock in 1730 the presbytery of Irvine concluded that they were 'of opinion that the Session should expend no more of the poor's money for Reparations', ensuring that heritors met their obligations.[65] The presbytery of Linlithgow found when it returned to Falkirk in 1740 that their previous advice had been ignored:

> they are advised by the Presbytery not to imploy any of the Poors Money for reparations of Church or Manse without the advice & Consent of the Presbytery had thereto, and yet they have been in use to depurse Sums of money for the said purposes frequently afterwards.[66]

This shirking of responsibilities was an irritant to presbyteries, but of more significance were attempts to assert control over the activities of the session itself. These predate the Humbie judgement. The position with poor relief was that half of the collections of the church were to be subject to the joint management of heritors and session. This was, as Cage notes, purely a conceptual distinction: there are no examples of separate accounting practices.[67] In practice, many heritors were content to let their session do all the administrative work. They were invited to an annual meeting for the settling of accounts, but many chose not to attend. In many parishes this was uncontroversial and the issue of joint management was never raised. Where churchmen had concerns was not only with their ability to distribute money on an occasional basis, but also with what they saw as dangerous Erastian tendencies – that is, especially against the backdrop of opposition to patronage, the encroachment of secular powers on matters of church governance. In 1740 the presbytery of Stirling discussed the concerns of the minister of Alva that Sir Charles Erskine, 'by virtue of a legal Right vested in his person as Patron and Sole Heritor of the Parish of Alva', was claiming the right not only to meet with the session but also ' that the poors Money cannot be dispos'd of without his Special Advice and Direction or his Deputs'.[68] The presbytery declared their opposition to this, forbidding the minister and session to accede and writing to Erskine accordingly, opposition 'which in a consistency with the Regard they Owe to the Rights and priviledges of the Church they could not avoid'. What happened is not clear; presumably Erskine did not pursue his demand. In the following year several members of the presbytery of Dumbarton reported that, as a consequence of a recent decision by the justices of the peace, they were being threatened with joint administration of poor funds. Matters came to a head in one parish, Kilmaronock, where the minister refused to allow inspection of session accounts as a matter of principle.[69] The intervention of the presbytery following a parochial visitation resulted in a negotiated settlement, but it was this matter of principle that was at the root of the Humbie and Cambuslang affairs.

The other common feature was an obdurate and litigious heritor. In both parishes, despite their claims to the contrary, the dissident heritors represented no one but themselves. At Cambuslang, John Hamilton of Westburn had paid no interest for a period of twelve years on a bill for nearly £30 sterling, despite the urgings of members of the session. What might have enraged him was the decision of the session in November 1748 to return to their minutes following the death of their session clerk and insert a new minute detailing his failure to pay and its consequences for the poor.[70] At Humbie the key actor was the Laird of Humbie and the dispute between him and the minister went a good deal further back. The tale is a torturous one, but involved legal processes against the laird for the recovery of money owed to the poor and his refusal to part with documents belonging to the session. In 1730 this was followed by attempts by Humbie (who was the chief, but not the only heritor) to have his candidate for schoolmaster and session clerk accepted.[71] The session, however, stood on their dignity and their right to appoint their own candidate. This led to considerable tensions between the minister and the rejected candidate, which saw the process, according to the presbytery, being 'wakened' by the schoolmaster Robert Young. In both cases attempts were made to secure compromises, attempts that foundered on the obduracy shown by both sides.

In Cambuslang much of the dispute revolved round the custody of the session's registers. While they agreed to allow Westburn to inspect their register in the presence of their clerk, he was refused permission to make notes from it. This was because, the session declared, 'we would not tamely throw up any thing we conceive to be any of the Rights of the Church'.[72] Following negotiation, Westburn was allowed to make notes, and in 1750 offered to drop his process in return for the right to attend the annual agreement of accounts; a practice which was entirely uncontroversial in other parts of the church. Here the session overplayed its hand, by insisting both that Westburn refund their expenses and, more provocatively, that he insert an advertisement in the *Edinburgh Gazette* declaring that:

> tho' thro' Mistake or Misinformation, he had raised a Process against us at Edin[burgh] yet he saw no ground to insist, and that he is now Satisfied with our care, Honesty, and good Management of the poor's money intrusted to us.[73]

Given what we can glean of Westburn's character from the records, this was likely to be regarded as an insult and so he proceeded with the process. In this event, as we have seen, certain items of spending were declared to be *ultra vires*. In the case at Humbie the same resistance to secular interference by one heritor, especially one who seemed relatively isolated in the parish, lay behind events escalating as they did. As Mitchison puts it, the process was 'a legal "try on". That it worked was a surprise'.[74] The decision was that all the financial affairs of the church were to be subject to joint management. In both cases the decisions were widely ignored. In the Hamilton presbytery it is true that the Cambuslang accounts for 1790 show spending on poor relief to be 100 per cent of expenditure, but other parishes in the presbytery continued to pay fees out of their collections. The same was true across the rest of the country. While the Humbie decision may have encouraged some sessions to start separate books of account, as we have seen this was by no means a uniform response. It is also misleading to see it as the start of a practice that had been in place in some parishes from the early seventeenth century. The idiosyncratic nature of both of these cases means that, colourful though they are, their impact was rather localised. They can distract our attention from the broader patterns of accountability revealed through a detailed examination of local records. We are now in a position to join our consideration of financial accountability practices to those of broader record keeping, and to place them in the context of other aspects of Scottish society; that is the task of the next chapter.

CHAPTER 6

Scottish Systemic Accountability

We have seen over the past three chapters some of the operation of the practices of accountability of the Church of Scotland in the eighteenth century.
This chapter brings these threads together and places them in a broader
context. It looks at three types of contrast: that between the policies promulgated in documents printed at the national level and the practices at local
level; that between practices at the beginning of the century and those which
had emerged by its close; and that between practices in different areas of the
country. The broad system of accountability that emerges from these
contrasts, which is characterised by an emphasis on detailed record keeping
and a systemic rather than a personal form of accountability, is then placed
in a broader context. In particular, we look at the complementary and reinforcing role of law and education, the other two great Scottish institutions
that endured after the Union. The strands are brought together in a detailed
examination of another case that has received less attention in the subsequent
historiography than Humbie or Cambuslang, that of Monymusk. Its bitterly
contested stand-off between a determined heritor and an equally determined
minister illustrates the tactical use of some of the practices we have seen
already, as well as the impact of changes in university education and the status
of the clergy.

Our initial contrast is between the practices advocated by the framers of
the various printed guidance manuals of the early century and before: the
Overtures of 1696, the modified *Overtures* of 1704 and Pardovan's *Collections*.
Part of these documents, extracted as the *Form of Process* in 1707, did indeed
endure, although its operation occasioned considerable debates over its application, especially in attempts to discipline ministers.[1] As we have noted, Clark
argued that it gave an enduring legalistic cast to church governance that is of
considerable relevance later in the chapter. However, our investigation of the
detailed operation of practice across the eighteenth century should convince us
that Pardovan is not a reliable guide to church governance in practice. We saw
the tenor of his suggested questions about ministerial conduct in Chapter 2.
As a reminder of their flavour, he went on to ask 'Is he at variance with any?
Is there any that reproaches him? Or, is he well beloved of all? And upon what
ground is that variance or good liking of the people is?'[2] This formulation
gives reason to suspect that Pardovan was concerned as much with a popular
minister as with one who had disagreements with his flock. As Clark observes
of these questions 'to pass in all [...] successfully should have qualified him

for canonisation among the saints. The system was an encouragement to men to show up one another's faults.'[3] However, there is no evidence of these questions being put in visitations. While, of course, the inquisitors of the presbytery may have had their copy of Pardovan in hand, ready to catch out one of their brethren, it has to be remembered that they then had to work with the same person. While they were certainly ready to discipline those guilty of gross dereliction of duty, especially at the beginning of the century, the standard that was applied was more that of the 1704 *Overtures*. This was still challenging and, as we saw, all the guidance placed strong emphasis on the 'walk and conversation' of the minister both at home and abroad. However, Pardovan is better seen in the context of suspicion among the godly of the rise of a priestly caste in the church. Fuelled by the bitter conflicts of the seventeenth century and refined by time in Dutch exile, Pardovan seems to have reflected the disappointment and anguish of those who felt that their sacrifices had been betrayed by the failure to purge the church of those who had temporised, in their view, with prelacy.[4] Pardovan, after all, had opposed the Union in the name of Presbyterian purity, seeking to prevent debate in parliament before he had secured additional guarantees for the Church's independence.

Theory and practice

The 1704 *Overtures*, therefore, seem a more appropriate guide to governance practice, but they illustrate the profound gap between those designing a system free of considerations of local contingency and those who had to deal with such contingencies on the ground. In particular, they profoundly underestimated the sheer volume of work that had to be undertaken by presbyteries. The clear impression is that the framers of the guidance hailed from those areas in which the infrastructure of Presbyterian government could be relatively swiftly rebuilt after the restoration of Presbyterian church polity in 1690. However, even in such areas the business of recruiting, certifying and placing ministers involved time-consuming routines. This was on the assumption that the process went smoothly, and envisaged a smooth articulation between the parties, which rarely happened in practice. It was not to factor in, for example, heritors not of Presbyterian persuasion whose Episcopalianism was accepted under the Toleration Act of 1712. Still worse followed after the reinstatement of patronage in 1712. While this was seen as a clear breach of the Treaty of Union, engineered by High Church Anglicans, it added the potential for time-consuming processes. Even, that is, if we bracket off theological disputes, the practices envisaged for national application by the framers of the 1704 *Overtures* were easily derailed by the sheer volume of presbyterial work. This is clear in the fate of parochial visitations. It was always ambitious to imagine a round of annual visitations of parishes, especially given the material conditions of transport infrastructure and parochial geography. The smaller parishes around the shore of the Forth might be one thing, but the large upland parishes of a presbytery such as Ayr were quite another. In addition, to get through all the business envisaged required a full day for each visitation; with an average of fifteen parishes to consider this was a huge burden, especially when one considers the detail with which the early visits were written up. Then there were the issues to follow up, especially when it involved cajoling recalcitrant heritors into meeting their obligations. It is not surprising, therefore, that the detail of such visitations gets steadily attenuated, with a move to what might be termed 'exception reporting', rather than the recording of every detail. Questions shifted from a detailed inquiry to a general invitation to express any concerns. In many areas parochial visitations moved fairly quickly after about 1720 from a system of regular structured visits (if one had ever been established) to a more opportunistic response to local concerns. Even where there was more persistence with the practice, which seems to have been the case in the Ayrshire presbyteries, what it foundered on was the opportunity it gave for dissent. The causes of such dissent often seem, as in Kilwinning in 1743, lost in the murk of local politics, but they might involve local heritors, especially those with smaller holdings, and a mixture of theological dissent and financial considerations. Whatever the detail, which might require more local excavation but is likely to be impossible to discover, the impact of long-running disputes such as that engendered by the Kilwinning visitation might have persuaded presbyteries that any gains were outweighed by the opportunities provided to those with an axe to grind.

What is also noticeable in examining local practice in detail is the extent to which widespread practices were not evident from a reading of the policy guidelines. This again suggests that they are not always a reliable guide to what happened on the ground. This is clearest when we look at accounting for financial transactions. There were, at best, only a handful of scattered hints about both the requirement to exercise financial accountability and the practices that might facilitate this. And yet the surviving local records were marked above all by attention to such matters. While one index of this was the gradual emergence of separate money registers, even where this practice did not obtain books of discipline were generally scrupulous in their recording of financial transactions. Careful reconciliations at regular intervals, employing not only written records but also the poor's box, were evident across the country. While formats might vary from place to place, as did intervals for balancing written records to the cash in the box, detailed book-keeping was a feature of all well established sessions, despite not being mentioned in the guidance collections. The fact that in presbyteries such as Linlithgow such practices were well established by the end of the seventeenth century might have meant that the framers of the guidance simply assumed that all their readers would be familiar with such practices. They have nothing to say, for example, on the matters that exercised the Court of Session in the Humbie and Cambuslang cases. Here kirk sessions had simply been following long established practice in, for example, paying the fees of their session clerk and kirk officer from the money they collected. They generally continued to do so after the Cambuslang judgement, which cast doubt on the validity of such a practice. Again, the printed decisions prove to be a poor guide to what happened in practice. Does this mean, then, that they had no impact?

This would seem to be overstating the case, for the impact of the guidance collections seems to have been two-fold. The enduring impact seems to have been in the strictures about record keeping. While having registers with a clear margin might seem like a mundane matter of administrative detail, it was actually of significance in the operation of systems of accountability based on the quality of record keeping. As Todd notes for a much earlier period, clear margins facilitated the indexing of entries, which in turn formed a system of reference, which enabled the course of a particular issue to be followed.[5] The diffusion of such practices by recommendations following the revision of session registers and parochial visitations was a key legacy of the practices enjoined by the various *Overtures*. The second impact was the very compilation of such guidance, continuing as it did a distinctive practice of attempting to build comprehensive governance systems. Drawing on practice in France and Geneva, but also on the systematic approach of Calvin, with his legal training, the Scottish church was distinguished by attempts to use the relatively new medium of print to establish blueprints for governance systems.[6] That there was a considerable gap between such blueprints and practice is hardly surprising; it is an enduring feature of such attempts. What is of significance is that the attempt was made and as such formed part of a broader 'culture of organisation'; that is, it provided part of the sense that organisation could and should be consciously designed, as opposed to simply emerging from practice.

Of course, the examination of detailed practice also indicates that governance was never a completed event but rather a continuing process, in which practices evolved out of experience and modified the formal policies of the church.[7] This seems to be clearest in the evolution of the content of the privy censure. Here, while the practice continued to be animated by concerns with spiritual health, it also changed with the realisation that physically going out to parishes was both potentially divisive and relatively expensive of limited resources. It was much easier, as it were, to bring the parish to the presbytery, in the form of an expanded list of questions to be posed to ministers. This was shaped in part by broader debates in the church, as illustrated by attempts to encourage more frequent celebrations of communion. These were broadly unsuccessful but did focus attention on the regular celebration of communion in the majority of parishes. What also seemed to happen over the century was a reduction in the use of monitoring practices, such as the revision of registers, in a regular and structured fashion, but always with the potential of their being used. In this way the attention to the quality of records that had been fostered by the guidance and visitations became a taken-for-granted practice, facilitated by the broader improvement in levels of education. Although it is difficult to establish an easy measure, the general standard of record keeping improved, in form if not in content. That is, registers of discipline became, in general, better organised, with clearer recording over the course of the century. At the same the level of detail tended to diminish. In part this reflected changes in the nature of discipline, with public humiliation being replaced by sessional rebukes towards the end of the century. In combination with such changes there was less focus on detailed witness statements. At the same time as this relative attenuation of detail there was a steady rise in the volume and quality of the recording of financial transactions. In some parishes, as we will see below, there was almost a correlation between the quality of the financial records and the paucity of records of discipline. This broad picture at national level conceals some considerable regional differences.

Regional differences

From the detailed examination of local records at both parochial and presbyterial levels three broad patterns can be identified. Of course, it has to be reiterated that this examination focused largely on rural areas and excludes some areas of the country. The presbyteries examined were all Lowland ones and important areas of the country, such as Fife and the southwest, were excluded. However, the broad patterns that emerged seem worthy of consideration, especially for what they reveal about the northeast, which is often relatively neglected in this context. The first of such patterns is that to be found in the presbyteries of Linlithgow and Haddington, that is, those in the hinterland of Edinburgh. Shaped by both landlord-led agricultural improvement, especially around Haddington, and recruitment into the ranks of local landlords from the professional, especially legal, classes of Edinburgh, this saw what one might term the formation of 'polite' sessions. We have seen the increasing recruitment of advocates, writers and landowners to the ranks of sessions. There were occasional episodes of resistance to this, as in Gladsmuir, but this was associated with particular ministers. In general, sessions in this area functioned as executive committees of the heritors, putting into motion the decisions they had arrived at, collecting and distributing assessments. An indication of this trend is the marked decline in the extent of recording. At the opening of the century this area contained some of the most thorough sessions, where decisions and their supporting evidence were recorded in great depth. Over the course of the century, and certainly by mid-century, the volume of recording diminished noticeably. We noted above the stark decline in the recording of affairs in Gladsmuir in 1790; the financial registers are kept at the same time with very clear details of transactions. Similar observations could be made about many of the Lothian parishes, as mirrored in the sharp decline in the number of pages per year towards the end of the year.

One marker of the difference between practice here and in more western parishes was the public punishment of sin. In Abercorn, which we might recall was the home parish of the Earl of Hopetoun as well as other landowners, the session in February 1794, after 'their most serious consideration', decided to abandon the practice of public rebuke before the congregation for the sin of fornication. As well as calling into question the efficacy of the practice, they noted that such appearances 'were extremely disagreeable to several of the most respectable persons in the parish, who had requested information before they took place that they and their families might not be present'.[8] By contrast, the minutes of Dailly in Ayrshire record the public rebuke of two separate offenders, male and female, for the same offence in August 1798.[9] The Abercorn decision is recorded in immaculate copperplate writing, that in Dailly in a rather more sprawling, albeit clear, hand. Some other records suggest the tone of radical conservatism that marked the more western parishes, bolstered as they were by the rhetoric and myths of their Covenanting past.[10] Scottish church services featured a distinctive practice whereby the precentor read out a line of a psalm before then leading the singing of the same line. This catered for an illiterate population, but advances in literacy led to some questioning the practice. In 1768 the session of Saltoun in the presbytery of Haddington, responding to a memorial from the 'principal inhabitants', resolved that, as it was 'much more decent to omit reading the Line in Time of the singing Psalms in the Church', the practice be ended with immediate effect.[11] When the minister of Dalrymple in Ayrshire tried to effect the same change in 1797 he was faced with determined opposition from his session, who declared unanimously that they were representing the majority of the congregation. They appealed to the presbytery and in the end a compromise was reached.[12] Pardovan would have appreciated their resistance to 'innovations' in church worship, as he would the extensive declaration of opposition to Catholic relief by the session of Dundonald in 1779. Again having given the matter their 'most serious consideration' (a favourite phrase of session clerks), they declared that they 'would be exceedingly sorry to see the popish religion publickly tolerated in this Kingdom'. With mention of the dangers of 'cunning Jesuits', with their 'insidious arts' propagating a 'detestable Superstition', they deplored any weakening of opposition to the 'Apostles of Antichrist'. While accepting private liberty of conscience, they drew on their Covenanting past to declare their resolute opposition to 'the spread of that Superstition which has caused so much Blood to be shed in this land'.[13] Their declaration extended to a page and a half; while the polite sessions of the east were reducing their minutes to simple brief mentions of routine business, some in the west were not only maintaining extensive records of discipline, but also at local level making such policy directives as this.

I have termed this a more 'plebian' culture of organisation, where major heritors, unless aligned with a more radical tradition, tend to withdraw and the session is dominated by the concerns of smaller heritors and tenants. This produces minutes which are not always as tidy in appearance as those in the east, but which have considerably more content. Another pattern that produced a distinctive form of record keeping is to be found in the northeast of the country. The religious historiography has tended to focus on the endurance of Episcopalianism, stressing the conservatism of the area. However, it is arguable that such a focus is misleading, and does not explain the subsequent radicalism associated with Free Church figures such as William Alexander.[14] A closer examination of the local records indicates the growth, especially after the discrediting of Episcopalianism following its close association with the failed rising of 1715, of the same traditions of detailed record keeping that mark the Presbyterian tradition elsewhere but with distinct regional inflections. One such inflection was the production of records that have the form of books of account but turn out on closer inspection to contain records of discipline. This was an area in which the emergence of separate money registers proceeded at a much slower pace than elsewhere, with only 22 per cent of parishes in the synod having adopted them by the end of the century. Rather than constructing separate records, perhaps as a response to the price of paper for very poor sessions, the response was to combine the two using the columnar format of the ledger. Incorporated into these records were details of the texts preached by ministers, which are carefully recorded right through the period in a manner that is not found in the more southern parishes, but was surely more in line with the objects of the framers of discipline. The inspection of session registers, while patchy, also appears to have continued longer in this area, and was a weapon in the armoury of presbyteries that we will see was deployed in Monymusk. This was a profoundly conservative area with a very structured approach to record keeping, which did not exhibit the same spirit of challenge that comes through the western records, but was far more attentive to the details of church governance than the eastern parishes were. It is arguable that here, as in other aspects of Scottish historiography, that examples drawn from the central belt give a misleading impression of practices.[15] This is a theme that we will return to when we consider the Monymusk case in more detail. Before that, however, it is helpful to set the practices we have examined so far in the context of other traditions, notably those connected with the law and education.

Law and education

The Victorian historian Thomas Henry Buckle in his survey of *Scotland and the Scotch Intellect*, published in 1861, argued, from a close study of an extensive range of Scottish books, that Scottish thought had a deductive cast to it.[16] He attributed this to the dominance of theological considerations in Scottish thought of the seventeenth century. He was disparaging of that century in Scotland, seeing it as dominated by a narrow clerical spirit of fanaticism and intolerance, redeemed only by what he saw as a religious tradition of a 'democratic and insubordinate tone, which eventually produced the happiest results, by keeping alive, at a critical moment, the spirit of liberty'.[17] He was prepared to admit that Scottish theological thinkers in 'dealing with their premises after they obtained them … were extremely skilful; how they obtained them, they were very heedless'.[18] However, he concluded that Scotland produced little of merit in the seventeenth century, needing the Union with England to release the work of thinkers such as Smith, Hume and Reid from the toils of theological debate. However, Karin Bowie provides a more nuanced judgment, that findings 'in theology, science, literature, and law point to forms of dynamism and moderation that complicate the stereotypically negative picture of a benighted century'.[19] One of the important books published in this period was one which, had Buckle considered it, might have extended and supported his argument about a distinctively Scottish form of argument. This was the publication in 1681 of the first edition of Stair's *The Institutions of the Laws of Scotland*.[20] It argued from theological premises to present a comprehensive system of civil law as operated in Scotland, perhaps drawing some of its careful and structured form of organisation from familiarity with Calvin's *Institutes*. Drawing also on his exposure to Dutch legal education, especially the work of Grotius, he founded a tradition that 'believed law to be a rational discipline, capable of being set out in a scientific form deduced from natural first principles'.[21] This attachment to deduction shaped by theological commitments can be seen to support Buckle's argument by the provision of a much earlier example. However, it also extends it by pointing to a tradition of systematic exposition that seems to have influenced the framers of the guidance contained in the *Overtures*. Pardovan was explicit about this influence, noting:

> [he] thought it not improper to add, here and there, some hints of civil laws, which I hope the reader will not find unuseful or impertinent, seeing there are some circumstances concerning the worship of God, and the government of his church, common to human actions and societies, which are to be ordered by the light of nature and Christian prudence.[22]

His chief source for such 'hints' was Stair, whose work he cited eleven times. The format of his work, with short numbered paragraphs, also has echoes of the form of Stair's work. Stair also included, drawing on a longstanding

Scottish tradition, considerations on a form of process.[23] We noted in Chapter 2 that the committee appointed to revise the 1696 *Overtures* included three senior lawyers in their number. The emphasis on the rules of procedure for the production of witnesses and evidence that resulted in the *Form of Process* of 1707 and the ensuing legalistic cast to church affairs can be seen to owe a good deal to Stair's example. Harvie notes the intertwining of church and legal system, arguing that not only did this give a legalistic cast to church proceedings but that, 'legalism is flesh of Scottish flesh, bone of Scottish bone'.[24] Be that as it may, the practice that we have seen engendered by this legalistic tradition produced a focus on the written word and the recording of decisions in great detail.

The extensive form of those records also mirrored a focus in the Scottish legal tradition on the written word. It is surely significant that solicitors were known as Writers to the Signet. As James Boswell observed:

> Ours is a court of papers. We are never seriously engaged but when we write. We may be compared to the Highlanders in 1745. Our pleading is like their firing their musketry, which did little execution. We do not fall heartily to work till we take to our pens, as they do their broadswords.[25]

This tradition caused Scottish legal proceedings to be subject to inordinate delay while judges sought to pick out relevant facts and arguments from voluminous and dense written pleadings. This might provide a goldmine for later historians, but it also provided an example that some sessions were only too willing to follow. Jealous of their status as courts, sessions and presbyteries employed often long-winded presentations of facts and decisions that they took to be legal best practice.

The production of such written records depended on widespread literacy. The claims made for Scottish education, both in the terms of the extent of such literacy and their social reach, have been subject to considerable debate.[26] For our purpose, however, the extent to which Scottish educational opportunities were available to the full population is somewhat wide of the mark. As we have noted, kirk sessions were largely made up by the middling sort. We have noted that in the first half of the century that such men might be illiterate, as expressed for the elders of Cambuslang and the treasurer of Abercorn. However, as the century progressed such men might be more likely to be able to read and keep accounts, forming the audience for the widespread circulation of agricultural books that Holmes notes in the last quarter of the century.[27] These advances in basic literacy were produced as a side effect of the focus on education in the Presbyterian system from the early days of the Reformation. The aim here was not to produce success in secular matters, but to provide the basic ability to read the bible in English among broader numbers of the population and to provide for recruits for the ministry.[28] The focus of much education was on a very basic curriculum for the many and one oriented to the biblical languages of Hebrew, Greek and Latin for the talented few. In 1740, five members of the presbytery of Peebles, accompanied by 'several Gentlemen of Distinction and Learning', descended on the school at Innerleithen. There they heard boys reading from Homer's *Iliad*, from Livy and from Horace and approved their translation of a passage from English to Latin. As a by-product they 'observed they learned a good fashionable hand'.[29] Fifty years later the *Statistical Account* recorded that at the same school about thirty pupils learned Latin, English, writing and arithmetic.[30] Some of these pupils might have made their way to university and so on to the ministry; many more would acquire basic numeracy and literacy.

Again as a by-product of this system, elements of vocational education more suitable for secular activities began to creep in. In 1661, Mann notes, the town council of Edinburgh licensed a school in Leith to teach, as well as reading and arithmetic, how to 'keep a compt book and to teach Dutch'.[31] At Ayr, the school offered bookkeeping as a course of instruction in 1716. A new master, John Mair, joined the school following his graduation from St Andrews in 1727. He added navigation and geography from 1729, the council supplying 'maps and globes, the knowledge of which … is highly necessary for forming the man of business'.[32] In 1746 Mair took over as head teacher and persuaded the council to convert the school into an academy, of which he became rector. His vision was:

> a sort of academy where almost every sort of the more useful kinds of Liter-ature will be taught and the want of College education will in great measure be supplied to boys whose parents cannot well afford to maintain them at Universities. Gentlemen in the County will be encouraged to send their children to Ayr, considering that the school will by this means have no rival.[33]

He continued to teach 'arithmetic, book-keeping, geography, navigation, surveying, Euclid's elements, algebra and other mathematical sciences, plus some natural philosophy, as well as taking the top class in Latin'.[34] In 1736 he published his *Book-keeping Methodised*, which went through nine editions in the course of the century and was the leading text on bookkeeping.[35] Edgar tells us that the presbytery of Ayr appointed an inspection visit of the academy in 1738, although that volume of minutes has unfortunately gone missing since his use of it.[36] By the end of the century, when the presbytery of Hamilton was testing the credentials of a proposed teacher at Bothwell, the two elements, classical and vocational, both came in for scrutiny:

> He was then asked if he professed the latin language? To which he answered, that he did not profess to teach it. He was asked if he professed Book keeping and Mensuration? To which he answered, that he had studied the principles of both these sciences, but never had occasion to teach either of them.[37]

The education system overseen by the church thus developed to produce not only the learning necessary for the reproduction of its ministerial cadre, but also the skills to keep the records on which its governance depended. As we have seen, many of these skills were deployed by the schoolmasters, who acted as session clerks. They were frequently divinity students who hoped to progress to the ministry and so would have shared the university experiences of their ministerial colleagues. That experience changed during the century, with the shift from the regenting system, where one master took students through their whole course of study, to a model of specialised lecturers. This began under the influence of Dutch models with the reforms of William Carstares at Edinburgh. Generations of Scots had gone to the Netherlands to study at university, with law at Leiden being particularly influential. This had been reinforced by the exile of many Presbyterians, including Carstares, in the Netherlands in the 1680s. Carstares introduced specialised teaching in place of regents at Edinburgh in 1708, followed by Glasgow in 1727. The success of this change was seen in the decline in the numbers of students going abroad; by mid-century there was 'no reason for an annual exodus of budding lawyers to Holland unless they happened to be Jacobites under a cloud'.[38] Change was slower in coming to Aberdeen, with Marischal College changing in 1753, and King's not until 1799.[39] This gave a very different feel to the two institututions, with Emerson concluding:

> King's stagnated throughout much of the eighteenth century, unable to rise above the mediocrity to which its recruitment policies confined it. .,. The recruitment process at Marischal College was rather typical of that at Edinburgh and Glasgow Universities. It shows us why those institutions also flourished, and why King's, and the St Andrews arts colleges which resembled it, did not.[40]

What this suggests is that those educated at Glasgow, Edinburgh and Marischal would have been exposed to the new ideas of Hutcheson, Reid and others, and we will see the significance of this in the clergy involved in Monymusk. They will also have been educated alongside those studying more vocational subjects, with subjects such as agriculture being subject to the spirit of scientific investigation. This equipped them to take a considerable interest in the improvements that were taking place often under the guidance of university-educated factors and lawyers.[41] These aspects of the legal and education systems thus complemented aspects of the church governance system, especially its focus on detailed record keeping. The convergence of these factors can be illustrated by a closer examination of the events in one Aberdeenshire parish, that of Monymusk.

Monymusk

Monymusk occupies the fertile banks of the River Don, twenty miles west of Aberdeen. It belonged to the presbytery of Garioch, although physically separated from the other parishes by the bulk of Bennachie, which looms over the north. This feeling of separation, with the fertile haughs of the parish surrounded by significant hills, must have been far more telling given the limited means of transport in the eighteenth century.

The parish is now a fertile, intensively farmed and well-wooded one, but that owes much to improvements set in train in the eighteenth century. This, and the survival of extensive estate records, has given the parish an important place in the annals of Scottish agrarian history.[42] At the heart of the parish is the distinctive estate village and kirk. In a region dominated by the plain heritors' preaching boxes of the late eighteenth century, the kirk of Monymusk is a rare rural survival of elements of a pre-Reformation church.[43] Where most of the churches of the presbytery have simple belfries on their gables, Monymusk announces its presence with a tower dating from the early thirteenth century. Inside, the church is small and the number of internal reorganisations means that there is no trace of the laird's loft that one graced it. The influence of the Grant family in the parish is clear in the memorial tablets to family members that ornament the walls. To get an indication of the impression a laird's loft might have created one has to go north to Rose-hearty on the northern edge of the shoulder of land that pushes into the cold North Sea. There, in a now redundant nineteenth-century church, is the magnificent Pitsligo loft of 1634.[44] Of Dutch origin, its splendid carving (some of the best of its time in Scotland, thinks McKean) must have created an overwhelming symbol of power and wealth in an extremely poor country. Whatever the appearance of Monymusk's equivalent, the small scale of the church must have provided an impressive theatre for the exercise of power that took place in May 1792. The minutes record: 'Said day, A. Grant appeared in his fathers Loft, and after the blessing was pronounced, read a paper, commanding the Elders to relinquish the seat set apart for them in the Church'.[45] This must have been a moment of profound discomfort for the elders, jealous as they were of the respect due to them by virtue of their ordination: an ordination that had already marked them out as among the most respected members of a relatively small, relatively isolated farming community.

The occasion of this pronouncement was an ongoing and increasingly bitter legal dispute between the Grant family, sole heritors of the parish, and the church. The case ran at the Court of Session in Edinburgh from 1794 to 1825, but the dispute had been running since at least 1787.[46] The tensions that the case reveals about the system of governance are the main interest for our purposes, but first it is helpful to give a brief outline of the key features of the case. We will then look at some of the key actors in more detail. The dispute centred on the administration of a 'mortification', or trust created by the first Grant owner of the estate, Francis, Lord Cullen in 1713. His bequest was for his successors to provide two chalders (a measure of grain volume equivalent to some two and three-quarter tons) of meal or the equivalent in money to support schools in the parish. The fund was to be managed by the kirk session, subject to the overview of the presbytery. The dispute centred on both the scale of the funds subsequently supplied and their application. The details are tortuous and often confused with questions about the ordinary expenditure of the session, but they boil down to allegations that Lord Cullen's successors failed to provide the full value of the bequest. When a monetary equivalent was provided this was to be calculated at the ruling fiars price for the county, that is, the price set each year for various grains. In 1741, with an accumulated and unallocated fund of £1,220 Scots, the heritor, Sir Archibald Grant, fixed the price at the then ruling fiars price and stuck with this for twenty years. In 1761 this was renegotiated at 200 merks a year. No interest had been paid between 1741 and this date and there was an accumulated fund of £250 sterling.[47] By these means, it was alleged, the bequest had been severely under-funded. Moreover, those funds that had been supplied had been applied to the wrong purposes. The consequence, it was alleged, was that:

> instead of 4 Charity Schoolmasters there is only 1, who has got all the Salary and both he and the Parish Schoolmaster, whose Salary is also raised above the plan, have charged College fees for 4 boys from the Session funds since that time.[48]

They also found that the funds from the trust had been turned to other purposes, such as the provision of medical support. In the 1761 settlement, provision had been made for:

> an additional Salary to a Better than Ordinary Schoolmaster for the Improvement of the Youth of the Parish and Indeed of the Whole Country, Especially as the Heritor is to Give Large Accommodations and other Important Benefits for the Same purpose.[49]

This could certainly be interpreted as being part of efforts to attract more substantial tenants to take on the newly improved farms and so falling outside the charitable provisions of the mortification. As the Society in Scotland for the Propagation of Christian Knowledge (SSPCK) argued, it was an 'evident perversion of the fund in order to serve the heritor and the Inhabitants of higher rank, instead of being a benefit to the Poor'.[50] Even more contentious was the provision of a 'singing loft'. The second baronet was an enthusiastic advocate of choral music in church and led the way in introducing it to the county (later earning the approbation of John Wesley).[51] Not only was this against the inclinations of some members of the presbytery, but also spending on fittings in the church was properly the responsibility of the heritor. However, in 1748 a singing loft was erected in the church at the cost of £486 Scots, which 'was instead of being in any sense a charitable distribution of the funds in reality a donation to the heritor by saving him so much of what ought to have been paid by himself'.[52] Following the investigations that led to these conclusions (of which more below), local negotiations to put the fund on a better footing failed. This led to an initial court case, in which the allegations were substantially confirmed, with a decision in favour of the church. However, thanks to intransigence on both sides, the case was not settled for twenty years. The eventual settlement resulted in a substantial fund for educational provision, which continued until it was consolidated with other charitable bequests in 1933.

Francis Grant was a lawyer who attended Leiden in 1684 after study at King's, Aberdeen and Edinburgh.[53] This means that he was in the Netherlands at the same time as many Presbyterian exiles, although he returned to Scotland in 1687 for his admission to the Faculty of Advocates. Described by Wodrow as, 'a man of great piety and devotion, wonderfully serious in prayer and hearing the word', he was of a similar milieu to Steuart of Pardovan, although they had contrasting views over the Union.[54] Both were members of the Committee for Public Affairs of the Scottish Parliament, but Grant was convinced of the need for Union to preserve the Protestant faith. They also disagreed over societies for the reformation of manners, the Edinburgh Society for the Reformation of Manners holding its founding meeting in Grant's house in 1700. Pardovan thought such societies unnecessary and a threat to the established bodies of the church.[55] In this he was a far more conservative figure than Grant and thus out of step with some key figures in the mainstream of devout lay Presbyterians.

There was little doubting Grant's devotion to Presbyterianism. He authored pamphlets warning against scepticism about witchcraft. However, to Wodrow he 'seemed a little ambulatory in his judgment as to church government'. He was raised to a baronetcy in 1705 and took the title of Lord Cullen when he was appointed to the Court of Session in 1709. His title derived from estates in Banffshire, which he sold to purchase the estate of Monymusk in 1713. (He retained land around Ballintomb on Speyside, where he was born in about 1658.) One of his first steps was to create his fund to support education. On his death in 1726 he was succeeded by his son Archibald, who had acted as his factor since 1716.

Archibald Grant, the second baronet, is a key figure in Scottish agrarian history, although a controversial one. He followed his father into legal training, being accepted as an advocate in Edinburgh in 1714. He served as Member of Parliament for Aberdeenshire for ten years, but his parliamentary career came to a spectacular end when he was expelled following charges of fraud and neglect in connection with financial speculations involving the York Buildings Company and the Charitable Corporation for the Relief of the Industrious Poor.[56] His retreat to his Monymusk estate was accompanied by considerable indebtedness. A schedule of his debts in 1732 indicates that he owed nearly £28,000 to a wide variety of creditors, a fact that may well have influenced his conduct in relation to the mortification (which is listed as a debt due from his estates).[57] His view of the Monymusk estate when he entered it was a jaundiced one:

> The whole land raised and uneven, and full of stones, many of them very large, of a hard iron quality, and all the ridges crooked in the shape of an S, and very high and full of noxious weeds and poor, being worn out by culture, without proper manure or tillage. Much of the land and muire near the house, poor and boggy; the rivulet that runs before the house in pitts and shallow streams, often varying channel with banks, always ragged and broken. The people poor, ignorant and slothfull; and ingrained enemies to planting, inclosing or any improvements or cleanness; no keeping of sheep or cattle or roads but four months when oats and bear, which was the only sorts of their grain, was on ground. The farme houses, and even corn millns and mans and scool, all poor dirty hutts, pulled in pieces for manure or fell of themselves almost each alternate year.[58]

He devoted much of the rest of his life to the twin task of clearing his debts and improving his estate. He was a dedicated planter of trees, which Hume thought was 'the only laudable thing he has ever done'.[59] Posterity has judged him more kindly. Thanks to the extensive estate papers he left behind his role in agricultural improvement, introducing new crops and farming techniques to the northeast, has been central in the historiography. He sought to create consolidated holdings and to attract farmers from the Lothians, not just for the capital they needed to stock and run the new holdings but also for the knowledge they brought with them, which was to act as a role model and a prompt to local farmers. His marriage to his first wife, Anne, daughter of James Hamilton of Pencaitland, might have reinforced his knowledge of agricultural improvements in the Lothians. His administration of the funds of his father's bequest might have been shaped, therefore, by the competing demands of debt reduction. On the one hand, providing a monetary equivalent lower than was strictly required would preserve money in the estate for other purposes; on the other, application of those funds for purposes that might attract new tenants would aid the improvement process. Sir Archibald was in a strong position to get his way as he was the sole heritor in the parish and the kirk session, and indeed the presbytery, as we will see, was pliant and accommodating in the middle years of the century.

Sir Archibald died in 1778 and was succeeded as third baronet by his son, also called Archibald. This Sir Archibald had an army career and, it would appear, did not share his father's interest in agricultural matters. The agricultural writer Wight noted in 1783 that 'the present Sir Archibald, who had been long in the army, has no notion of bestowing his whole time upon husbandry'.[60] This was the father mentioned in the announcement of 1792, and his army career seems to have given him something of an autocratic character, to judge by the progress of the case. He in turn was succeeded by his son, also, confusingly, Archibald, in 1796. If the father was intransigent when faced by the power of the kirk, his son, an Edinburgh lawyer, was even more so. It was his manipulation of the legal process, featuring objections at every turn, which frustrated attempts to bring the affair to an end.[61] In 1802, for example, the presbytery approved in principle a new scheme of management, but insisted that Sir Archibald pay all the arrears due at that date, which included a sum of £15 sterling owed to the charity schoolmaster. This was agreed, but Sir Archibald continued to delay the process by objecting to specific items. Each time the court found against him, but he was determined to grind out what the Society termed in 1808, 'the very long and obstinate litigation of Sir Archibald Grant'.[62] As we will see, this was probably due to the breakdown of relations in the parish. Later in the same year he had still not made any payments and the court ordered the immediate interim payment of £100.[63] Following further objections, in exasperation the court ordered Sir Archibald Grant to pay a bond of £700 to Edinburgh bankers. However this was still not sufficient, as Sir Archibald continued to object to the settlement of the costs of the case, even seeking to deduct his own costs from the accumulated fund. This is where he finally overstepped the mark with the court. In 1810 he argued that:

> instead of the presbytery of Garioch, his real antagonists are the persons intrusted with the funds belonging to the Church of Scotland. That the funds of the latter of these venerable bodies have paid all the expenses hitherto incurred under the name of the presbytery, there is no doubt; and the respondent would, therefore, submit it as a point requiring some consideration, Whether the persons above mentioned are entitled, at their own discretion, and without authority, to use the names of this or that presbytery, for the purpose of harassing individuals with litigation in this Court, which, having no persona standi, they could not do in the name of the general body?[64]

This was too much for the court, which ordered this passage to be struck from the record. However, the case was not brought to a close until after the death of Sir Archibald in 1820. Then the trustees for the new heir, Sir James (fifth baronet of Monymusk), showed a willingness to compromise and to settle on a plan of management. Under this plan, the fund was to be managed by the heritor and the ministers of Monymusk and Chapel of Garioch. This gave status as chair to the heritor, but effective power, in terms of a voting majority, to the church. This was finally agreed in 1825, although in the interim arrears of pay of £198 to the village schoolmaster and £109 to the charity schoolmaster were agreed and the building of a new schoolhouse financed. After this expenditure, the accumulated fund stood at over £1,259, an indication of just how much the trust should have been worth.[65]

This gives an indication of how far heritors could depart from the vision of harmony between the spiritual and secular interests envisaged by Pardovan and Cullen in the early years of the century. Indeed, in establishing his bequest, Cullen expected 'the exact discipline of Presbyteries over ministers in what relates to religious ends' to ensure that its terms of his bequest were met.[66] This was found to be a somewhat sanguine expectation. The session, which of course was composed of estate tenants, agreed to expenditure, such as that on a public clock and bell, that was strictly the responsibility of the heritors. The presbytery, too, acquiesced in a revision of the terms of the bequest in 1761, which was later agreed to have been to the detriment of its aims. The minister for most of the first Sir Archibald's ownership was Alexander Simson. Ordained in 1729, he was a graduate of Marischal and thus a product of the regenting system. He died in 1781 as 'father of the church', having served his parish for fifty-two years.[67] In his later years he was assisted by the parish schoolmaster, William Marr, another Marischal graduate and the husband of Simson's daughter Jean. He, however, died before Simson and so Alexander Duff, a graduate of King's, was ordained in 1781. Duff struggled with his financial affairs, having to go to court to get full and proper payment of his stipend. He also appears to have suffered from Sir Archibald's (this was the third baronet) autocratic rule, in which we see echoes of the attempts to control parish administration that we noted as happening elsewhere in the 1740s. In 1784, for example, Sir Archibald wrote to Reverend Duff:

> the Kirk Treasurer & Session should be personally liable for any misapplication of the same, particularly if any distribution of poors money should be made from these funds without a Session regularly intimated and legally called, which had been attempted to be done of late without any such regular notice.[68]

What this seemed to imply, as later became apparent, was that any such distribution was invalid without Sir Archibald's participation and approval. Duff, however, was not the person to stand up unaided to Sir Archibald. As he lamented in 1797:

> his situation, as Minister of this parish, has been singularly hard, and that with the commands of the Presbytery, on one hand, and the interference of the Heritor on the other, he has found it impossible to obtain that quiet and satisfaction which his neighbouring clergymen enjoy, and to which neighbouring and respectable Gentlemen contribute.[69]

The key personage in the dispute, one as intransigent for what he saw as the church's rights as both the third and fourth baronets were for their rights of ownership, was the Reverend George Skene Keith. In the view of the fourth baronet it was Keith who orchestrated what he saw as a campaign against his family. 'I am informed', he wrote to his man of business in 1797, 'by several members of the pby that ... Mr Skene Keith acts in concert with Mr Duff, and is the only member of the pby who visits him'.[70] Keith graduated from Marischal in 1770, thus being a product of the more specialised lecturing system. Here he was particularly influenced by the work of George Campbell, who later became his friend. Campbell is now best known for his work on rhetoric, which continues to be cited in the field, but he was a key part of the Aberdeen Enlightenment, and a member of the Aberdeen Philosophical Society alongside Thomas Reid.[71] He presented a set of lectures on ecclesiastical history, which were later published with a biographical introduction provided by Keith.[72] In these lectures Campbell stressed the importance for his theology students of understanding the development of church governance structures. He was sceptical of any scriptural warrant for these but was supportive of Presbyterian arrangements, with particular emphasis on the ways in which they could control the conduct of ministers. Keith had therefore been exposed to recent teaching, informed by Enlightenment principles of reason and systematic investigation, about the importance of church governance. Like many of his contemporaries he provided the entry on his parish of Keithhall for Sir John Sinclair's *Statistical Account*, but he went beyond this. In 1811 he authored *A General View of the Agriculture of Aberdeenshire*.[73] He also carried out a series of experiments on distillation that led to the *Glasgow Herald*, reporting his call to the Perthshire parish of Tulliallen in 1822, to describe him as 'so well known in the scientific world'.[74] He was to prove a formidable and determined proponent of what he saw as the church's rights.

He was ordained to the parish of Keithhall in 1778 and so was a member of the presbytery when Simson died in 1781. Quite what prompted the subsequent investigation is unclear, but it appears to have been Keith who instigated an examination of the registers of Monymusk. This appears to have been a tactical revival of the power of presbyteries to call for session books. The investigation took an inordinate amount of time, partly because of illness and changes among those appointed to do the revision, partly because of the confused state of the records. The final highly critical report was presented to the presbytery by Keith and Patrick Davidson, minister of Rayne, in 1790. (Davidson, son of an Insch farmer, had been a schoolmaster in Keithhall and then minister at Kemnay before being ordained at Rayne in the same year, 1778, that Keith entered Keithhall.) They found much to censure in the conduct of the previous minister and session, but reserved their main fire for the management of the Cullen bequest. As they noted:

> The visitors observe that the Poor of Monymusk are worse supplied than those of any other parish in the Country, Altho' the Session Funds were much better. The principal cause of this appears to be that the Interests of Lord Cullen's & Sir A. Grant's [second baronet] Bonds, amounting together to 1600 pounds Scotch were paid irregularly.[75]

The initial response from Sir Archibald (the third baronet) was a mixture of defensiveness and compromise. In his defence, he argued that the state of the records was such that the precise details of the visitors' findings could never be clearly verified. In addition, the presbytery had approved explicitly of the arrangements in some cases. Their failure to raise any concerns until this date, coupled with the long delay in analysing the records, was held to condone implicitly the management of the fund.[76] However, there was also evidence of a willingness to establish the management of the fund on an agreed basis for the future, provided that the past was closed to further investigation. Sir Archibald's 'man of business', Isaac Grant (kinsman but no relation), wrote to Keith in 1789 suggesting a process of negotiation.[77] This exchange shows little of the acrimony that was to mark later exchanges. It is not entirely clear why this mood of compromise broke down, but break down it did. It resulted in the court case that we have outlined above, full of claims and counter claims. This caused considerable tensions in the parish, with allegations of malpractice coming from both sides. In 1792, soon after the elders had been ordered from their seats, Alexander Duff's son Lewis, student of divinity, was appointed as schoolmaster and, as was the procedure in most parishes, also appointed as session clerk.[78] In 1795, Sir Archibald refused to allow a meeting of the session to proceed until Lewis was removed as clerk, and proposed that one of his servants act as clerk.[79] Following this, Lewis was turned out of his school, resulting in yet another court case to secure his reinstatement.[80] In 1814 the unfortunate Alexander Duff died, aged seventy and having served the parish for thirty-three years.[81] That his funeral sermon was preached by George Skene Keith might have exasperated Sir Archibald (the fourth baronet), for the presbytery minutes record, 'a petition from the Misses Duff representing that Sir Archibald Grant would not pay the stipend due to their late Father, alleging that the manse & office houses had been dilapidated and requesting a visitation of the same'.[82] Until the end, therefore, the bitter contest continued.

Part of the bitterness of the Monymusk case stemmed from personal relations, part from the intransigence of the two main actors. However, it can also be related to the struggle for control over parish affairs that we have seen in a number of parishes, a struggle that animated the Cambuslang and Humbie cases. In the presbytery of Garioch there was no tradition of assessments for poor relief. Regular meetings for the revision of balances were held and duly intimated to heritors, but few chose to attend. In general, they were also not active members of sessions and matters were generally left to the minister and the core members of the session. The concern minuted by the session of Monymusk was that adherence to the fourth baronet's demand to be chair of any meeting discussing poor relief would seem to prevent them from making such ad hoc distributions. As a consequence the elders gave notice that they would demit that part of their office concerned with poor relief. However, what also underlay this dispute was the control of session meetings. In a previous meeting this had come to the fore. Sir Archibald relied on an interpretation of the distribution of poor relief in which the minister and elders only had control over the distribution of half of the money collected for poor relief. In doing so, he was explicitly resting on the Humbie decision, something he would be familiar with from his practice of law in Edinburgh. It is instructive, however, that this example carried no weight in the court proceedings. In part this was because he was confounding two issues: the activities of the session qua session in the distribution of standard poor relief, and the actions of the same body as trustees of a bequest, which was subject to the rules of that bequest, not to precedents that may or may not have mandated certain practices. In part, also, however, the Monymusk case shows the limited impact of the Humbie decision.

What the case also shows is the parlous position of kirk elders in a parish dominated by one heritor. In 1795 Duff wrote to the SSPCK asking how they could ensure 'that my Elders, who are but plain country men may not be involved in distress thro the overbearing interference of Sir Archd Grant'.[83] As we have seen, they were all tenants of the estate, drawn from the ranks of those with smaller holdings. They would all be aware of their potential to be victims of the consolidation of holdings by the estate. None of them was among the ranks of the larger tenants who were most closely associated with agricultural improvement. In 1824, following the settlement of the case, the session minutes carefully and deliberately record:

> The Session considering that the seat in Church, next to the Pulpit on the east side, had been set apart for their accommodation, but being too small for this purpose, as at first finished that they had, with consent and permission of Robert Grant Esq on behalf of the Heritor, enlarged the same at their own private expenses for their own accommodation and that of their successors, Members of the Kirk Session, resolved that a record of this transaction should be preserved in their Register.[84]

Restored to their place of honour and respect, this symbolically marked the end of the affair. The case had illustrated just how much a determined heritor could frustrate the process of church governance. But it also demonstrated how a determined clergy could enforce the independence of the church. Much turned in the case, as it had in some of the other cases, on the right of the church to run its own affairs, subject to its own disciplinary mechanisms. In Cambuslang and Humbie they had not been able to prevent secular interference. The difference now was perhaps in the changing nature of the educational experience of ministers and the confidence that this gave them. Of Keith's fellow members of the presbytery in the key years of the controversy between 1780 and 1800, educational details are available for twenty-four of the twenty-seven ministers who served.[85] Sixteen of these had graduated from Marischal College, eight from King's. The presbytery was staffed, therefore, by men sharing a common educational background, supported in their work by schoolmasters, serving as session clerks, who had also generally had, or were undertaking (as with Lewis Duff) education in divinity. Five of the minsters were themselves the sons of ministers and a number had sons, like Alexander Duff, who aspired to or had achieved the same status. The success in providing a fully graduate clergy provided men shaped in turn by changes in university education. These changes produced a more self-confident body of men, willing at times to resist what they saw as challenges to their authority. The deference to secular authority that was seen at mid-century, when the presbytery was willing, with relatively little scrutiny, to adhere to the wishes of a powerful heritor, was diluted.

CHAPTER 7

Contrasts and Consequences

In his survey of the agriculture of Aberdeenshire, the Reverend George Skene Keith did not restrict himself to matters purely agrarian. An observation that Adam Smith would have probably approved of was as follows:

> [the] clergy of the church of Scotland are placed in that happy mediocrity between opulence and poverty, which calls on them to look for the respect of their people, only from the purity of their morals, and the cultivation of their intellectual powers.[1]

He was keen to stress that assessments for poor relief were not a feature of the county's life and then moved on to an important aspect, as he saw it, of church governance:

> The Elders, or Church-wardens, receive no recompence – not even a *dinner* from the *funds of the Church Session*, which are applied solely to the relief of the poor. The parochial clergymen, in country parishes, generally give them their dinner twice or thrice a year: and the only reward of these worthy men, who manage the poor's funds in Scotland, arises from the general esteem of their neighbours, and the approbation of their own minds.[2]

This passage was clearly designed with a British audience in mind. This was not just the translation of elders into an English equivalent, but was also the unstated contrast between the sociability associated with churchwardens and the more sober Scottish approach. Other hints in the book, such as references to Holt's contemporaneous survey of Lancashire farming, also indicate that Keith was writing for a British audience who he would expect to appreciate these contrasts. The lack of a paid-for dinner might seem to be an extremely mundane matter and not one expressive of significantly different approaches to governance and accountability. The same might be said for many of the practices we have examined so far. Taken individually, equivalents might be found in other systems. However, the point is that the contrast need not be between individual items on their own, but as part of an overall system. When we undertake such a contrast then the distinctiveness of the Scottish system becomes apparent.

Personal accountability in the Church of England

The contrast essayed in this chapter is with English practice. Given that the two countries were part of a united state from 1707, which was premised in large part on the need to defend a shared Protestantism against the 'other' of Catholic Europe, the contrast seems worth undertaking. However, it is fraught with difficulties. The term 'contrast' is used rather than 'comparison' in part because, as will be seen, the two systems are so different. Poor relief, for example, so central to Scottish church governance, was more of a secular matter in England (although the lines were blurred).[3] It can be difficult, therefore, to compare practices directly. This is also because of the limitations of evidence. Writing on the English church is particularly concerned with debates about ideas and competing structures, notably the clash between Anglicanism and various forms of Dissent.[4] The focus in what follows is primarily on the Anglican experience. This is because the Church of England was a national body and, especially in rural areas during our period, was the main or only form of church governance. Even where forms of Dissent existed, they were subject in some forms to the particular governance of the established church. Of course, the existence of a growing body of Dissent adds another layer of complexity to contrast, and this point will be returned to later in the chapter. Where writers considering the eighteenth-century Church of England attend to matters of organisation this tends to be at national level; observations about the types of practice we have been examining tend to be made briefly and in passing. However, there are some local studies that enable us to glean some hints – hints that can be supplemented by the use of published diaries from the period.

The challenge in investigating English church practice is the scale of the country, the profound regional differences and the devolved nature of record-keeping and archiving. Scotland was and is a small country with a centralised system of archiving, certainly for the Church of Scotland. By contrast, and it is an instructive contrast, the survival of records from the local operations of the Church of England is a matter of considerable chance. Because of the way in which churchwardens held office, records often became almost personal property. The Hickling, Nottinghamshire, parish book is annotated thus on its inside back cover:

> This book having been held for many years by the late Mr William Collishaw, formerly Churchwarden, and on his death having come into the custody of his son, Mr Thos Wm Collishaw, was handed by the latter to the Rector, Revd Canon Skelton, for preservation in the Church Chest this 8th day of May 1895.[5]

John Collishaw was noted as a warden from 1764, and in 1785 he is noted as having been out of pocket to the tune of £14 1s 5d. This continuing family connection extending for well over a century indicates the extent to which the office of churchwarden and the material artefacts associated with it were attached to a small number of actors. If they were deposited in an archive, that archive would be a county one. Although advances in cataloguing make it easier to identify the existence of such records, their consultation requires

a physical visit. Accordingly the observations that follow are based on one
area in Nottinghamshire, supplemented by the secondary literature and
published diaries from the eighteenth century. This is obviously a profound
limitation, given that we are contrasting evidence on a national scale with one
particular locality in a very much larger national system. However, if we
accept such caveats, the contrast still seems instructive; it might, perhaps,
encourage further investigations of the English experience in order to provide
a more refined approach.

The area examined in detail is that of the deanery of Bingham in south
Nottinghamshire. The centre of this largely pastoral area was the market town
of Bingham. Close to Nottingham, particularly where land was owned by a
single proprietor, enclosure took place early and land was converted to pasture
for stock rearing. During the eighteenth century enclosure of the remaining
open fields, together with developments in stock breeding, saw considerable
conversion to stock grazing.[6] During the eighteenth century domestic stocking
weaving spread to several villages such as Bingham and Ruddington, and the
churchwardens' accounts bear testimony to the spread of putting out.[7] However,
the economy remained a predominantly agrarian one. Despite Nottingham
being a centre for 'Old Dissent', the rural area remained predominantly
Anglican in complexion until Methodism started to make some inroads late
in the century.[8] There were fifty parishes in the deanery during the eighteenth
century, but usable records survive in the county archives for only twenty
parishes.[9] These records are often fragmentary, with few substantial runs. In
addition, they are largely accounts, with very few surviving minutes. We
already have a stark contrast to record survival in Scotland. This is not just a
matter of archiving policy; the records themselves reflect a very different
system of church governance and accountability.

The Church of England was the established church of the English state,
with its bishops sitting in the House of Lords. Such a practice was anathema
to Scottish Presbyterians, with their dual conception of church and state and
determined resistance to Erastianism, that is, the intrusion of the secular into
the spiritual. Because of the conditions of its emergence the Anglican Church
carried forward many of the organisational arrangements and practices of the
pre-Reformation period. This also meant that churchwardens, along with
other parish officers, were vital to state formation, giving the remarkable
'social depth' that characterised the early modern English state.[10] These
arrangements were constructed in the absence of a national blueprint for
church organisation and practice. Arrangements were both imposed by
central legislation, more or less successfully, and emergent from local practice.
There was no equivalent of centrally sponsored books of procedure, with
such guides being produced by individual, commercial interests. So the
appeal of the *Compleat Parish Officer*, published in 1734, was that parish
officers would have 'so many valuable Informations communicated in so small

a Compass'.[11] The book is a collection of references to statutes and decided cases but with no sense of proceeding from first principles that characterises the Scottish books. The church was hierarchical in structure, but with diffused power centres. Bishops were approved by the state, but their dioceses were staffed by clerical incumbents, who owed their positions to lay patrons. The control that bishops could exercise over men who possessed livings as personal property was limited. The practice of visitations was to be found in the Church of England, but with very different content to the same practice in the Church of Scotland. There was no physical visit to the parish, but a meeting hosted by an archdeacon where churchwardens presented their response to questions circulated in advance. Several writers on the church in the eighteenth century have commented on the ineffectiveness of church discipline as expressed in the annual archdeacon's visitations. They note the frequent recording of 'omnia bene' in churchwardens' returns to the questions posed by archdeacons before their visitations.[12] William Cole, vicar of Bletchley in Buckinghamshire, was scathing of his archdeacon, recording after the visitation dinner in 1766 that he 'ended, most quaintly (in the State of the Church Wardens' Presentments, to which he alluded), that he was very glad to find, as he hoped he always should do, That All was well'.[13] The surviving presentment books for Nottinghamshire have a standard formulation that is subscribed to without comment in most cases. In 1740 it reads:

> We the Churchwardens there Whose names are here unto Subscribed having diligently perused the Book of Articles which for our direction was delivered unto us by Virtue of our Oaths do say that we have nothing to present.[14]

Churchwardens were expected to present inhabitants (or, indeed, incumbents) for offences against church discipline. In 1740 only four parishes in the Bingham deanery presented any offenders for consideration, all mothers of illegitimate children. There were good reasons for churchwardens failing to present, notably the opprobrium they might face in small rural communities if they presented any other than the relatively defenceless or outrageous. It was not that controversial presentments could not be made; in 1731 the wardens of the neighbouring parishes of West and East Leake presented their rector for being an absentee and not providing a curate.[15] However, such examples are extremely rare. We have noted that the Scottish visitation system was never fully implemented and gradually fell into disuse. However, it was always far more thorough than the English equivalent, and even the sparsest of records are fuller than those surviving in England. This might, of course, be an artefact of record survival as Scottish visitations might leave their mark in both kirk and presbytery registers. The contrast between the content of the two practices does suggest the greater local autonomy of the English parish, subject to much lighter scrutiny than their Scottish equivalent and this is confirmed when examining local practice.

While the Scottish minister had to be moderator of his kirk session (without which it could not meet), English incumbents seem to have had more distance from the details of parochial administration. This is suggested by clerical diaries. In his study of lay involvement in the church in the eighteenth century, Jacob notes that the vestry 'was chaired by the incumbent', but evidence for this is very patchy in both the Bingham sample and in the broader diaries.[16] This is not to say that incumbents were completely absent. In East Bridgford at mid-century the 'Rev. Peter Priaulx was an active rector in many ways, as a man of business and a disciplinarian. He insisted on full and precise details in the parochial accounts of overseers, constables, and churchwardens at the vestry meetings'.[17] The Sussex churchwarden Thomas Turner noted the presence of Thomas Porter, the incumbent, at three of the fourteen meetings he recorded, but none of these was the parish meeting at which accounts were approved.[18] Some accounts were signed by incumbents in the Bingham sample, but very few. In Somerset the vicar of Over Stowey, Willliam Holland, recorded calling a number of vestries to do with concerns about parishioners. In 1803 he recorded an Easter Monday vestry:

> After dinner the Parishioners met. I represented the Altar in the Chancel and the Cloth that covered the Communion Table as shabby and rotten and proposed repairs and a new one. Farmer Morle agreed to rectify them at once. Mr James Rich objected with some warmth. I told him that I would present them, which fired him still more. I believe he had been drinking, however I gave him some strong replies and appointed Farmer Morle for my Church Warden and he partly declining for the other Church Warden, Farmer Dibble was chosen in his stead.[19]

Eleven years later he noted, 'I had Prayers in the afternoon to take in the Farmers who were coming to settle Parish matters. They retired to my house where we signed and I gave them a Jug of Strong Beer'.[20] Cole in Bletchley also notes two Easter meetings both held after Matins at which wardens were chosen.[21] However, by contrast, many of the other clerical diaries are simply silent about parish matters. Benjamin Rogers of Carlton in Bedfordshire notes his son losing his way back from a fair on Easter Monday, but nothing of a parish meeting.[22] The strongest evidence for the lack of clerical involvement comes from the famous diaries of James Woodforde, incumbent of Weston Longville in Norfolk from 1776 to 1803, and it is worth looking at this evidence in more detail.[23]

In his first full year of office he noted that he 'could not attend our Parish Meeting to day, but desired Mr Dade to nominate John Bowles my Church-warden'.[24] This was followed in the next year by a similar passage. There is then a two–year gap until the note of 'a Parish Meeting at the Hart to day. I did not attend, but nominated Mr Mann to be my C. Warden'.[25] This is the last mention of the selection of churchwardens. Woodforde's diaries are famous for their attention to mundane detail, but parish matters are rarely featured. The only detail of involvement comes in 1784, when two meetings are recorded. On 26 May that year he attended a meeting in the church 'held for examining things belonging to the Church'.[26] Two months later another meeting was held in the church about 'moving the Singing Seat'. Eight parishioners attended and there was some debate:

> Mr Peachman with some others were for letting of it remain where it is – but they all said they would agree to have it placed wherever I pleased – Accordingly I fixed to be a proper place for it behind the Font and so inclose the Belfry – was concluded on and so the Vestry was dissolved – They all behaved extremely obliging to their Rector.[27]

This is the only comprehensive entry about parish business and afterwards notes are restricted to Woodforde's provision of extracts from the registers that the wardens needed for visitation purposes. That parish meetings continued is seen from the entry in January 1789:

> Mr Howlett & Mr Forster called here this Afternoon as they were going to a Parish meeting at the Heart to speak to me respecting the Rent due for the Poor Cottage where Dick Buck &c live, which belongs to the Widows Charity – I told them that I expected the Parish would pay the arrears.[28]

But there is no sign that Woodforde had any interest in or desire to be involved in parochial affairs. This perhaps supports the lack of mention in other clerical diaries, where the emphasis is more on ecclesiastical preferment than parish business.[29]

On 20 April 1778 Woodforde noted in his diary, 'I sent a note to the Gentlemen at the Heart at their Easter meeting, nominating M. Burton my Churchwarden'.[30] This brief note encapsulates much of the 'ideal type' of the selection of parish officers – the meeting at Easter and the selection of two churchwardens, one for the incumbent and one for the people. In the Sussex parish of East Hoathly Turner records a clear pattern for the selection of parish officers: churchwardens and the overseer of the poor at Easter and surveyors for the upkeep of roads in the parish in December. He does not mention the other parish officer, the constable, perhaps because this office was regarded as of much lower status and was most likely to be occupied by those below the rank of farmer. In the hierarchy of office the churchwarden was at the apex, although in many cases the role was blurred with other functions, notably the care of the poor. The main functions were maintaining Church discipline, caring for the fabric of the church and supporting the incumbent in the provision of materials (such as those for communion). However, in many cases these functions overlapped with others. Many churchwardens' accounts in Bingham record matters such as provision for the poor, most notably in the supply of materials for the poor to work on. This was taken furthest in the parish of Shelford, where from 1729 the separate sets of accounts were replaced with one unified set under the control of a 'parish officer' who combined the roles of churchwarden, overseer and surveyor. Here, too, accounts were presented every six months. This was atypical, but it reminds us that it is dangerous to assume that the 'typical' pattern obtained everywhere. A closer examination of practices across a particular set of parishes and over time enables us to test this pattern.

For Tate, the post-Reformation church settled on a pattern of annual office holding, with two wardens being selected at a vestry of the substantial inhabitants at Easter.[31] Although not specifically laid down in the legislation, by custom one of the wardens represented and was selected by the incumbent, the other by the people. They served for a year and presented their accounts to the meeting in the following year. They were responsible for getting agreement to the setting of a church rate, if needed, to cover expenditure, and for its collection. They were confirmed in office by the archdeacon at his half-yearly visitation, which they were required to attend. At the next visitation they were to present any concerns about parishioners, the fabric of the church or the conduct of the incumbent. They in turn faced the possibility of presentation by the incumbent if he felt they were neglecting their duties. In the Bingham deanery some of the smaller parishes departed from this pattern, with five having only one warden. One parish, Langar, had three churchwardens. The majority of parishes, therefore, had two wardens but the patterns of selection could be complex. In only four of the parishes was there a classic pattern of single-year office holding. In many there emerged extensive periods of office holding by one warden with others serving shorter periods. In Bingham, for example, William Petty served as warden from 1771 until past the end of our period. Because of disputes in the parish we know that he was the incumbent's warden. In this case his counterpart generally served an annual term of office, until George Baxter, his bitter rival, served a six-year spell. In this case we know that Petty 'had refused to have anything to do with him [Baxter] since his appointment and "always turned away from him"'.[32] Other parishes also had long-serving wardens. Richard Watt, for example, served single handed at Stanton in the Wolds from 1780 to 1815; in Flintham, John Jebb's term of office as what appears to be the incumbent's warden of six years was followed by the ten-year tenure of Charles Neale.[33] Their counterparts over the same period generally served two-year terms. In Wiltshire Spaeth notes that 'landholders shared the office of churchwarden between them, with each farm taking its turn, a procedure that ensured that the richest farmers did not monopolise parish office'.[34] We might see below that the motive for this practice, also noted in Tate, might be as much about the avoidance of office as a desire to occupy it. In 1757 Turner noted that William Piper was selected as overseer 'but as it was proved Will. Piper had served it very lately, it was agreed Ed. Hope should serve it'. This did not settle the matter, as six days later, 'Called a vestry to consult about the overseers that were nominated on Monday last, they both declaring they will not serve it, but (as is the custom of our vestries) we came to no resolution concerning it'.[35] This indicates some of the conflicts over serving, and customs of the rotation of office could help ease such conflicts. In the parish of Screveton, for example, examination of officeholding over the years 1761 to 1780 indicates two patterns. The first was a regular pattern of office holding, separated by about seven years. Within this, there was a practice of serving for two years, first as the people's warden, then for the incumbent. What emerges from this is the variability of practice across the deanery with the system employed being shaped by local custom, something Pitman also points out in relation to a much earlier period.[36]

It was noted above that vestry minutes are fragmentary for the Bingham parishes examined, but we might be able to glean some patterns from the dating of the accounts. In the same 1757 meeting on Easter Monday that Turner notes officers being selected he also records, 'I made up my accounts with the parish'.[37] Similarly, albeit for a period just beyond our timeframe, William Holland, incumbent of Over Stowey in Somerset, notes a parish meeting held in the rectory on Easter Monday, 1814, 'where we signed'.[38] However, analysis of the accounts from Bingham parishes does not confirm this pattern. Only 379 of 672 of the balanced accounts bear the date of agreement, perhaps reflecting the local nature of the accounts, as discussed more below. Of those which are dated, very few are in March or April, when Easter usually falls. A slim majority (199 or 52 per cent) were dated in May or June, but the rest were scattered through the year, with 15 per cent being signed in October and November. Of course, it may be that officers were chosen at the Easter meeting with accounts being approved later, but at the very least the Bingham sample indicates a considerable decoupling of the two events, with the lack of a smooth transition between the two. This mattered for wardens, given the likelihood that they were owed money at the end of their term of office. When Turner made up accounts following his term as overseer the result was that 'there remains due to me £25 14s. 10½d'.[39] This pattern of indebtedness was also demonstrated in the Bingham sample and it had considerable implications for those who held parochial office. Of the 672 balances, 53 per cent were negative, that is, wardens were owed money at the end of their term of office. This varied considerably from parish to parish, with 81 per cent of the unfortunate officers of Shelford being owed money. In Langer, Gervas Howe served with Mathew Dextor in 1756; when accounts were settled two years later he was owed £22 16s 2d. Despite this (or perhaps to ensure he recovered his money) he served another two years term of office with Dextor, at the end of which he was still owed £10. Despite having this balance agreed in December 1760, he was not reimbursed by his successors until June 1762.[40] It would be only the wealthier inhabitants who could stand this level of indebtedness.

These practices thus stand in sharp contrast to those obtaining in

Scotland. One distinction was the form of communion. In the Church of England, communion was, by the late seventeenth century, an 'open' sacrament with nothing of the closure aimed at in Scotland; a key concern of clerical debate was the desire for more frequent and more widely shared communion.[41] Historians have used churchwarden accounts to trace the pattern of sacraments, through, for example, the purchase of communion wine.[42] However, a detailed recording of the annual communion season and the preparations that accompanied it are totally absent from the English records. Another difference is length of office. While some churchwardens served for extended periods, the English vestry did not have the corporate form of the Scottish kirk session. We lack the minutes necessary to observe the workings of the vestry because in many cases it did not operate as a formal body. Its core officers, the churchwardens, often operated on a rotating basis. This is not to deny that there was a core group of inhabitants who constituted in practice an organising committee for the parish, but its visible form changed from year to year. In particular, the form of accounting was in practice far more sporadic than in Scotland. In Scotland, the enduring existence of the session meant that funds were accumulated. The key difference here was in the level of indebtedness. We noted in Chapter 5 that approximately 4 per cent of balances recorded in Scottish accounts were negative. This stands in sharp contrast to the picture gleaned from the Bingham records. It is not that negative balances, such as that suffered by Gervas Howe, cannot be found in the Scottish records. In Saltoun in 1800, for example, the session recorded its obligations to 'Mr Park their Treasurer not only for the attention which he continues to give to the affairs of the Poor, but also for having so kindly advanced so much money to carry on their necessary supplies'.[43] He was owed over £38 sterling, largely because the interest on a bond had not been paid. This was a parish with £700 lent out on bond and so dependent on interest. It was also a polite parish dominated by its landowner and so an example of those Lothian parishes that were tending towards a more English model, albeit with immaculately kept accounts.

Contrasts with Scotland

It is in comparing those sets of accounts that the differences between the two systems become more apparent. The marks of this uneven practice are clearly visible in the Bingham parish accounts, where there was a bewildering range of account formats. In many cases, especially at the beginning of the century, there was a simple record of the amount either owing to or due from the wardens. As an example, in the Bingham parish of Shelford, in common with a number of other parishes, in the early years of the century this was given in textual form:

> The Accounts of Jo: Palethorp taken this 30 day of May he being Church

warden & Overseer for the Poor for the year 1704 he having Rec'd 16£=8s=6d and hath Disburst 17£–17s-0d so there remains due to the Accomptant 1=13=6 as Apears by his Account.[44]

It was not until 1720 that this information was presented in a tabular as opposed to a textual form, but it was still restricted to the bare details of summary balances. That is to say, there were no means by which observers could query the nature of transactions in detail.[45] Although there was a clear process of greater detail during the course of the century, so that many more accounts gave full details of transactions and when they were incurred, this was by no means a linear process. So for 1799, for example, there was still the bare statement in Wysall, 'William Case in Hand on the Church account 15s 7d'.[46] Coding these transactions on the same basis as for Scotland in Chapter 5, Table 7.1 shows average values during the century, indicating that as a whole the area was well adrift of Scottish practice.

Table 7.1 Transaction details in Bingham parishes

Period	Average value	Average number of parishes
1700–24	4.22	6
1725–49	5.52	8
1750–74	6.45	12
1775–99	7.61	15

Source: Mutch, 'Custom and personal accountability', p. 80.

That is, even towards the end of the period, as the example of Wysall indicated, accounts could be presented with a minimal level of detail. This suggests the local nature of accounts, where details were conveyed orally and were approved at the time, with participants not seeing the need to record details for further scrutiny. After all, the accounts did not go elsewhere for scrutiny. There was just one mention of accounts at the annual visitation of the archdeacon, when in 1777 William Hutchinson, late churchwarden of Bingham, was presented for, 'not passing his Accounts of all and Singular his Receipts and Disbursements of Money by him received and Disbursed as Churchwarden of the said Parish in 1775'.[47] Unfortunately, a settlement was reached and the case dismissed before proceeding to a hearing, so we have no further detail. This exception does rather point up the lack of scrutiny that these accounts were subject to outside the circle of the parish elite. However, this did not preclude the keeping of records, at the centre of which was 'the book'. In Hickling in May 1800, for example, William Mann's accounts for the year 1799 include the sum of 2s 6d, 'spent when I Received the Book'.[48] Wardens frequently charged sums of money for entering up their accounts. In Orston, for example, in May 1783 there was a charge of 1s 'for Transferring the Accounts into the Book'.[49] Turner records in 1758 that he attended the parish meeting where 'I made up the accounts between Mr Joseph Burges the present overseer and the parish, and there remains due to the parish £11 7s 6d'.[50] His skills from keeping his shop seem to have been transferred for the assistance of his less able peers. What we have therefore is a process in which much of the conduct of the churchwardens was in their hands during the course of the year, with them maintaining records in whatever manner they found suitable until they were to be transferred into the accounts book. This also meant that their stewardship of money during the year was relatively opaque, with little recorded connection between their actions, perhaps as agreed by a vestry, and the transactions they recorded.

These details also suggest a further significant difference between the two countries, one of which Keith alluded to. This was the nature and place of presenting accounts and holding meetings. As we have seen, Scottish meetings were always on church premises, except for the meeting to which heritors were invited, which was usually held in the manse. By contrast, the public house was central to the practices of the churchwarden, and sociability was a key feature. We have noted above the 'giving up' of accounts for Orston and this phrase is often encountered, suggesting the oral nature of some of these events (as in the Latin root of the 'audit'). It was combined with the social nature of the occasion as at Edwalton in 1725 when the accounts note, 'Paid for ale when these accounts was given up'.[51] This continued late into the century and in other parishes, so in Willoughby on the Wolds in September 1786 we have 2s 6d 'Spent when the accounts was gave up'.[52]

This is where Turner's diary is so valuable in giving us an insight into the conduct of such meetings. From his records, they were often fractious affairs, fuelled by considerable volumes of alcoholic drink. All the vestries he recorded took place at 'Jones's', otherwise the village inn, the Crown (until at the end of the period concerned Jones failed and the vestry moved to the Maypole). We get here confirmation of the social nature of these occasions conveyed by the spending on ale and food recorded in the Bingham parish accounts. In October 1756, Turner noted that a number left a vestry meeting that had already run from 4.30 until 7.00 as 'they found if they stayed they must spend their own money and not the parish's. ... The rest of the company stayed on until gone 11 having spent 3s 6d of the parish's money and a 1d of their own'.[53] This sociability often had predictable results, with Turner frequently bewailing the poor behaviour that too much drink led to. At Easter 1760 he records that 'we had several warm arguments at our vestry today and several volleys of execrable oaths oftentime resounded from almost all sides of the room, a most rude and shocking thing at public meetings'.[54] Not all meetings ended this way and Turner does record more agreeable and sociable events. In April 1764 he records a meeting that started in the afternoon and continued 'till near 3 o'clock in the morn before we broke up and spent 10s allowed out of the poor book and a halfpenny each'.[55] His diaries confirm the focus on the inn that we get from other records. Woodforde noted parish meetings at the (variously recorded) Hart or Heart public house in Weston Longville. In East Bridgford in the Bingham deanery the 'giving up' of accounts frequently happened at John Hose's inn.[56]

What we see in the English experience was variation in local practice and the impact of custom.[57] In the absence of detailed blueprints, central monitoring or the intervention of people trained outside the parish, and strongly influenced by the patterns of office holding, forms of record keeping varied wildly. Structuring of the records was a contingent matter that depended on local expertise, as in the case of Thomas Turner. There was no equivalent to the university-educated Scottish session clerk. In 1800 Holland recorded in his diary, 'Wm Frost and the Clerk are at it mowing in the Paddocks'.[58] His function as parish clerk seems to have been largely chasing farmers for their tithe contributions. Some aspects of this account therefore bring in those considerations of the legal and education systems that we observed in Scotland.

From a legal perspective, the complex mix of customary practices and the absence of system was complemented by the primacy in England of common law practices, in which law emerged from precedent and so was dependent on issues being brought to court. The first attempt to systematise this body of law came with Blackstone's *Commentaries* of 1765.[59] This tends to parallel the focus on custom that we have seen above, in which practices emerged from local traditions, producing a form of accountability that rested heavily on the personal characteristics of those holding positions. This was mirrored in the longstanding execution of the law at local level by justices of the peace, their ranks dominated by the gentry but joined from the late eighteenth century by increasing numbers of Anglican clergy. By contrast, in Scotland the sheriff, a trained official paid by central government, was a key figure. This meant that there was no alliance between ministers and the gentry. They were not seen, argues Whetstone, 'as members, or allies, of the landed classes. They rarely came from the gentry and rarely did the gentry share their religious beliefs'.[60]

In England clerical incumbents and local gentry frequently shared a common educational background in the colleges of Oxford and Cambridge, a common background that emphasised their distance from the parish elite with whom they had to deal. However they could so deal at something of a social distance. Some revisionist accounts in church history have sought to defend the classics-based education offered by the English universities from the criticism of its irrelevance and ineffectiveness that has been offered, but examples such as that of James Woodforde seem to militate against this.[61] As Winstanley concludes of Woodforde's time at Oxford, 'in a way, his attitude was rather like that towards his parish work. In each case, he did what was required of him, but without enthusiasm. The fire and spirit that come from a sense of vocation were missing.'[62] This could be taken as a personal, rather than a systemic failing, but another judgement came from Adam Smith. He won an Exhibition to support attendance at Balliol College in 1740, but found it full of 'exploded systems and obsolete prejudices'.[63] His unfavourable comparison of his experience of the English system to his time at Glasgow University was mirrored in his preference for the organisational arrangements of the Scottish church due to their more favourable impacts on government and society.[64]

This does suggest a contrast between a systemic form of accountability in Scotland, in which a system of checks and balances, in part laid down centrally, in part emergent from local practice conditioned by that central guidance, was dependent on the clear specification of roles and the keeping of detailed records, and a personal form of accountability in England, in which the focus was on character and leadership. The central notion was that of the gentleman, who was to be trusted because of his character, not because of his place in a system. Of course, it could be argued that there were other places for the English to learn to practice accountability. This study has not, for example, examined the account books of overseers of the poor. Unfortunately, the work, which has looked at poor relief at a local level, does not present us with much detail as to practices. Hindle, for example, notes that parish officers, in drawing up accounts, 'made only the haziest of distinctions between payments disbursed by churchwardens on the basis of collections at communion and other times, and those made by collectors for the poor out of funds raised by assessments'.[65] He warns against drawing generalisations from isolated examples of careful record keeping, but detailed consideration of what these formats might be is missing. It could also be argued, of course, that it is not to the Church of England that we should look for the development of practices of accountability, but to the various nonconformist denominations. There is a longstanding historiographical tradition of regarding chapels as schools for learning organising techniques to be used in other spheres, most notably in the case of nineteenth-century agricultural trade unionism. Again, we lack detail on this, but it is interesting to note the connection to Scotland that Ashton stresses in his study of the industrial revolution. He notes the large numbers of Nonconformists, denied entry to Oxford and Cambridge, who studied at Scottish universities. He also points to Scottish educational traditions as an inspiration to the Dissenting Academies, which, he argues, 'did for England in the eighteenth century something of what the universities did for Scotland'.[66]

Consequences

The contrast with England points up the distinctiveness of the Scottish system of church governance, but what were its consequences? It seems implausible that, given the pervasive influence of the Scottish kirk throughout the period, it did not have consequences for secular activity. This has often been painted in terms of its negative impact, in that the triumphs of the Scottish Enlightenment are seen in terms of an escape from the tendrils of dour and literal scripturalism. There is a danger here of reading too much into the later estimation of the work of sceptics like Hume. At the time, men like George Campbell and Thomas Reid, with their attachment to Presbyterianism shorn of its fundamentalism and enriched by the broader ideas of the Enlightenment, were considered just as influential.[67] This was to continue into the next century, with the work on ritual by the Free Churchman William Robertson Smith being a profound influence on Durkheim.[68] These cultural influences, especially the attachment to deductive modes of thought as identified by Buckle, were of profound and lasting importance. However, there were also consequences outside the ranks of academe and it is on these that the rest of the chapter focuses. As noted already, Scotland at the beginning of the eighteenth century was a poor and underdeveloped country, prone to crises of subsistence and dependent on basic commodity exports. By the end of the century the country was in the van of agricultural and industrial developments. An interesting point about such developments is the extent to which they were landlord–led and dependent on the expertise of professional management. Devine has pointed to the importance of the legally trained estate factor in giving shape to aspirations to agricultural improvement.[69] Cooke notes the importance of the manager or managing partner in the Scottish cotton industry, in the context of different legal arrangements for multiple partnerships.[70] The rest of this chapter looks at the influence that the system of Presbyterian church governance examined so far might have had on economic developments, both in Scotland and further afield. We start with the more local examination of practices of lending on bond to business. This is followed by a consideration of the embodiment of the stress on accountability of the Scottish system in the form of the cadre of accountants it produced. Finally, we look at the broader dissemination of these ideas through print, with a particular focus on the fledgling United States of America.

Bonds

We noted in Chapter 5 the importance of interest received by many kirk sessions, but not the source of that interest. What is significant here is the corporate form of the kirk session. This gave it the ability, as we have seen, to accumulate balances as contrasted to the English approach where, in general, finances were raised and expended in the same period. We noted the appearance of an item for the receipt of '@rent' or interest in the earliest separate accounts of 1608. It is instructive, therefore, to examine how lending at interest for the benefit of the poor operated in the eighteenth century. By this time the practice was not only widespread, but indeed was enjoined upon parishes by presbyteries. When, for example, the presbytery of Hamilton inspected the session registers of Bothwell in 1750 they 'recommend it to William Meek to find a sufficient hand & lend out on Interest the 200 Merks now in his hand & not let it lye dead by him as it has done too long already'.[71] They were also concerned that sessions should not lend money without sufficient security. In 1702, for example, the presbytery of Haddington instructed their clerk to write to the session of Saltpreston recommending them not to 'lend any of the poors money, either to Heritors or others, without good and sufficient securitie'.[72]

It is clear, therefore, that in exercising stewardship over the money they collected for the benefit of the poor, sessions were expected to accumulate balances and to invest these balances, against appropriate security, in order to augment their funds. Their challenge, at a time when secure banks were in their infancy, was to find a sufficiently 'good hand' for their funds. One response was direct investment. Some sessions built 'lofts' or galleries in the church, which could be let out annually. This, however, was a relatively low yielding investment and one that could involve the session in disputes over seat rents. Another approach was to invest in land or houses. In 1721, for example, the kirk session of Abercorn near Edinburgh agreed to buy six acres in Queensferry from the Earl of Roseberry for £1,905 Scots, the purchase money being that which the session had accumulated plus some that the minister managed to borrow.[73] Subsequently the neighbouring parish of Dalmeny bought an adjoining acre of land in 1726.[74] The session of Abercorn held their land for nearly fifty years, selling it back to the Earl in 1770.[75] Dalmeny, by contrast, seemed to hold on to their land, granting James Ponton a nineteen-year lease in 1780.[76] Other sessions chose to invest in housing. In 1721 the session of Inverurie in Aberdeenshire purchased some land in the burgh and had houses built on it.[77] The aim was to use the rental income for the benefit of the poor, but by 1763 the houses had themselves become part of poor relief, being let free to some on the poor roll.[78] Direct investment also meant a continuing need for expenditure on maintenance and the problem of chasing tenants for arrears.

Accordingly, many sessions looked for secure homes for their money that would guarantee them steady annual interest. The natural port of call was the local landowner. In some cases, in a poor and underdeveloped country that had only the stirrings of agricultural improvement before about 1760, this was seen as more of a duty by landowners than as an opportunity to secure investment funds. In Chapel of Garioch, Aberdeenshire, in 1758, a parish with a number of heritors, Sir Archibald Grant felt that heritors should take it in turns to hold the session's money and suggested that they approach Clark of Balquhain.[79] This does suggest that in many cases heritors perhaps saw themselves more as holders of deposit than active investors. Landowners were not always the secure home for money that their appearance might suggest. In 1768 the session of Insch lent £81 sterling to John Grant of Rothmaise, 'a Gentleman of undoubted Credit'.[80] Ten years later, however, he was declared bankrupt and the session had to join other creditors in receiving eleven shillings in the pound.[81]

Joining local landowners as common destinations for investment were local farmers and tradesmen. Here the loan of money was even riskier and sometimes seemed to amount to a form of deferred poor relief. In 1753 for example, the session of Culsalmond, Aberdeenshire, lent forty merks to William Ellemont in Putwhile, but two years later, despite having a cautioner, he was unable to repay. The session wrote the debt off, 'at the same time they notified to him that he was not to expect for a considerable time after this any more supply from them'.[82] In other cases, loans seemed to be more for the working capital of recipients, but even here their security was precarious. In the same parish, a review of outstanding loans in 1770 found that of five small loans with accumulated interest ranging from three to thirteen years,

> excepting James Mackie alone, the other persons who granted the above Bills are in the most indigent Circumstances, and as for this reason they have no ground to expect full Payment without depriving them of the little subject they are presently professed.[83]

These problems meant that some sessions, especially those closer to developing urban centres, took a more adventurous course of lending money to those developing new investments. Loans to housing developers, because they could be secured on the property, were a popular choice. In 1761 the session of Bolton in Lothian was advised that 'there was one Deacon Brown in Edinburgh who wanted to borrow about eighty pounds sterling to finish some buildings of a considerable Value, which he had been carrying on, and was willing to give Heritable security'. After realising some other loans the session lent £80 to Brown secured on the 'Lands & Houses in Bruntsfield Links'; in this way the session both contributed to and benefited from the expansion of Edinburgh.[84] Houses, however, were not always a reliable investment. The session of Gladsmuir, Lothian, had loaned money to Edward Baillie, an Edinburgh merchant, secured on houses in the Canongate. However, in endeavouring to recover their money in 1753 they discovered that the houses were in poor condition. Legal process ensued, with the session deciding three years later that, as the houses were in ruinous condition that they would accept the offer of an Edinburgh merchant to buy their debt from them, 'the Session being desirous to avoid & get free of a Tedious Law Suit which has already depended for many years'.[85]

Other more industrial enterprises, however, were also homes for funds. In 1753 the session of Bolton lent £20 sterling to William Hamilton, a brewer in Edinburgh. A further £10 was added to the loan in 1760. The loan proved a good one, continuing until it was redeemed on Hamilton's death in 1770.[86] In 1782 the same session lent £90 to 'John Blair, Merchant in Edinburgh and William Cheap Linen Manufacturer there at 5%'.[87] Sessions near Edinburgh were able to take advantage of the legal infrastructure in which advocates and Writers to the Signet (respectively the equivalent of barristers and solicitors) acted as brokers for clients in search of funds. In 1761 the session at Dirleton lent £200 sterling to 'James Campbell of Arkinglass Esq, John Livingston Merchant in Edinburgh and Adam Cleghorn Merchant in London'.[88] In similar fashion, through the mediation of David Anderson WS, Edinburgh, the session of Saltoun lent £400 sterling in 1769 to James Wilkie esq and Mr William Tod junior, 'merchant in Edinburgh'.[89] On the other side of the country, meanwhile, the session at Dundonald, Ayrshire lent £45 sterling to the Tannery Company in Kilmarnock in 1760. These commercial loans continued with loans to James Wilson and Company, repaid in 1778, and to the merchant John Parker and Company from 1779.[90] Another tannery company, that in Glasgow, was also the target of investment by the session of Cambuslang, which had a bond of £68 with them from 1737 until 1743.[91] For a short period all of their available money was lent secured on land in the conventional way, until £130 was lent in 1747 to Messrs Crawford, merchants in Glasgow.[92] This was followed by the loan in 1749 of £100 to another Glasgow merchant partnership, that of Connell and Campbell, whose loan continued until 1776.[93] Meanwhile, the Crawfords' loan was redeemed in 1758 and promptly lent out to Glassford and Ingram.[94] John Glassford and Archibald Ingram were two of Glasgow's most famous 'Tobacco Lords'.[95] Glassford started trading in tobacco in 1750 and, based on a system that involved the provision of credit and the direct purchase of the crop in America, accumulated a considerable fortune. It is interesting to note that in 1739 he and Ingram, together with two other Glasgow merchants, published a reprint of *Prima, Media & Ultima: the First, Middle and Last Things* by the English Presbyterian divine Isaac Ambrose.[96] His loan from the session had increased to £170 by 1762 and was renewed to £200 in 1768. This continued, by now just in Glassford's name, until repaid in 1787. The sum was then lent on a series of notes to Henderson, Gordon, Riddel and Co., another firm of Glasgow merchants whose counting house was behind Glassford's premises. The connection continued when £270 was lent to Glassford and Riddel in November 1797.[97] Thus for the better part of the eighteenth century the session of Cambuslang had significant sums lent out to the elite of Glasgow's merchants.

However, the most interesting commercial investment was that by Old Monkland session in the developing sugar refining industry of Glasgow.[98] Based on trade with Scottish plantation owners in the Caribbean, the King Street sugar house was founded by Colonel McDowall on his return from St Kitts in 1727. The session invested all its accumulated funds in this new venture in November 1727, adding a further £11 13s 4d Scots in 1735.[99] In 1743 the accounts recorded:

> Received from United Company of Wester & King Street Sugarhouses the sum of one hundred & three Pounds ten shillings Scots as a year and half's interest (viz from Martinmas 1741 to Whitsunday 1743) of the Principal Sum of 2300 Merks Scots contained in a bond granted by Sd Company.[100]

The bond was still extant in 1750, when it had been joined by a bill for £29 sterling to Messrs Coats. The sugar house bond appears to have been redeemed in 1755 when a consolidated bond of £200 sterling was invested in Richard and John Coats, merchants in Glasgow.[101] Although the details are not clear, it would appear that the Coats were later involved in Glasgow's fledgling textile industry. They were certainly part of the city's flourishing trade with North America.

Devine has pointed to the ability of Glasgow's businesses to consolidate small investments in order to facilitate commercial development, especially of the tobacco trade, which gave such a boost to industrial development. He notes that:

> The main medium for transmission of credit was the loan secured on bond. The basic advantage of the bonded loan was that it produced a higher return than government stock. Most of the bonded loans studied were for the full legal limit of 5 per cent of interest between 1750 and 1775. If necessary, further security for the lender could be obtained by guaranteeing them against heritable property, and although bonds were commonly drawn up for six months or a year, they endured in most cases for much longer periods.[102]

What an examination of church records indicates is how important the practice of lending on bond was to the local bodies of the church. Their corporate form gave the potential to accumulate credit balances that could in turn be lent out, in some cases to new commercial enterprises.

Accountancy

The success of Glasgow's merchants in first of all dominating Atlantic trade and then investing in manufacturing enterprises created a demand for book-keeping skills. Murray noted an advertisement in the *Glasgow Mercury* of 1788 for 'a Manager for a considerable Manufacturing Company near Glasgow. None need apply who is not a good Accountant, thoroughly acquainted with business, and the managing of servants'.[103] This demand created an infrastructure of academies dedicated to training in bookkeeping and other commercial skills; and it built on earlier initiatives, such as the one already noted for Leith in 1661. The town council of Edinburgh appointed John Dickson, merchant, as their approved teacher of accounting, considering 'how necessary the Science of Book-holding is for the Advantage of Trade and Commerce, especially when the same is carried on in Co-partnery'.[104] We have already noted the teaching of bookkeeping at Ayr Academy in 1716; similar courses were also to be found in Stirling and Perth.[105] In Glasgow several private academies 'provided advanced courses in arithmetic and mathematics, bookkeeping and accounts, in the course of trade and business, in geography and history; in short, their aim was to provide a commercial education'.[106] However, the impact was felt more broadly, with Murray noting that in 'the parochial schools in Scotland arithmetic was well taught in all its branches, and both girls and boys left these schools with a sound knowledge of all the ordinary rules, and with much facility in computation'. That teaching, he argued, was based largely on commercial models: 'the examples of the ordinary rules are mostly of a commercial nature, while a large portion of the course is devoted to the special rules which constitute commercial arithmetic'.[107]

All this activity produced a cadre of skilled bookkeepers who were in much demand with the expansion of industry and commerce. Writing of his travels through England in 1845, the Free Churchman Hugh Miller recorded a Dudley landlady observing that 'the Scotch became overseers and book-keepers, sometimes even partners in lucrative works, and were usually well liked and looked up to'.[108] The most famous example of the Scottish book-keeper in the eighteenth century was Robert Burns, who was preparing to leave for a post as bookkeeper on Charles Duncan's plantation near Port Antonio in northeast Jamaica when he learned of the success of his first collection of poems, which enabled him to stay in Scotland. Scots dominated the ranks of plantation bookkeepers. Hamilton notes that this was a two-way arrangement, with many of the funds employed to establish Inverness Academy, with its courses in writing arithmetic and bookkeeping, coming from the West Indies.[109] In similar vein, Andrew Wedderburn, a member of the Governing Committee of the Hudson Bay Company of Canada in 1810, introduced new accounting practices that, with their emphasis on detailed accountability and individual responsibility for income and expenditure, prefigured (argue Spraakman and Margret) practices that are more closely associated with developments in the United States over 150 years later. Edward Ellice, the London-born but Marischal College, Aberdeen-educated son of an émigré Scot, introduced similar practices into the rival North West Company at the same time.[110]

Scots were also much in demand as land agents, drawing on the expertise they had acquired in landlord-led improvement in their own country. Here men such as John Burrell, chamberlain to the Duke of Hamilton and a leading 'improver', used detailed work journals to keep control of all aspects of the process.[111] Eric Richards and Monica Clough's account of estate management on the lands of the Earl of Cromartie argues that 'land agents were the lynchpin of the managerial class which emerged strongly during British industrialisation'.[112] These land agents were heavily influenced by Lowland Scots.[113] Men like James Loch, agent for the Sutherland estates, and Francis Blaikie, steward to the pioneering Holkham estate in Norfolk, were widely called upon for advice and held up as models of advanced practice.[114] A detailed focus on accountability through information characterised the work of James Loch. Spring reports of Loch's work for Lord Egerton:

> He proposed that the administration be divided into distinct departments; that the profit and loss of every unit, down to the last coalpit, be clearly accounted for; and that agents be allowed to keep in their hands only such moneys as were remitted to them for authorized expenditures.[115]

This focus on detailed accounting, facilitated by careful record keeping, draws not only on the practices that we have examined but also on a more individual practice fostered by Presbyterianism, that of diary keeping. 'May we ever keep in mind,' wrote the Aberdeenshire farmer and merchant Adam Mackie in January 1826, 'that we are accountable creatures'.[116] The turn of the year was a time for self-examination. The purpose of the diary was to record, 'what manner I have spent my time whether in labour, study, business, pleasure or idleness. Also to be a taskmaster which I may suppose asks the question every night: What have you done this day?'[117] This built on a long tradition of self-examination. The Glasgow merchant George Brown recorded his concerns on reviewing his life in December 1746:

> My predominants have been an inordinate love of worldly riches, and excess of affection to one I wanted to be settled in m—d state in the world (with). These evils have led me to others, viz., wandring in duty, publick, private and secret, fretting and murmuring at disappointments, joined with excessive wrath at the causes of these disappointments; but my leading sin has been pride and unbelief.[118]

This habit of diary keeping for accountability was taken to its apogee in the remarkable diary of Charles Cowan, managing owner of the family paper-making business at Penicuik outside Edinburgh. Using a printed proforma produced by his company, Cowan recorded in extraordinary detail the time he spent on business and spiritual matters, with the latter being divided between personal and church affairs. Cowan was ordained as an elder at just 29.[119] He was active at the session and was selected as the presbytery representative within two years.[120] Cowan was joined on the session in 1833 by another papermaker, Robert Blyth of Eskmills, and the bleacher John Reid.[121] It is not possible to know whether Cowan's family ancestors, who originated from Crail in Fife, played a formal part in church affairs there, although they are recorded as having been devout Presbyterians. However, it is possibly of significance that in 1782 the church accounts there record the repayment of a bill for £13 12s 6d by David Cowan Junior, indicating again the significance of lending to businesses by local sessions.[122] Cowan's experience suggests two things. One is the growing participation of industrialists in the local affairs of the church. The other is the reinforcement of habits of detailed record keeping in both public and private spheres.

A further consequence of this background was the propensity to publish. Francis Blaikie, the Holkham steward and native of Bowden in the Borders, was the writer of a number of pamphlets on agricultural matters; he considered it 'a duty incumbent upon man to diffuse to his fellow-men the fruits of his experience in this life. All men have not the same advantages of acquiring information. Those advantages are bestowed upon us by the prov-idence of God'.[123] His father, Andrew, is noted as having 'chiefly furnished' the materials for the *Statistical Account* of Bowden, and was thus a represen-tative of those literate farmers who formed the audience for texts on agricul-tural matters.[124] In the parish school, he records, about fifteen pupils were taught arithmetic, bookkeeping, and mathematics. Publications for farmers built on the strong infrastructure of printers and publishers that had been built up on the production of religious tracts.[125] These factors were particu-larly important in the widespread influence of Scottish accounting texts. Mepham has demonstrated that Scotland was a world leader in the production of accounting texts in the eighteenth century.[126] In particular, the work of John Mair was, writes Sheldahl, based on an analysis of sales cata-logues and library listings, 'easily the most popular accounting text in the major American cities during the latter half of the eighteenth century'.[127] His *Book-keeping Methodiz'd* and subsequent *Book-keeping Moderniz'd* went through twenty-nine printings and eighteen numbered editions between 1736 and 1807.

This connection with America becomes still more significant if we consider the career of James Montgomery. The Glasgow cotton industry was marked, in contrast to England, by the employment of salaried managers to run the enterprises funded by the profits of transatlantic trade.[128] One of these managers, James Montgomery, rising from a humble background, wrote what has been termed the 'first management text', *The Carding and Spinning Master's Assistant*, published in Glasgow in 1832.[129] Based on the success of this book and his comparative work on American and British productivity, Montgomery moved across the Atlantic to manage mills in New England. He retired as a pillar of his local Presbyterian church and a respected mill manager in South Carolina.[130] His book was published in Glasgow by the book-seller John Niven, who specialised largely in Presbyterian tracts. However, Niven was also the publisher in 1824 of Robert Brunton's *A Compendium of Mechanics, or Text book for Engineers, Mill-Wrights, Machine-Makers, Founders, Smiths, &c*, which also ran into several editions. In this way not only did Scots bring traditions of accountability strongly shaped by religious practices into their working lives, but they also diffused such traditions through publication.

America

There is, however, a problem with this account. Accounts of comparative management styles in the late twentieth century suggested that, compared to other European countries, British management was characterised by a focus on leadership and character.[131] A study of the religious commitments of British business leaders at the end of the nineteenth century found that the majority of the business elite were Anglicans.[132] To return to the contrast with which we started this chapter, it does rather appear that the personal mode of accountability that we have associated with Anglicanism won out as the dominant British style. The career of one businessman is a good illustration of the process. In 1846 Andrew Barclay Walker was granted a licence for a public house on Brownlow Hill.[133] His father, Peter, variously brewer, inventor (credited with devising the famous Burton Union system of brewing) and coal owner in Ayrshire had moved to Liverpool at some point in the decade.[134] It was Andrew who appears to have been the force behind the business, and particularly behind the retailing side in Liverpool. He acquired many properties; the majority were run as managed houses, as opposed to being tenanted.[135] It would seem that the running of these houses under direct management might have been partly as a result of Andrew drawing on family experience in the coal business and partly a response to conditions in the town.[136] The company was later to claim that it was the originator of the 'managerial system'.[137] This development, at a time when most brewers owned few, if any, public houses, and ran those that they did own under tenancy, was a distinctive one.[138] This system was run on the basis of annual profit and loss accounts for each public house.[139] These accounts are fragmentary and scattered among both business and personal papers, but their existence suggests a focus on the detailed monitoring of managerial activity in the pubs, made possible by an elaborate accounting system and embodied in a managerial hierarchy involving house inspectors at the lowest level reporting to the head of a dedicated Managed House Department.[140]

Walker served two terms as Mayor of Liverpool, on the second occasion being knighted by Queen Victoria on a visit there. He provided the funds to build the art gallery that bears his name, as well as being a significant contributor to the university. In 1866 he took up a £25 share in St Andrew's Church of Scotland on Rodney Street in the city and joined the Committee of Management.[141] It is possible to see his success as owing much to the traditions of detailed record keeping and careful accountability that we have been examining. However, in 1884, for approximately £250,000, he purchased Osmaston Manor in Derbyshire. Three years later he married his second wife, the Honourable Maude Okeover, the twenty-six-year-old daughter of Haughton Charles Okeover of Okeover Hall, Staffordshire. When he died in 1893, after the successful flotation of the company, he left a fortune worth well over two million pounds and was buried at the Anglican Church near his Liverpool residence at Gateacre. His sons, who ran the business rather unsuccessfully, were firmly integrated into British ruling circles. One, Colonel William Hall Walker, 'being himself *persona grata* at Court is, needless to say, a member of the most exclusive of Social Clubs, the Marlborough, to which only personal friends of His Majesty have the *entrée*'.[142] While Walker fits into the pattern of careful and detailed accountability that we have associated with Scottish traditions, his trajectory suggests the absorptive capacity of the English model. It may be that to see the lasting impact of the Scottish tradition we have, as Montgomery did, to head west.

By the end of the eighteenth century a dense network of connections through both trade and settlement had built up between Scotland and North America. Following the earlier development of the trade in sugar between the Caribbean and Glasgow, merchants from that city came to dominate the transatlantic trade in tobacco by the third quarter of the century. The so-called 'Tobacco Lords' received a check to their fortunes from the War of Independence, but transatlantic trade meant enduring connections between the city and the emergent United States of America. Woven into these relationships were spiritual links that mutually reinforced the position and influence of Presbyterianism on both sides of the Atlantic. The Cambuslang Revival was widely commented on in America. Indeed, Murdoch has argued that, 'in many ways the Scottish revivals of 1742 marked a turning point in Scottish contact with America far more important than the defeat of Scottish Jacobitism in 1746 which has attracted so much more attention in Scottish History'.[143] Schmidt has shown how the Scottish communion season provided an organising template for the development of American revivalism.[144] Exchanges of ideas and personnel continued throughout the century.

Undergirding such exchanges were the governance practices that we have been examining. Tiedemann has suggested that not only did Presbyterianism provide a useful 'to-hand' template for organising in frontier conditions, but also that lessons learned prepared congregants for actions in secular arenas, in his case for participation in the revolt against Britain.[145] American Presbyterians, in the forms of their 'books of order', drew on Scottish exemplars. In particular, the work of Pardovan had an enduring influence. Coldwell notes the way in which American Presbyterians used the book as an authority in developing their own standards, citing one minister, Ashbel Green, as recalling that, 'when I was preparing for the gospel ministry, I was directed to read the Scotch collections of Steuart of Pardovan, as a book of authority on the government and discipline of the Presbyterian Church'.[146] Pardovan, for example, was extensively cited in a court case in Vermont in 1846 concerning the discipline of a Presbyterian Associate church congregation.[147]

We may recall that James Montgomery, author of *The Carding and Spinning Master's Assistant*, ultimately settled in South Carolina, where he was a stalwart of local Presbyterianism. He left Scotland in 1836 to run cotton mills in Maine. In 1840 he published *A Practical Detail of the Cotton Manufacture of the United States of America and the State of the Cotton Manufacture of that Country Contrasted and Compared with that of Great Britain*.[148] He left Maine in 1843 to work in New York State and thence on to South Carolina, always managing cotton mills. His work appeared significant enough to the doyen of American business history, Alfred Chandler, for him to have Montgomery's first work reprinted as a 'Precursor of Modern Management'. Little is known of Montgomery's early life in Blantyre, although his father William worked in the cotton mill there. In 1809 Mr James Wightman from the mill was an elder on Blantyre session.[149] James must have received a sound education there, for by the 1830s he was working as a mill manager for MacLeroy, Hamilton & Co. of Calton, Glasgow. His career therefore suggests the capacity of the educated Scot not to only organise work but also to write about it. It might also suggest that the lessons learned were more easily put into operation in the conditions of the United States. Another Scot who achieved great success on leaving his homeland for America was Andrew Carnegie. In 1868, in the style of the diary keepers we have already observed, he drew up a balance sheet of his activities during the year. He 'had never accepted the Calvinist view of either man or God', writes his biographer, 'but the ethos of Scotland had been bred into him. With all the introspection of an Edwards or a Knox, he took a hard, unpitying look at himself'.[150] Supported by the accounting practices, which gave him an obsessive level of detail on costs and 'the fullest minutes of board meetings that probably ever existed in business history', it was such habits, rather than belief, which were then transferred to managerial capitalism.[151] Hall has used the term 'culture of organisation' to examine the predilection of some groups in the United States to form voluntary associations for the management of all sorts of activities. He isolates in particular the influence of evangelical Protestants:

> This subculture of individuals, trained to autonomy and accommodated to modes of corporate and proto-bureaucratic activity, would prove of immense importance not only in organizing the Civil War mobilization but also in creating and staffing the large-scale organizations that emerged after the war.[152]

While the Scottish influence was only one strand of several, the impact of the organising practices that we have examined provided formidable support for this particular culture of organisation.

Scottish historians have been cautious and concerned about some of the triumphalism that seems to accompany accounts of Scottish influences on the United States, especially as manifest in Arthur Herman's *The Scottish Enlightenment: The Scots' Invention of the Modern World*.[153] That caution is well merited, but examining practices as opposed to just beliefs, especially as stated in the printed word, indicates where some of the more enduring influence might lie. It is the development over time of a particular culture of organisation, which has two aspects. One is the explicit development of blueprints for organisation as seen most clearly in Pardovan's work. That practice diverged from such blueprints should not divert our attention from the importance of seeking to work from first principles to lay out rules for organisation. Working from first principles in this manner would influence the accounting texts that Scottish authors were so prolific in producing in the eighteenth century. The second aspect is belief in the value of organisation as a good in its own right. Drawing ultimately on Paul's injunction to the Corinthians, this raised adherence to the value of orderliness in church affairs to a good to be valued in its own right. This might be seen more clearly if we draw some broader contrasts, which we will do in the next, and concluding, chapter.

CHAPTER 8

Conclusion

What are the implications of the practices we have been examining for Scotland and the wider world? This chapter examines these implications in two ways. We look first of all at the wider picture, setting the practices we have examined in the context of other belief systems. This allows us to suggest some of the ways in which a focus on religion as a social practice revives and redirects the debate raised by Weber's Protestant Ethic thesis. We then turn to look at the consequences for our understanding of the formation of particular forms of Scottish national identity. Some of the limitations of this work are acknowledged, but looking at the legacy of Presbyterian practices, it is argued, forms a valuable corrective and supplement to approaches that have focused on other aspects of Scottish history.

Religion as a social practice

We left the last chapter with Hall's observations about the importance to the United States of Protestant organising practices. Hall goes on to point out that there do appear to be distinctions between the propensities of groups with particular religious traditions to engage in voluntary organised activity. He notes, for example, that voluntary organisation is central to Judaism. Recognising the dangers of ethnic stereotyping, he suggests:

> it does appear that 'national' traditions (in the sense of familiarity with particular technologies of collective action) have a good deal to do with where particular groups locate themselves in the polity and, of course, with their propensity to occupy formal trusteeship roles.

He notes, for example, that in Irish Catholic traditions much organisation 'tended to be left to ecclesiastical authorities'.[1] A problem here is with the lack of detailed attention to the sort of organising practices that we have been examining for other major belief systems. To take the example of Catholicism, which was the focus of Foucault's lament about the lack of attention to religion as a social practice, there are some limited investigations of particular practices. Foucault himself, in his partial excavation of the techniques of pastoral power, paid particular attention to the confessional.[2] He looked, for example, at the advice given to pastors about the types of question they might ask and on the material artefacts, such as the confession box, that accompanied such guidance. However, it is noticeable that he was heavily dependent in this endeavour on a massive work by the American writer Henry Charles Lea.[3] Drawing on an extensive range of sources, this seems thorough, if not exhaustive, in its approach, but it can hardly been see as an impartial account when one notes observations such as the 'history of mankind may be vainly searched for another institution which has established a spiritual autocracy such as that of the Latin Church'.[4] More recent work has examined some practices with parallels to those we have seen in Scotland. Paulo Quattrone, for example, in his study of accounting practice in the Jesuit Order in Sicily in the seventeenth century, examines the use of a box for holding money and papers with two keys, one held by the Procurator, in charge of economic affairs, the other by the rector, responsible for spiritual and missionary matters.[5] What seems interesting here is that we have a similar artefact and a similar process inserted into a different structure of accountability, one in this case that is internal to the hierarchy.

Another investigation of an earlier practice within Catholicism reminds us that the Scottish Presbyterians (and for that matter the English Anglicans) did not fashion all of their practices from new cloth, but built on existing practices. This is hardly surprising, given both that the early reformers were trained in the old church and that they saw their task as to remove what they perceived to be the accretions of centuries of misdirected effort. This practice was that of the visitation. It appears to have been particularly associated with reform movements. In the diocese of York in the fourteenth century there was a determined effort to visit nunneries in a response to perceived misdeeds. Guided by lists of questions, this was an internal church matter conducted by the Archbishop.[6] By contrast, visitations in the diocese of Ferrara in Italy in the following century that were also inspired by reforming impulses and featured detailed lists of questions, additionally featured other stakeholders. Two of these were of particular importance. One was that a notary, whose tasks included writing up a detailed report and compiling a detailed inventory of church property, was present at visits. The other important feature was the involvement of a group of laymen or 'massari': appointed following the visit, they were to update the bishop on the changes made after the visitation. Selected from the wealthier inhabitants:

> [they] also had an important role in keeping all the buildings of the parish in a good state which often required them to contribute financially to repairing church buildings and helping the priest to collect the rest of the required resources from the local parishioners.[7]

They were also to keep account books, which were to be referred to during subsequent visitations. Elements that we have seen in Scotland – direct parochial visitations, the taking of minutes, the involvement of laypeople, the keeping of books of account – all appear in this configuration. However, it is perhaps significant that 'at the local village level no parish account books appear to have survived, even though the minutes of the pastoral visits often refer to the liber introituum et expensarum ("book of incomes and expenses")'.[8] Some of this could be due, of course, to the vagaries of record survival, but it is perhaps also related to the lack of organisational form for lay involvement. Other studies of later Catholic practice do tend to be suggestive of a lack of lay involvement with, for example, participation in brotherhoods running in parallel with church structures.[9]

These are only hints in the absence of any detailed studies of practices, as opposed to belief or organisational form. For other major belief systems the picture is even less clear. Weber spent much of his effort on elucidating what he saw to be the prescriptions for economic activity of the major world religious traditions, but his hints on the importance of practice have not been followed up.[10] Limited comments in the sociology of religion suggest, for example, that within Islam 'the mosque lacks a sense of full-blown congregational solidarity' that might generate practices analogous to those outlined above.[11] Even more, Hindus practice a home-based form of religion evincing the observation that 'there is nothing two Hindus do together that one Hindu cannot do alone'.[12] So the secondary literature is poorly developed beyond the consideration of national organisational forms.[13] This suggests that there are two ways in which the practice-based approach essayed here might be taken forward. One is that in the United States, where much has been made of the Scottish contribution, there could be much value in tracing further the influence of writers such as Steuart of Pardovan. That is, much attention has been paid to the transatlantic trade in doctrinal matters, but attention to matters of governance might also be valuable. The second is to look at other major belief systems through the lens of governance practices, with particular attention being paid to the involvement of lay people in such practices.

Of course, a key distinction here might be in the availability of source material. It has been seen that this is particularly rich in Scotland, a fact not unrelated to the emphasis on detailed record keeping. We also have to recognise the propensity of Scots, as Devine observes, to publicise 'their achievements widely in the press and in books'.[14] We have noted this in a number of circumstances, a number of them related to religious predilections. There was, for example, Francis Blaikie's stated belief that it was his duty to share his insights into agricultural management. James Montgomery codified his experience of managing cotton mills in book form and Scottish authors dominated the market for accounting texts in the eighteenth century. Building on a history of publishing religious tracts, Scots seemed to have both the capacity and the willingness to share ideas on not only a theoretical but also a vocational level. We noted the publishing activities of George Skene Keith in agricultural matters. The apogee of such involvement was the production of the *Statistical Accounts* of Scottish parishes in the 1790s, the majority penned by ministers. 'Who is to say,' argues Withrington, that an enterprise such as the *Statistical Account*, and the fact of its successful completion, does not exemplify as effectively as any number of philosophical or legal treatises the longstanding inheritance of the Scottish Enlightenment, and at the same time clearly demonstrate its peculiarly Scottish character and achievement?[15]

The evidence presented in this book, the bulk of it from sources not designed for further dissemination, suggests both the religious shaping of this propensity to publish and that something more was involved than a talent for self-publicity. With this in mind as one of the enduring legacies of Scottish church governance, we now look at some other influences on the formation of Scottish national identity.

Scotland and Presbyterianism

It is as well to recognise some of the limitations of what has been presented before speculating on some influences on national identity. The evidence has been drawn substantially from five presbyteries, which, while they represent a good part of the country, cannot be claimed to stand for the whole. In particular, the focus has been on Lowland areas because of the later spread of Presbyterian forms of governance to the Highlands. Some of this focus is corrected by the attention paid to a greater range of presbyteries in looking at practices such as the parochial visitation, but there remains much to be done to quarry the riches in the archives at local level. This might encompass consideration of heritors' records. In addition, the focus has been largely on rural areas. Such areas were, as we will see, part of the ideal type of Presbyterian practice. They were also chosen, in part, to isolate practice from that which might have obtained in more urban areas. Of course, the boundaries were blurred. Several of the presbyteries had urban settlements at their heart and many parishes were connected with bigger urban areas by their strategies for investing money – in property in Edinburgh and industrial enterprises in Glasgow. However, it remains the case that the practices explored might not have obtained in the more complex urban settings. Here, too, were often strong dissenting Presbyterian congregations, whose practices have not been examined here. Their adherents seemed to have been particularly well represented in the ranks of Glasgow merchants. However, secession was over matters of doctrine rather than local governance, with seceding congregations adopting the same organisational forms as the parent church.[16]

What might be more important than the limits of evidence is the fact that national identity is a complex matter comprising a number of strands. There is a danger that too much weight is placed on Presbyterianism and its associated practices. To take one more recent example, here is the bass player of the group Jethro Tull, Glenn Cornick, on the frontman of the group, Ian Anderson: 'Even though Ian claimed to be an atheist or agnostic', he remembers, 'he retained that streak of Scottish Presbyterian Puritanism in him. He was very offended when we toured the States when I was off chasing girls'.[17] Cornick, whose parents hailed from Rothesay, had a clear view of what he understood the Presbyterian influence on Anderson to be. Anderson was born in Dunfermline and lived in Edinburgh until he was twelve, when he moved with his parents to Blackpool. He became known for his hard-headed approach to the business aspects of music, taking on the management of the band's activities from 1974. The living embodiment, one might think, of Presbyterian Scotland. And yet, although not investigated by numerous writers on the band's history, Anderson was brought up as an Episcopalian. So we have to be careful about attributing all the facets of what we might take to be Scottish characteristics to the direct influence of Presbyterianism.[18]

Yet, one could argue, that influence might be subtler. In an investigation of 'Puritan' Boston and 'Quaker' Philadelphia, Baltzell argued for the enduring impact of the founding religious influences of each city. Residents of the former, he argued, reflected 'Puritan traditions of educated and patrician leadership'.[19] He goes so far as to argue that this shaped the career of men like John F. Kennedy, despite their being from a completely different confessional background. In the same way, those, like Andrew Carnegie, who completely rejected their doctrinal heritage, were still shaped by its broader influence. A number of writers concur with such a judgement. Campbell, for example, argues:

> [T]here is no question that the influence of the religious tradition [in Scotland] was widespread, so that even those who rejected or actively opposed it were often as much its products as those who were among its supporters. The religious tradition may then have to be credited with much that might seem at first sight to have little contact with it.[20]

Likewise, McLean in his study of Adam Smith, argues (and it is his emphasis), '*Once a Presbyterian, always a Presbyterian, even if you reject the doctrines of the Church of Scotland*'.[21] Those influences have often been seen as relating to belief, especially with views about morality. Such views have been largely rejected, as has adherence to the beliefs themselves among a large section of the population. But if the thesis of this book is correct, that religious practice needs organising routines to put it into motion, and that those routines become relatively detached from belief over time, then it is these enduring routines that survive to shape identity. Let me take what seems to be a mundane indicator, but one to be taken in the context of McCrone's observation, repeated from the introduction, that 'people think of themselves as Scottish because of the micro-contexts of their lives reinforced by the school system'.[22] This is the survival, until reform of the Scottish school examination system in 1990, of a separate 'O' Grade in Arithmetic.[23] This might seem an unremarkable fact to those brought up exclusively in the Scottish system, but it had no equivalent in England. Is it too much of a stretch to see this as related to Murray's assertion in 1930 that, 'the Scots have for long had a genius for arithmetic and for higher mathematics, and have evinced special skill in bookkeeping and accountancy, and great aptitude for practical business'?[24] An examination of the *Statistical Accounts* would show the persistence of arithmetic, often linked to bookkeeping in parish schools. In turn, it would not seem far-fetched to link this not only to a tradition born out of Scottish mercantile education but also to Presbyterian exactness in recording financial transactions. After all, the combination did not seem strange to the Reverend James Clark, minister of the Tron Kirk in Glasgow, who published a series of sermons in 1703 entitled *The Spiritual Merchant: or, the Art of Merchandizing Spiritualized.* He had been inspired to do so, he explained, because, before he felt called to the ministry, as the son of a merchant he had been 'bred at Holland in Merchant Accounts, Bookkeeping and other parts of the Theorie of Merchandizing'.[25] He had put this into practice during 'the injuries and unsettlement of the late times', and so felt able to apply his practical knowledge to the spiritual sphere. He placed considerable emphasis on accounting for self-examination, urging his hearers:

> to keep Count books, noting down and posting all the particulars of your Soul concerns, and that for this purpose, that you may the more readilie view your profit and loss, and to understand if your stock grows or decreases, and what is your true and free estate.[26]

Here we have a link being drawn between secular and spiritual uses of accounting, by a minister who also authored tracts on Presbyterian governance.[27] This provides a link to those practices of diary keeping to aid self-examination that we explored earlier. Those examples were drawn from merchants and manufacturers, but their impact went wider. The diary of John Sturrock, millwright in Dundee in the 1860s, reveals similar practice by a member of the skilled working class. He, too, was an avid partaker of sermons and an advocate of self-examination, especially at the close of the year. His diary was kept:

> [as] a true and faithful record of how I spend and where I spend every evening, together with some of the more particular occurrences of my daily life, also my correspondence, thoughts and feelings, and any particular mood or frame of mind I may be in, I may be able to form an estimate of how I have spent my leisure time, whether I have been trifling it away or turning it to any particular advantage.[28]

This resolution was accompanied by a detailed income and expenditure statement. Of course, one isolated example can hardly be said to stand in for working-class practice more generally, but it adds to the enduring influence of one of the key Scottish myths, that of Presbyterian democracy. As with any myth, there were elements in this one that corresponded with practice. If we get beyond theological debates and procedure manuals, we have seen that practices of systemic self-governance and accountability characterised the Church of Scotland in parish after parish in the eighteenth century. This was hardly a democracy in our understanding of the term, and the devout in the eighteenth century would not have understood it in those terms. Participation was by a limited number on behalf of the great mass of people and the egalitarianism was of a moral rather than a social or economic type. However, the practices we have been examining spawned an extensive literature once the theological acrimony that accompanied the Disruption of 1843 had died down. Some of this followed the lead of Edgar in using the mass of the records that the practices of detailed record keeping had created to recreate the lives of individual parishes. This was explicitly the case, in the history of the Fife parish of Ballingry, of its minister, who observed that following Edgar's work, 'many ministers and session-clerks have been looking into their old Session Records with a keener interest than before, to learn what these have to tell of bygone days'.[29]

The apogee of this more scholarly use of the records was the *Fasti*. Compiled as his life's work by the Reverend Hew Scott, this massive work drew on presbytery and session records to provide biographical details, as we have seen, of all the ministers who served the church from the Reformation until the end of the nineteenth century. Scott was the son of an excise officer from Haddington, whose early death plunged the family into penury.[30] However Scott made his way to Edinburgh and Aberdeen universities and was licensed by the presbytery of Haddington in 1820. However, it was not until 1839 that he was ordained to the parish of Anstruther Wester after a series of assistant posts, during which he started the collection of material for the *Fasti*, which continued after his death in 1872. The first volume, covering the synod of Lothian and Tweeddale was published in 1866, and a further six followed.

This more scholarly attention to the records of the church blurred into a far more popular and anecdotal genre. In 1884 Nicholas Dickson published a series of books: *The Minister, The Precentor, The Elder at the Plate* and *The Kirk Beadle*. These proved popular enough to be reprinted with new material by D. Macleod Malloch in 1914 as *The Kirk and its Worthies*. Consisting largely of a series of couthy anecdotes, it was illustrated by pictures from artists such as J. H. Lorimer's 'The Ordination of Elders'. This carefully posed picture represents visually the serious and simple nature at the heart of this vision of Presbyterianism. The book relies on the memoirs and writings of ministers and a flavour of it is contained in the anecdote about the visit of a minster to a member of his congregation to fulfil his duty of examining the spiritual knowledge and health of the parish. '"Who made Paul a preacher?" an unpopular presentee asked of the head of a household, expecting, of course, the orthodox reply. But the reply came, snell and sharp, "It wasna the Duke of Queensberry at ony rate"'.[31] Such books fostered the notion of Presbyterian independence and in turn shaded into the most successful literary genre at the turn of the century, the so-called 'kailyard' novels. So named by later critics for their parochial focus on local affairs, these novels – most commonly associated with J. M. Barrie, S. R. Crockett and Ian McLaren – were predominantly about rural and small town life, in which church matters featured strongly. Undoubtedly sentimental, they were subject to coruscating criticism by later writers and by novelists such as Lewis Grassic Gibbon, who aspired to present a more robust view of Scottish life. However, it seems a little much to argue, as Donaldson does in his biographical note of William Alexander that, thanks to English domination of the book market, 'Scottish novelists, from Scott to Barrie and beyond, had to accommodate themselves to this fact, and present a view of Scotland and Scottish life that fitted English prejudices and expectations'.[32] As Islay Donaldson points out in her reassessment of the work of Samuel Crockett, his observations were based on direct experience of Scottish religious life from the inside (he was Free Church minister of Penicuik) and were often sharply critical of aspects of that life.[33] Rather, it seems that these works drew on the practices we have examined to present a view of Scotland that supported what Morton has termed 'Unionist Nationalism'; that is, a commitment to the shared enterprise of Britain and its Empire, accompanied by strong pride in distinctly Scottish institutions.[34]

Of course, that myth of Presbyterian independence, associated with democracy, literacy, liberty and progress, was to be replaced with another, one that focused on its grim repression of enjoyment and diversity.[35] New myths, fuelled in part by the literary abilities of Sir Walter Scott, presented alternative views that proved both more palatable and more capable of travel.[36] Thus, the dominant myths became romantic ones associated with Highlandism and the Celtic. As Devine notes with the extraordinary spread of 'Highland Games' far from their heartlands, complete with associated and often invented 'traditions', these myths are powerful and seductive ones, against which the dour virtues of the Presbyterian tradition rather pale into insignificance.[37] And yet the enduring elements of this are perhaps still of significance. Here is one marker: in a review of a book on the organisation of the Church of Scotland published in 1981 it was noted that:

> The whole system of courts, with lay representation from bottom to top, including therefore secular experience and expertise at every level of church life, makes for business-like completeness (a Calvinist carefulness?) in the returns made to the General Assembly. Since the data are there, one can have confidence in the analysis in a way that is not possible in some other Christian traditions.[38]

Some two hundred years or so earlier, Adam Smith had paid considerable attention to the Church of Scotland. This was not out of commitment to its theological tenets, but for its impact on government and society. He admired parish schools and the quality of the clergy, comparing both favourably to their English equivalents.[39] He was, as we have seen, scathing about the quality of the university education he had encountered at Oxford. Ian Carter has followed up on this contrast in his review of the depiction of universities in post-war British fiction, where he suggests the Scottish model, with its focus on the application of theory to vocational areas, is an alternative to what he terms the *Ancient Cultures of Conceit* that characterise the Oxbridge tradition.[40] It was perhaps these qualities that, Aspinwall argues, strengthened the connections between Scotland and America in the later nineteenth century. He notes American travel books as constantly recounting 'an antipathy to English hauteur, snobbery and ignorance'.[41] There is something, then, that endures in the contrast between the practices that I have termed as systemic accountability in the Scottish context, and personal accountability in England. To return to the contrast that Craig draws between the deductive cast of Scottish thinking and the inductive one that Buckle argued was characteristic of England, I would suggest that we move beyond theoretical statements to examine practice. When we do, this seems to confirm what I would suggest is a systemic cast to Scottish thought and practice, one that seeks to work from first principles and build elements into a coherent system. This approach, I have argued, is strongly conditioned by religious belief and practice. Craig and others are right to argue for the enduring impact of Presbyterianism, good and bad, on the Scottish character. My aim here has been to provide some material to support that argument, but also to finesse it. It seems, to me, to underplay a particular Scottish competence in administration, which has manifested itself historically in all sorts of ways. In particular, it supplied skilled people to manage the affairs of Empire. One can view the associated marriage of two different approaches to accountability and leadership in two different ways. You could argue that this marriage of convenience relegated Scots to a position of being the more competent junior partner, denied the opportunities deserved by their talents. Or you can view the approaches of the two as complementary, both drawing strength from each other and forming a powerful synthesis. One might also see an English genius for tolerance and coping with ambiguity as moderating some of the more adverse consequences of a Presbyterian attachment to system. That latter argument might well be outweighed by more powerful and romantic myths, now that the lure of Empire has gone.

Appendices

Appendix 1

Contrast of visitation questions

Q	1704	Q	1677	Q	1696
1	Hath your minister a Gospel walk and conversation before the people, and does he keep family worship, and is he one who rules well his own house?	4/7	His conversation was such [as to give satisfaction]/ Whither or not he did govern his own familie aright and made his families practice an example for the families of the congregation in following that [waxing] good and abstaining from evil	1	Hath your minister a Gospel walk and conversation before the congregation?
2	Keeps he much at home at his ministerial work, or doth he occasion to himself distractions and unnecessary diversions therefrom?	3	He did keep home or were found unnecessarily moving from his own house in affairs that were not [essential] to his calling	2	Keeps he much at home, giving attendance to Reading, Meditation, and Prayer, and study of the Holy Scriptures, or doth he occasion to himself distractions and unnecessary diversions therefrom?
3	Preacheth he sound doctrine, so far as you understand?			3	Preacheth he sound doctrine, so far as you understand?

Q 1704	Q 1677	Q 1696
4 Does he preach plainly, or is he hard to be understood for his scholastic terms, matter, or manner of preaching?		4 Studies he to be Powerful, and Spiritual in Preaching sensibly to your Consciences, Or, is he hard to be understood, for his Scholastick Terms, Matter, or Manner of Preaching?
5 Doth he faithfully reprove sin, especially such as most prevail in that parish?	2 Did he preach to the edification of the people and … [press] down sin especially those sins which did mightly abound in the congregation and if he were careful to reprove persons in private that did most abound in them	5 Doth he apply his Doctrine, with Authority and Wisdom, to the Corruptions of the time; especially such as most prevail in that Parish?
6 What time of day doth he ordinarily begin sermon on the Sabbath, and when doth he dismiss the people?		6 What time of day doth he ordinarily begin sermon on the Sabbath, and when doth he dismiss the people?
7 Spends he in his sermon too much time in repetition of what he had before?		7 Spends he in his sermon much time in repetition of what he had before?
8 Doth he visit the people and families, at least once a year, in a ministerial way, teaching and admonishing from house to house, and doth he visit the sick when it is needful, and pray over them?	9/10 Whither he were careful to visit the sick when acquainted and called thereunto/he did visit the families of the paroch [exhorting] them to [quiet] and to familie duties of praying reading … and such like	8 Doth he visit the people and families, at least once a year, and the sick when need is?

Q	1704	Q	1677	Q	1696
9	Does he lecture and preach in the forenoon, and preach again in the afternoon on the Lord's Day, and that both summer and winter?	1	If their minister did preach twice every Lds day		
10	Does he read a large portion of Scripture in public, and expound the same, as is enjoined by the Acts of the General Assembly?				
11	Does he preach catechetic doctrine ordinarily in the afternoon?	11	Whither he was diligent in catechizing and did take in the younger timeously to be publicly catechizing yt they may be ripened up for partaking of the Lords supper		
12	Does he administer the Sacrament of Baptism in an orderly way, when the congregation is convened, or does he it privately?			10	Doth he Administer both Sacraments according to the Directory for Worship
13	Doth he frequently catechize his parishioners, and administer the Sacrament of the Lord's Supper to them, and is he careful in keeping from that holy ordinance all who are known to be scandalous, grossly ignorant, or erroneous?	6	Whither or not he did administer the Lords Supper and how often	9	Doth he frequently Catechise, and Administer the Sacrament of the Supper?

Q 1704	Q 1677	Q 1696
14 Hath he weekday sermons, and at them collections for the poor?		11 Hath he week-days sermons, and Week-days collections?
15 Hath he a competent number of elders, and hath the deacons in the parish distinct from elders?		12 Hath he a competent number of elders, and hath the deacons in the parish distinct from elders?
16 If there be a magistrate in the parish for punishing vice, according to Act of Parliament?		
17 Doth he read termly the acts against profaneness from the pulpit?		
18 Does he keep sessional meetings frequently, and is he impartial in the exercise of discipline against offenders, and is the session's diligence thereanent recorded in a book?	8 Whither discipline were impartially exercised towards all offenders of whatsover qualitie	
19 If there be frequent meetings of the members of session for fasting and prayer, according to the 7th Act of the General Assembly, anno 1699		
	5 Whither he did resort to taverns and also ... keeping company and spending his time ... wise	

Q 1704	Q 1677	Q 1696
	12 Whither he was careful to promote peace among the people and were studious to remove differences so far as it was possible in him	

Sources: 1704 *Overtures*, 1677 Fordoun visitations and 1696 *Overtures*.

Appendix 2

Parochial visitations in four presbyteries, 1700–35

	Ayr	Haddington	Hamilton	Linlithgow
1700	4			
1701	3		2	1
1702	2	2		3
1703	5			
1704	5	1	4	1
1705				1
1706	4	1	1	2
1707	4			1
1708	1	1	1	1
1709	2	1		1
1710		2		
1711	3	1	1	2
1712				
1713	1			1
1714			1	
1715	1			
1716	1			
1717		1		
1718	3			
1719	2			
1720	2			
1721	1			
1722	6			
1723	2	1	1	
1724				
1725	2			
1726	5			
1727				
1728				
1729	2			
1730	2			
1731	1			
1732				
1733				
1734				
1735			1	

Source: Presbytery minutes.
Note: Blank cells indicate that no visits took place.

Appendix 3

Questions asked about ministerial conduct at parochial visitations in 1710 compared to 1704 Overtures

	1704	Haddington	Lochmaben	Cupar	Kirkcaldy	Stranraer	Edinburgh
1	Hath your minister a Gospel walk and conversation before the people, and does he keep family worship, and is he one who rules well his own house?	Is your Minr one of a Gospel walk that keeps family worship & rules well his own house?	Hath your Minr a Gospel walk before the people?	Hath your Minister a Gospel walk and conversation before the people?	If he hath a Gospel like conversation?	He hath a gospel walk & conversation before the people	Whether their Ministers have a Gospell Walk and Conversation before the people if they keep family Worship and enter well their own houses
2	Keeps he much at his ministerial work, or doth he occasion to himself distractions and unnecessary diversions therefrom?	Does he keep much at home at his Ministerial work & does not occasion to himself unnecessary diversions yr from?	Does he keep much at home at his Ministerial work?	Keeps he much at home at his Ministerial work?	If he keeps close by his work?	He keeps much at home at his ministerial work	If their Ministers keeps at home about their Ministerial work or did they occasion to themselves unnecessary diversions therefrom
3	Preacheth he sound doctrine, so far as you understand?	Doth he Preach sound doctrine so far as you understand & is he plain & Edifying in his sermons without unnecessary repetitions	Doth he preach sound doctrine so far as you understand?	Preacheth he sound Doctrine so far as ye understand and plainly		He preaches Sound doctrine, so far as they understand	Whether the Ministers preach sound Doctrine and plainly or are they hard to be understood by reason of Scholastick terms or manner of preaching

1704	Haddington	Lochmaben	Cupar	Kirkcaldy	Stranraer	Edinburgh
4 Does he preach plainly, or is he hard to be understood for his scholastic terms, matter, or manner of preaching?		Does he preach plainly or is hard to be understood for his Scholastick terms?			He preaches plainly	
5 Doth he faithfully reprove sin, especially such as most prevail in that parish?	Does he faithfullie reprove sin in all sorts of persons?	Does he faithfully reprove Sin especially such as most prevail in the parish?	Doth he faithfully reprove Sin especially such as is most prevalent in the parish?	If he exercise Discipline against delinquents?		If their Ministers faithfully and Zealously reprove Sin and preach against the same which prevail most in the place
6 What time of day doth he ordinarily begin sermon on the Sabbath, and when doth he dismiss the people?	Does he begin & end the publick worship timeous on ye Lords day?	What time does he begin Sermon and when does he dismiss the people?	What time doth he ordinarily begin Sermon on Sabbath and when doth he dismiss the people?		He is orderly as to the time of meeting and dismissing the people on the Sabbath dayes	What tyme of the Lords day they begin the publick Worships and when the people are dismissed
7 Spends he in his sermon too much time in repetition of what he had before?		Spends he much time in repetition of what he had before it was?				Whether the said Ministers spend much tyme in repetition of what they formerly delivered

	1704	Haddington	Lochmaben	Cupar	Kirkcaldy	Stranraer	Edinburgh
8	Doth he visit the people and families, at least once a year, in a ministerial way, teaching and admonishing from house to house, and doth he visit the sick when it is needful, and pray over them?	Does he visit ye [families] at least once a year, & carefully attend ye sick?	Does he visit the people at least once a year in a Ministerial way and pray over the Sick?	Doth he visit the people & families at least once a year in a Ministerial way?	If he be careful of Ministerial visits & if he pray in families when he visits?	He visits the parish once in the year and Catechises twice in the year for ordinary; and visits the Sick when it is needfull	Whether they Visit the people and families in the parish in a Ministerial manner once in the Year at least teaching and admonishing from house to house and if they visit the sick and afflicted when it is needfull or are called for and if they pray over them
9	Does he lecture and preach in the forenoon, and preach again in the afternoon on the Lord's Day, and that both summer and winter?	Does he lecture every Sabbat & read a large portion of Scripture?	Does he lecture and preach in the forenoon and preach in the afternoon both Summer and Winter?	Does he Lecture and preach in the forenoon, and preach in the afternoon on the Lords Day both summer and winter, and does he read a large portion of Scripture in publick and expound the same?		He lectures and preaches forenoon & preaches again in the afternoon Except in the winter time	Whether the Ministers does Lecture and preach in the forenoon every Lords day by turns and preach in the afternoon and that both Summer and Winter

	1704	Haddington	Lochmaben	Cupar	Kirkcaldy	Stranraer	Edinburgh
10	Does he read a large portion of Scripture in public, and expound the same, as is enjoined by the Acts of the General Assembly?		Does he read and explain a large portion of Scripture in publick?				Whether they read a Large portion of Scripture each Lords day and expounds the same as is enjoined by the Act of Assembly and if they have been preaching Catechetical doctrine
11	Does he preach catechetic doctrine ordinarily in the afternoon?	Does he preach Catechisal doctrine once in ye Lords day?	Does he preach Catechistical ordinarily in the afternoon?				
12	Does he administer the Sacrament of Baptism in an orderly way, when the congregation is convened, or does he it privately?		Does he administrat the Sacrament of Baptism in ane orderly way when the congregation is convened or does he it privately?	Does he administer the Sacrament of Baptism in an orderly way when the Congregation is convened, or does he it privately?			Whether they administer the Sacrament of Baptism in ane orderly way when the Congregation is convened
13	Doth he frequently catechize his parishioners, and administer the Sacrament of the Lord's Supper to them, and is he careful in keeping	Does he frequently administrate ye Sacrament of ye Lors Supper & is he careful to keep back ye Ignorant Scandalous & erroneous?	Does he frequently catechise the parishioners and administer the Sacrament of the Lords Supper to them?	Does he frequently catechise his parishioners and Administer the Sacrament of the Lords Supper to them, and is he careful in keeping		He administrates the Sacrament of the Lords Supper once a year for ordinary.	Whether they frequently Cathecise the parishioners and administrate the Sacrament of the Lords Supper and be carefull in keeping from that

1704	Haddington	Lochmaben	Cupar	Kirkcaldy	Stranraer	Edinburgh
from that holy ordinance all who are known to be scandalous, grossly ignorant, or erroneous?			from that holy ordinance all who are known to be scandalous, grossly ignorant or erroneous?			holy Ordinance all who are known to be Scandalous Ignorant and Erroneous
14 Hath he weekday sermons, and at them collections for the poor?						If the Ministers had week days Sermons and at them Collections for the poor
15 Hath he a competent number of elders, and hath the deacons in the parish distinct from elders?		Hath he a competent number of Elders?				Whether there be a competent number of Elders and Deacons and if they have Deacons distinct from Elders and if they have each their bounds assigned to them, which they have the Oversight of
16 If there be a magistrate in the parish for punishing vice, according to Act of Parliament?						Whether there be Magistrates in the bounds for putting into Execution the laws against Immorality

	1704	Haddington	Lochmaben	Cupar	Kirkcaldy	Stranraer	Edinburgh
17	Doth he read termly the acts against profaneness from the pulpit?						Whether the Minister reads termly the act and proclamation against profanity
18	Does he keep sessional meetings frequently, and is he impartial in the exercise of discipline against offenders, and is the session's diligence thereanent recorded in a book?	Does he keep frequent Sessional meetings, & is he Impartiall in ye exercise of Discipline?	Does he keep Session meetings frequently and does he punish offenders?	Does he keep Sessional meetings frequently, and is he impartial in the exercise of Discipline against offenders, and is the Sessions diligence thereanent recorded in a book?			Whether there be frequent meetings of the Session for the Exercise of Discipline and if the Ministers be Impartial therein against offenders and if their Session's diligence be duly recorded in a Book
19	If there be frequent meetings of the members of session for fasting and prayer, according to the 7th Act of the General Assembly, anno 1699						
		Does he frequently catechise his parishioners	Is there a Schoolmaster & precentor?	Does he keep family worship and is he one that rules well his own house?	If their Minister gave timeous intimation of this visitation?	He is powerfull & convincing in his Sermons and applies his Doctrine with Authority	

1704	Haddington	Lochmaben	Cupar	Kirkcaldy	Stranraer	Edinburgh
			Does he visit the Sick when needfull, and pray over them?		There were Collections made for the poor	
			Have you a Schoolmaster?			
			Have you a Bedel?			

Sources: 1704 *Overtures*, presbytery minutes 1710.

Appendix 4

Questions asked about sessions at parochial visitations in 1710 compared to 1704 Overtures

1704	Stranraer	Cupar	Edinburgh
1 If the session be rightly constituted, and all the elders and deacons duly admitted, according to the Acts of Assemblies?	That the Session is rightly Constituted and the Elders duly admitted	Have you a Session?	If their session be rightly constituted and members thereof all duly admitted
2 Do they all attend Gospel ordinances and diets of the session duly?	That they attend the session duly	Do they all attend Gospel ordinances and diets of the Session duly?	If they all attend Gospel ordinances punctually
3 Are they grave, pious, and exemplary in their lives and conversations?			If they be grave pious and Exemplary in their lives and conversations
4 Do they worship God in their families?		Do they worship God in their families?	Do they worship god in their families
5 Are they diligent, careful, and impartial, in the exercise of their offices?		Are they diligent and impartial in the exercise of their office?	If they be diligent carefull and Impartiall in the exercise of their offices
6 Do the elders visit the families within the quarter and bounds assigned to each?	That they attend the Minister when he visits the families and catechises and that they visit the families within their bounds		Do they visit the families of the bounds assigned to them and Dwell with them to Worship God therein

	1704	Stranraer	Cupar	Edinburgh
7	Have the elders subscribed the Confession of Faith?	That they had subscribed the Confession of Faith with the formula	Have your Elders Subscribed the Confession of faith?	Have the Elders signed the Confession of Faith
8	Have the elders their distinct bounds assigned them for their particular inspection?			
9	Are they careful to have the worship of God set up in the families of their bounds?			
10	Are they careful in calling for testimonials from persons who come to reside in the parish?		Are they careful in calling for testimonials from persons who come to reside in the parish?	Are they careful in calling for testimonials from persons who come to reside in their bounds?
11	Does the session always appoint a ruling elder to attend Presbyteries and Synods?	That the Session appoints a Ruling Elder to wait on the presbytery and synod	Does the Session always appoint a Ruling Elder to attend Presbyteries and Synods?	
		That there are no deacons distinct from elders	What number does it consist of?	
			Have your Session a Confession of faith, Church Bible, and overtures for Discipline?	

1704	Stranraer	Cupar	Edinburgh
		Have you a schoolmaster?	
		How are you pleased with your Schoolmaster?	
		Have you a Bedel?	
		Have you a competent Stipend?	
		Have you any Mortifications of money for the poors use?	

Sources: 1704 *Overtures*, presbytery minutes 1710.

Appendix 5

Questions at privy censures in presbytery of Cupar in 1730 compared to 1704 Overtures

1704	Cupar 1730
Hath your minister a Gospel walk and conversation before the people, and does he keep family worship, and is he one who rules well his own house?	
Keeps he much at home at his ministerial work, or doth he occasion to himself distractions and unnecessary diversions therefrom?	
Preacheth he sound doctrine, so far as you understand?	Are you careful to hold fast the form of sound words, and avoid novelties in Doctrine?
Does he preach plainly, or is he hard to be understood for his scholastic terms, matter, or manner of preaching?	
Doth he faithfully reprove sin, especially such as most prevail in that parish?	Are there any unpurged Scandals in your parish?
What time of day doth he ordinarily begin sermon on the Sabbath, and when doth he dismiss the people?	
Spends he in his sermon too much time in repetition of what he had before?	
Doth he visit the people and families, at least once a year, in a ministerial way, teaching and admonishing from house to house, and doth he visit the sick when it is needful, and pray over them?	Do you visit the families of your parish once a year in a Ministerial way?

1704	Cupar 1730
Does he lecture and preach in the forenoon, and preach again in the afternoon on the Lord's Day, and that both summer and winter?	Do you lecture and preach every Lords day both summer and Winter, and in lecturing read and expound a large portion of Scripture to your Congregation?
Does he read a large portion of Scripture in public, and expound the same, as is enjoined by the Acts of the General Assembly?	
Does he preach catechetic doctrine ordinarily in the afternoon?	Do you preach catechistical Doctrine to your Congregation ordinarily in the afternoon?
Does he administer the Sacrament of Baptism in an orderly way, when the congregation is convened, or does he it privately?	Do you administer the Sacrament of Baptism in an orderly way, when the Congregation is convened?
Doth he frequently catechize his parishioners, and administer the Sacrament of the Lord's Supper to them, and is he careful in keeping from that holy ordinance all who are known to be scandalous, grossly ignorant, or erroneous?	Is the Sacrament of the Lords Supper celebrated in your parish, at least once every year, and are you careful to seclude from it the ignorant, and do you act in Conjunction with the Session to exclude those who are prophane? Do you catechise your parish once every year at least?
Hath he weekday sermons, and at them collections for the poor?	
Hath he a competent number of elders, and hath the deacons in the parish distinct from elders?	Have you a competent number of Elders and Deacons in your Session?
If there be a magistrate in the parish for punishing vice, according to Act of Parliament?	
Doth he read termly the acts against profaneness from the pulpit?	Do you read publicly the Kings proclamation and the Abrieviate of the Acts of Parliament and assembly against Immorality, and exhort the people suitably thereupon?

1704	Cupar 1730
Does he keep sessional meetings frequently, and is he impartial in the exercise of discipline against offenders, and is the session's diligence thereanent recorded in a book?	Do you keep frequent meetings with your session for prayer and conference concerning the State of the parish, and the growth or decay of holiness and the success of the Gospel in it?
If there be frequent meetings of the members of session for fasting and prayer, according to the 7th Act of the General Assembly, anno 1699	
If the session be rightly constituted, and all the elders and deacons duly admitted, according to the Acts of Assemblies?	
Do they all attend Gospel ordinances and diets of the session duly?	
Are they grave, pious, and exemplary in their lives and conversations?	Are your elders and Deacons faithfull in the Discharge of their offices, and careful to maintain a Christian walk?
Do they worship God in their families?	
Are they diligent, careful, and impartial, in the exercise of their offices?	
Do the elders visit the families within the quarter and bounds assigned to each?	
Have the elders subscribed the Confession of Faith?	Have all your Ruling Elders signed the Formula contained in the tenth act of assembly 1694?
Have the elders their distinct bounds assigned them for their particular inspection?	
Are they careful to have the worship of God set up in the families of their bounds?	

1704	Cupar 1730
Are they careful in calling for testimonials from persons who come to reside in the parish?	Do you and your Elders call for testimonials from such as come to your parish?
New question	Are there any papists in your parish, and do you observe the Acts of Assembly particularly as to dealing with them for their Correction?
From visitation process	Have you and your Session all the acts of the General Assembly that are in print?
New question	Are you careful to observe fasts and Thanksgivings according to Act Seventh Assembly 1710 and act fourth, Assembly 1722?
From visitation process	Have you a Schoolmaster in your parish, and is he provided with a competent Salary?

Sources: 1704 *Overtures*, presbytery of Cupar minutes, 1730.

Appendix 6

Parish records examined for account formats

	1725	1750	1775	1799
Presbytery of Ayr				
Ayr		X		
Coylton	X			
Old Cumnock†			X	X
Dailly				X
Dalrymple*†	X	X	X	X
Dundonald			X	X
Galston	X	X		
Mauchline		X		
Monkton*†		X	X	X
Muirkirk				X
Ochiltree	X		X	X
St Quivox		X	X	X
Sorn†			X	X
Symington	X		X	X
Tarbolton				X
Presbytery of Garioch				
Chapel of Garioch*†	X	X	X	X
Culsalmond*		X	X	X
Daviot*		X	X	X
Insch*†	X	X	X	
Inverurie*	X	X		X
Keithhall*	X	X		
Kemnay†	X	X	X	X
Kintore†	X	X	X	X
Meldrum†	X	X	X	X
Monymusk	X		X	X
Oyne†			X	X
Rayne†	X	X	X	
Presbytery of Haddington				
Aberlady*	X	X	X	
Bolton*†	X	X	X	X
Dirleton†	X	X	X	X
Garvald †			X	X
Gladsmuir †		X	X	X

	1725	1750	1775	1799
Haddington †	X	X	X	X
Humbie	X			
Pencaitland		X	X	X
Prestonpans		X		
Saltoun	X		X	
Yester	X	X	X	X
Presbytery of Hamilton				
Blantyre		X		
Bothwell	X	X		
Cambuslang*†		X	X	X
Cambusnethan†	X			
Dalserf		X		
Dalziell	X			
Hamilton†				X
East Kilbride†				X
New Monkland	X			
Old Monkland*	X	X	X	
Shotts	X			
Presbytery of Linlithgow				
Abercorn*†	X	X	X	X
Bo'ness	X			X
Midcalder	X			X
West Calder			X	X
Carriden	X	X		X
Dalmeny†	X	X	X	X
Ecclesmachan		X	X	
Kirkliston*†	X	X	X	X
Livingston	X	X	X	
Muirvanside		X	X	X
Torphichen†		X	X	X
	34	37	37	39

Source: NRS.

Note: Parishes marked with * were those examined in more detail for balance figures. Parishes marked † were analysed in detail for 1790 income and expenditure.

Appendix 7

Coding structure for analysing the recording of financial transactions

Summary form

1   Summary total of disbursements only in textual form

2   Summary of amounts of expenditure and disbursements in textual form

3   Summary of amounts of expenditure and disbursements in tabular form

Limited transaction detail

4   Accounting transactions given in words in the body of minutes

5   Accounting transactions in figures in the body of minutes

6   Not used

Transaction detail

7   Accounting transactions given as figures in margin with no separation of income and expenditure

8   Not used

9   Separate columns for income and expenditure alongside minutes

10   Separate recording of accounting transactions at rear of minutes

11   Separate recording of accounting transactions in a 'money register'

Note: Codes 6 and 8 were employed for comparisons to English experience and are not used in this analysis.

Appendix 8

Account formats across five presbyteries

Consolidated

	APO	AYC	AYO	BPC	BPO	BYC	BYO	CPO	DPO	DYM	DYO	E	EM	ET	Totals
1725	2	4	7	1	4	2	3	0	0	0	0	3	4	4	34
1750	0	4	15	0	2	2	1	1	0	1	0	3	1	3	33
1775	2	4	13	0	0	2	4	0	1	4	1	1	2	1	35
1799	11	2	11	0	1	3	2	0	0	4	1	1	1	2	39
Totals	15	14	46	1	7	9	10	1	1	9	2	8	8	10	141

Source: Calculated from parochial records as indicated in Appendix 6.

Codes

Page format

A: one page
B: two columns per page
C: continuous (probably memo book)
D: two mixed columns
E: embedded in register
EM: margin of register
ET: columns in register

Order of entries

Y: full year
P: periodic (month/quarter)

Position of entries

O: charge/discharge face each other
C: charge first, then discharge (consecutive)
M: mixed in date order

Notes

Introduction

1   Colley, *Forging the Nation*.
2   Clark, 'Protestantism, nationalism and national identity', p. 262.
3   Jeremy Gregory, 'For all sorts', pp. 29–54.
4   McIntosh, *Church and Theology*; Whitley, *Great Grievance*.
5   Jack Whytock, *Educated Clergy*.
6   Robert Anderson, 'Lad of Parts'; Mitchison, *Old Poor Law*; Mitchison and Leneman, *Sexuality and Social Control*.
7   See especially Whitley, *Great Grievance*.
8   Whatley, *Scottish Society*, p. 81.
9   Ibid., p. 3.
10 On the problematic aspects of Braveheart see Gallagher, *Illusion of Freedom*, p. 14.
11 McIlvanney, *Burns the Radical*.
12 Alan Taylor, 'James Robertson', p. 5.
13 Craig, *Crisis*, pp. 121–2.
14 Fox, *Watching the English*.
15 Craig, *Crisis*, pp. 104–5.
16 David McCrone, 'A new Scotland?', p. 684.
17 David McCrone, 'Cultural capital', p. 74.
18 Allan Megill, *Historical Knowledge*, p. 251.

Chapter 1

1   Gorski, *Disciplinary Revolution*.
2   Weber, *Protestant Ethic*.
3   Campbell, 'Today's sociologists', pp. 207–23.
4   Published by Clarendon Press, Oxford, 1980.
5   Smout, *History*, p. 88.
6   David McCrone, *Understanding Scotland*, p. 56.
7   Todd, *Perth Kirk Session Books*, p. 32.
8   McKinstry and Ding, 'Alex Cowan', pp. 721–39.
9   Munro, *Maritime Enterprise*, p. 33.
10 Jeremy, *Capitalists and Christians*, p. 112.
11 Gorski, 'The little divergence', pp. 165–91.
12 Marshall, *Presbyteries and Profits*, p. 145.
13 Chalcraft, 'Bringing the text back', pp. 16–45.
14 Gerth and Mills, *From Max Weber*, p. 312.

15   Ibid., p. 316.
16   Hennis, *Max Weber*, p. 181.
17   Hindle, *State and Social Change*, p. 114.
18   Foucault, *Discipline and Punish*.
19   Foucault, *Security, Territory, Population*, p. 150.
20   Ibid., pp. 171–95.
21   Foucault, *Abnormal*, p. 191.
22   Gorski, *Disciplinary Revolution*, p. 24.
23   Hall, 'Religion', p. 113.
24   Ranson, Bryman and Hinings, *Clergy*, p. 165.
25   Beckford and Demerath, *Sociology of Religion*.
26   Demerath and Schmitt, 'Transcending sacred and secular', p. 322.
27   Durkheim, *Elementary Forms*.
28   Published by Routledge, London, 1997 [1889].
29   Friedland, 'Institution, practice, ontology', p. 60.
30   Schmidt, *Holy Fairs*.
31   Whitehouse, *Modes of Religiosity*, p. 8.
32   Asad, *Genealogies of Religion*, p. 62.
33   Whitehouse, *Modes of Religiosity*, p. 17.
34   Anne Clark, 'Two modes theory', pp. 125–42.
35   Whitehouse, *Modes of Religiosity*, p. 69.
36   Ibid., p. 93.
37   Baltzell, *Puritan Boston and Quaker Philadelphia*, p. 367.
38   MacCulloch, *Reformation*.
39   Martha Feldman, 'Organizational routines', pp. 611–29; Feldman and Pentland, 'Reconceptualizing', pp. 94–118; Pentland and Feldman, 'Organizational routines', pp. 793–815.
40   Feldman and Pentland, 'Reconceptualizing', p. 95.
41   Feldman, 'Organizational routines', p. 613.
42   Ibid., p. 612.
43   Yates and Orlikowski, 'Genres of organizational communication', p. 301.
44   Ibid., p. 300.
45   Stinchcombe, 'Social structure', p. 149.
46   Wuthnow, *Communities of Discourse*, p. 149.
47   Brown, *Diary of George Brown*; Stevenson, *Diary of a Canny Man*.
48   National Records of Scotland (NRS) CH2/310/5, Rayne session minutes 1744–70, 25 July 1750, 71.
49   Hindle, *State and Social Change* p. 229.
50   Yates, *Preaching, Word and Sacrament*.
51   Schmidt, *Holy Fairs*.
52   Zahniser, *Steel City Gospel*, p. 5.
53   Donald Withrington, 'New university tradition'.
54   Camic, *Experience and Enlightenment*, p. 185.
55   Jeremy, 'Important questions', p. 11.
56   Black, 'Confessional state', p. 73.

57 Spaeth, *Age of Danger*, p. 5.

58 Hindle, *State and Social Change*, p. 23.

59 Brown, *Religion and Society*; Drummond and Bulloch, *Scottish Church*.

60 Brown, 'Costs of pew-renting'.

61 MacLaren, *Religion and Social Class*.

62 McIntosh, *Church and Theology*; Whitley, *Great Grievance*; Jeffrey Stephen, *Defending the Revolution*.

63 For example, NRS CH2/121/10 presbytery of Edinburgh minutes 1718–21, 16 March 1720, 279; CH2/1132/2 presbytery of St Andrews minutes 1714–23, 16 March 1720, 225.

64 McCrie, *John Knox*; McCrie, *Andrew Melville*.

65 Edgar, *Old Church Life In Scotland*, 2 volumes.

66 Graham, *Social Life*, p. 286.

67 Ibid., p. 334.

68 Edgar, *Old Church Life*, vol. *1*, p. 233.

69 Henderson, *Ruling Elder*, p. 5.

70 Clark, *Church Discipline*, p. 178.

71 McPherson, *Kirk's Care*, p. 26.

72 Gregory, 'Book of Common Prayer', p. 29.

73 Walker, 'Religious factor', p. 595.

74 Jenny Wormald, 'Godly Scotland?', p. 205.

75 Anderson 'Lad of parts'; Mitchison, *Old Poor Law*; Mitchison and Leneman, *Sexuality and Social Control*.

76 Todd, *Culture of Protestantism*, p. 83.

77 Ibid., p. 77.

78 McCallum, *Reforming the Scottish Parish*, p. 66.

79 Hanham, *Sinners of Cramond*.

80 Raffe, *Culture of Controversy*; Stephen, *Defending the Revolution*.

81 Christopher Whatley, 'Reformed religion', pp. 66–99.

82 Gorski, *Disciplinary Revolution*, p. 154.

83 Snell, *Parish and Belonging*, p. 492.

84 Ibid., p. 14.

85 Veyne, *Writing History*, p. 7.

86 Anon, *Overtures*, 1696.

87 Mitchison, *Poor Law*, pp. 60 et seq.

88 McPherson, *Kirk's Care*, pp. 61, 85.

89 Edgar, *Old Church Life*, vols 1 and 2.

90 NRS CH2/201/3 Keithhall session minutes, 1744–78, 22 January 1777, 426. See similar problems in Monymusk NRS CH2/1399/2, Monymusk session minutes, 1763–96, 15 January 1789, 115, 13 July 1792, 129; in Insch NRS CH2/189/4, Insch session minutes 1771–92, 18 April 1777, 37; and in Stewarton, NRS CH2/197/3 presbytery of Irvine minutes 1710–30, 13 December 1720, 342.

91 *Overtures*, 1696, p. 4.

92 Ibid., p. 4.

93 Edgar, *Old Church Life*, vol. *1*, p. 2.

94 CH2/189/4, Insch, 18 April 1777, 37. Cf CH2/1399/2, Monymusk, 17 February 1780, 66, 'when the minutes are transferred from the loose sheets into the Register'.

95 NRS CH2/527/3, Chapel of Garioch session minutes 1766–1804, 4 December 1783, 200.

96 NRS CH2/189/2, Insch session minutes (1720–1732) and accounts (1720–1728), 21 November 1721, 16.

97 NRS CH2/295/7, presbytery of Peebles minutes 1699–1716, 10 August 1710, 223.

98 NRS CH2/393/2, presbytery of Hamilton minutes 1695–1719, 22 March 1710, 395.

99 NRS CH2/532/6, presbytery of Ayr minutes 1746–56, 6 March 1750, 58.

100 Henderson, *Ruling Elder*, examined the records of eighteen sessions from across the country. McPherson, *Kirk's Care*, used a wide range of session records from the northeast, but did not specify the selection of these. Lindsay, *Scottish Poor Law*, specifies the 22 session records that she examined, but not the basis of their selection. Cage, *Scottish Poor Law* (p. 19), discusses the need for a systematic sample in selecting two sessions from each county (where available) across the country, but this does not meet the need for statistical validity that he espouses. Mitchison, *Old Poor Law*, examined 'parts of the registers of nearly 300' (p. 2) parishes but she does not present the results in a comparative fashion.

101 *OSA*, Edinburgh, 21 volumes, 1791–9.

102 Scott, *Fasti Ecclesiae Scottianae*, 7 volumes.

Chapter 2

1 NRS CH2/263/6, presbytery of Meigle minutes 1718–22, 15 September 1720, 127.

2 For a general overview, Yates, *Preaching, Word and Sacrament*. For Abercorn, McWilliam, *Buildings of Scotland*, p. 70.

3 'Midmar', *OSA*, vol. 2, p. 524.

4 NRS CH2/35/8, presbytery of Biggar minutes 1734–53, 16 April 1740, 197.

5 NRS CH2/157/5, presbytery of Fordoun minutes 1739–51, 1 October 1740, 53.

6 McPherson, *Kirk's Care*, 36.

7 NRS CH2/189/3, Insch session minutes 1732–71, 7 April 1768, 158; CH2/322/7, Saltoun session minutes 1760–95 and accounts 1759–94, 8 November 1775, 46.

8 Ryrie, *Origins*, p. 204.

9 As Kyle notes, 'Though John Knox did not write a treatise on ecclesiology per se, church considerations occupied an important, if not dominant, position in his writings': Kyle, 'Nature of the church', p. 485.

10 Kirk, *Second Book of Discipline*, p. 105.

11 Ibid., p. 82.

12 Hazlett, 'Scots Confession', pp. 41–66.

13 Knox, *History*, p. 352.

14 Hazlett, 'Scots Confession', p. 55.
15 Reid, *Reformation*, p. 134.
16 Calvin, *Institutes*, p. 434.
17 Kirk, *Patterns of Reform*, p. xix.
18 Weatherhead, *Constitution and Laws*, p. 37.
19 Calvin, *Institutes*, p. 330.
20 Knox, *History*, p. 403.
21 Ibid., p. 379.
22 Ibid., p. 402.
23 Ibid., p. 395.
24 Todd, *Perth Kirk Session*, p. 17.
25 Ibid., p. 33.
26 Ibid., pp. 319, 321, 323, 326, 329.
27 Kirk, *Second Book of Discipline*, p. 177.
28 James Kirk (ed.) *Stirling Presbytery Records 1581–1587* (Edinburgh: Scottish History Society, 1981), p. 253.
29 Ibid., p. 253.
30 McCallum, *Reforming the Scottish Parish*, p. 66. See also Stevenson, *Booke of Kirkcaldie*, p. 165.
31 Todd, *Culture of Protestantism*, p. 21.
32 McInnes, *Charles I*; Stevenson, *Scottish Revolution* and *Revolution and Counter-Revolution*.
33 Davidson, *Inverurie*, pp. 313–15.
34 Ibid., p. 313.
35 Ibid., p. 314.
36 Ibid., p. 313.
37 Ibid., p. 313.
38 Ibid., p. 314.
39 Ibid., p. 314.
40 Ibid., p. 314.
41 Jackson, *Restoration Scotland*.
42 Gardner, *Scottish Exile Community*.
43 NRS CH2/157/13, presbytery of Fordoun minutes of visitations 1677–88.
44 Raffe, 'Presbyterianism, secularization', pp. 317–37; Graham, *Aikenhead*; Alasdair Raffe, 'Scotland restored', pp. 251–67.
45 Skoczylas, *Mr. Simson's Knotty Case*', p. 118; Wodrow, *Analecta*, pp. 12, 18, 19.
46 Patrick, 'Kirk, Parliament and Union', pp. 94–115; Stephen, *Scottish Presbyterians*, p. 45.
47 Stephen, *Defending the Revolution*, p. 111 et seq.; Whitley, *Great Grievance*, p. 106; Raffe, *Culture of Controversy*, pp. 208–33.
48 *Overtures*, 1696.
49 Ibid., p. ii.
50 Ibid., p. 5.
51 Ibid., p. 3.
52 Ibid., p. 29.

53 Church Law Society, *Acts of the General Assembly*, pp. 258–9 (1697).
54 Ibid., pp. 272–3 (1698).
55 Ibid., pp. 323–4 (1703).
56 Ibid., p. 336 (1704).
57 Ibid., p. 336 (1704).
58 Ibid., p. 338 (1704): 'Overtures concerning discipline and method in ecclesiastical judicatories'.
59 *Overtures*, 1696, p. 11.
60 Ibid., p. 37.
61 *Acts of the General Assembly*, 1704, p. 358.
62 Fry, *The Union*; Patrick, 'Kirk, Parliament and Union'; Whatley, 'Reformed Religion'; Whatley and Patrick, *Scots and the Union*.
63 *Acts of the General Assembly*, pp. 403–20 (1707). On the implications for practice, see Skoczylas, *Simson's Knotty Case*.
64 Ibid., p. 430 (1708); 438 (1709).
65 Ibid., p. 449 (1710).
66 Ibid., p. 524 (1718).
67 NRS CH2/1132/1, presbytery of St Andrews minutes 1705–13, 19 April 1710, 224.
68 Drummond, *Kirk and Continent*, p. 104.
69 John Erskine, 6th Earl of Mar considered him, 'a foolish fellow': Patrick, 'Kirk, Parliament and Union', p. 98.
70 Published by Andrew Anderson, Edinburgh.
71 Steuart, *Collections*, p. xi.
72 Ibid., pp. 60–1.
73 Although we will see later that in practice Pardovan's strictures were not followed, there are distinct echoes of his views in a complaint against the minister of Kilmacolm, in the presbytery of Paisley, in 1720, a complaint which was, in the words of the parish historian, 'a curious medley of pharisaic piety, malicious bitterness, and narrow-minded zeal'. Murray, *Kilmacolm*, p. 136.
74 Steuart, *Collections*, p. 177.
75 Ibid., p. 45.
76 Ibid., pp. 94–5.
77 Peterkin, *Compendium*, p. 569. Interestingly in the light of connections with Scottish legal traditions that are explored later, he regarded the standing of Pardovan's work within the church as being on a par with 'the Commentaries of any Institutional writer on the municipal law'. Referring here to authors such as Stair, Peterkin is referring to the particular status in Scottish law of certain authoritative collections of legal commentary.
78 CH2/393/2, presbytery of Hamilton, 26 July 1709, 381.
79 CH2/197/3, presbytery of Irvine, 12 December 1710, 19, 'The presbyterie appoints Pardovan's book to be bought by each Member'; CH2/234/5, presbytery of Lanark 1709–17, 14 December 1710, 58, 'Several Copies of Pardovans books anent Church Government were laid before the presbytery, and such Ministers as have not provided themselves with that book were desired to take one of them'.

80   NRS CH2/169/3/1, Gladsmuir session minutes 1775–1804, 3 April 1786, 119.

81   Clark, *History of Church Discipline*, p. 130. On such legalistic tendencies, see Harvie's observation that the Scottish church had 'a religious ideology both legalistic in its Talmudic attitude to scriptures and deeply preoccupied with church government and social discipline': Harvie, *Travelling Scot*, p. 63. He follows this up with a connection to Stair's work.

82   Graham, *Social Life*, p. 333

83   Ibid., p. 334.

Chapter 3

1   NRS CH2/526/4, presbytery of Kirkcudbright minutes 1734–41, 6 August 1740, 409, containing a report of a meeting at Kells on 31 July.

2   Ibid., 4 July 1739, 359.

3   NRS CH2/165/3, synod of Galloway minutes 1713–46, 16 April 1740, 377.

4   CH2/526/4, presbytery of Kirkcudbright, 4 June 1740, 399.

5   The following account is drawn from the minute of 6 August, 409–17.

6   CH2/526/4, presbytery of Kirkcudbright, 5 August 1740, 419.

7   Ibid., 419–31.

8   CH2/165/3, synod of Galloway, 21 October 1740, 282–3.

9   CH2/526/4, presbytery of Kirkcudbright, 3 December 1740, 331.

10   NRS CH2/202/2, kirk session minutes of Kells 1731–73, 31 March 1741, 54.

11   Scott, *Fasti*, vol. 2, 'Synods of Merse and Teviotdale', Dumfries and Galloway, p. 310.

12   Ibid., p. 285.

13   NRS CH2/224/6, presbytery of Kirkcaldy minutes 1724–42, 28 August 1740, 331.

14   NRS CH2/82/5, presbytery of Cupar minutes 1715–23, 9 February 1720, 185.

15   On the grounds for this selection, see below.

16   CH2/532/6, presbytery of Ayr, 10 January 1750, 57.

17   NRS CH2/166/5, presbytery of Garioch minutes 1732–52, 30 July 1740, 251.

18   NRS CH2/299/14, presbytery of Perth minutes 1736–41, 2 January 1740, 195.

19   Scott, *Fasti*, vol. 4, Synods of Argyll, and Perth and Stirling, p. 200.

20   NRS CH2/198/9, presbytery of Jedburgh minutes 1733–43, 3 September 1740, 391.

21   CH2/263/6, presbytery of Meigle, 31 August 1720, 124.

22   NRS CH2/722/13, presbytery of Stirling minutes 1738–45, 4 June, 3 July 1740, 142, 148.

23   NRS CH2/298/4, presbytery of Penpont minutes 1736–45, 19 June 1740, 168.

24   NRS CH2/424/11, presbytery of Dalkeith minutes 1719–26, 5 April, 5 July, 6 September 1720, 25, 45, 73.

25   NRS CH2/263/4, presbytery of Meigle minutes 1708–13, 18 January 1710, 156.

26   *Acts of the General Assembly*, 1708, p. 430.

27   Struthers, *History of Relief Church*, pp. 300–1.

28   NRS CH2/234/8, presbytery of Lanark minutes 1732–49, 17 September 1740, 274.

29   Graham, *Social Life*, p. 334.
30   Stephen, *Defending the Revolution*, pp. 108–9. Cf Camic, *Experience and Enlight-enment*, p. 28.
31   Withrington, 'What was distinctive', p. 12.
32   *Acts of the General Assembly*, 1706, p. 395.
33   Ibid., 1713, p. 480.
34   NRS CH2/185/10, presbytery of Haddington minutes 1698–1716, 6 September 1706, 249.
35   NRS CH2/105/5, presbytery of Dunfermline minutes 1718–29, 28 September 1721, 70; CH2/105/6, presbytery of Dunfermline 1729–45, 1 October 1730, 36.
36   *Acts of the General Assembly*, 1704, p. 358.
37   NRS CH2/424/9, presbytery of Dalkeith minutes 1705–11, 16 May 1710, 284.
38   NRS CH2/242/9, presbytery of Linlithgow minutes 1701–10, 26 June 1706, 221.
39   NRS CH2/171/8, presbytery of Glasgow minutes 1707–13, 5 July 1710, 57.
40   CH2/234/5, presbytery of Lanark, 20 April 1710, 35.
41   NRS CH2/247/2, presbytery of Lochmaben minutes 1708–18, 25 July, 26 July 1710, 117, 119.
42   NRS CH2/103/6, presbytery of Dundee minutes 1706–10, 3 January 1710, 18 January 1710, 22 February 1710, 1 March 1710, 15 March 1710, 31 March 1710, 21 April 1710, 147, 154, 155, 161, 175.
43   CH2/234/5, presbytery of Lanark, 23 May 1710, 37.
44   NRS CH2/82/4, presbytery of Cupar minutes 1708–14, 23 August 1710, 77.
45   NRS CH2/121/7, presbytery of Edinburgh 1708–11, 28 June 1710, 329; CH2/82/4, presbytery of Cupar minutes 1708–14, 23 August 1710, 77.
46   CH2/103/6, presbytery of Dundee, 3 January 1710, 147.
47   NRS CH2/546/6, presbytery of Dumbarton 1704–14, 25 July 1710, 233.
48   NRS CH2/224/4, presbytery of Kirkcaldy 1705–13, 20 September 1710, 247.
49   NRS CH2/341/3, presbytery of Stranraer minutes 1716–26, 8 March 1720.
50   CH2/263/6, presbytery of Meigle, 13 November 1720, 142.
51   NRS CH2/393/3, presbytery of Hamilton minutes 1719–57, 25 October 1720.
52   NRS CH2/723/7, presbytery of Dunblane minutes 1716–22, 1 September 1720, 239.
53   CH2/234/5, presbytery of Lanark, 23 May, 21 June 1710, 37, 41.
54   CH2/247/2, presbytery of Lochmaben, 25 July 1710, 117.
55   CH2/103/6, presbytery of Dundee, 18 January 1710, 154.
56   Ibid., 21 April 1710, 188.
57   CH2/247/2, presbytery of Lochmaben, 26 July 1710, 119.
58   Ibid., 1 August 1710, 123.
59   CH2/393/3, presbytery of Hamilton, 12 November 1735, 271.
60   NRS CH2/546/10, presbytery of Dumbarton minutes 1740–47, 21 January 1742, 113.
61   Ibid., 22 February, 21 December 1743, 7 March 1744, 166, 235, 315.
62   NRS CH2/197/4, presbytery of Irvine minutes 1730–43, 28 April 1742, 511.
63   Ibid., 8 June 1742, 529.

64 Ibid., 14 June 1743, 8.
65 Ibid., 12 July 1743, 15.
66 NRS CH2/197/5, presbytery of Irvine minutes 1743–59, 12 June 1744, 76.
67 CH2/197/4, presbytery of Irvine minutes 1730–43, 13 September 1743, 35.
68 Whatley, 'Reformed religion'.
69 *Acts of the General Assembly*, 1704, p. 366.
70 NRS CH2/113/7, presbytery of Duns minutes 1739–49, 1 April 1740, 15.
71 NRS CH2/82/7, presbytery of Cupar minutes 1730–36, 386.
72 CH2/546/10, presbytery of Dumbarton, 5 March 1740, 8. See also CH2/157/6, presbytery of Fordoun, 18 June 1740, 37 and CH2/103/12, presbytery of Dundee minutes 1739–57, 30 April 1740, 9.
73 *Acts of the General Assembly*, 1713, 'Act containing Directions to the Visitors of Synod Books', p. 480.
74 Ibid., 1704, p. 370.
75 CH2/224/4, presbytery of Kirkcaldy, 29 September 1709, 188.
76 NRS CH2/99/4, presbytery of Dunbar minutes 1704–20, 13 April 1710, 172; CH2/185/12, presbytery of Haddington minutes 1730–96, 6 November 1734, 43; See also CH2/327/6, presbytery of Selkirk 1736–55, 21 April 1742, 107: 'it being found that a Reference was given in with Depositions of Witnesses & abstracts of them mentioned but neither of them recorded, that several References are not inserted, & other material papers besides many Mistakes & Omissions in Clerking, Therefore the Synod declared their Dissatisfaction with the Sd Records, and appoint the Presbyterie to be more careful in revising their Minutes before they be insert in the Book & more exact in Clerking for the future'.
77 NRS CH2/242/11, presbytery of Linlithgow minutes 1716–21, 5 May 1720, 461.
78 McIntosh, *Church and Theology*, pp. 99–102.
79 CH2/242/11 presbytery of Linlithgow, 5 May 1720, 461.
80 Ibid., 3 May 1721, 525.
81 CH2/185/12, presbytery of Haddington, 21 August 1735, 80.
82 CH2/546/6, presbytery of Dumbarton, 12 December 1710, 251.
83 CH2/121/7, presbytery of Edinburgh, 22 February 1710, 290.
84 NRS CH2/121/12, presbytery of Edinburgh minutes 1726–32, 21 October 1730, 332.
85 NRS CH2/835/4, Abercorn session minutes 1718–33, 17 April 1721, 54, 395.
86 CH2/532/6, presbytery of Ayr, 25 April 1750, 63.
87 NRS CH2/532/4, presbytery of Ayr minutes 1719–32, 8 September 1730; 21 January 1730, 404.
88 NRS CH2/37/3, Bolton session minutes 1683–1745, 21 April 1719, 196; CH2/242/13, presbytery of Linlithgow minutes 1731–42, 28 May 1740, 323.
89 CH2/82/4, presbytery of Cupar, 7 July 1713, 202; 9 March 1714, 249; 30 March 1714, 250; 31 August 1714, 258; CH2/82/5, presbytery of Cupar, 22 March 1715, 31; 20 March 1716, 35; 16 January 1717, 68.
90 CH2/82/5, presbytery of Cupar, 30 September 1719, 64.

91 NRS CH2/99/5, presbytery of Dunbar minutes 1720–34, 5 October 1720, 12; 7 June 1721, 40; CH2/113/4 presbytery of Duns 1707–16, 3 October 1710, 93; 29 May 1711, 121; 4 December 1711, 140; 1 April 1712, 151; CH2/393/3, presbytery of Hamilton, 27 March 1750, 495; 28 August 1750, 501.

92 NRS CH2/299/7, presbytery of Perth minutes 1705–10, 8 January 1710, 294.

93 CH2/121/7, presbytery of Edinburgh, 28 June 1710, 329.

94 CH2/82/4, presbytery of Cupar, 16 May 1710, 65.

95 Ibid., 23 August 1710, 80.

96 NRS CH2/266/2, Midcalder session minutes 1691–1761, 1 June 1710, 162.

97 NRS CH2/392/2, Dailly session minutes 1711–59, 'Remarks on the Session book of Dailly from page 59 to 96 , 78.

98 CH2/242/9, presbytery of Linlithgow, 25 June 1707, 279.

99 CH2/266/2, Midcalder, 1 June 1710, 162.

100 Ibid., 238.

101 NRS CH2/464/3, synod of Glasgow and Ayr, 1715–60, 3 April 1750, 394; CH2/252/12, synod of Edinburgh, 1747–61, 1 May 1750, 134.

102 NRS CH2/840/5, synod of Aberdeen minutes 1787–1816, 13 October 1790, 44.

103 NRS CH2/166/6, presbytery of Garioch minutes 1752–92, index.

104 Ibid., 3 December 1783, 386.

105 NRS CH2/415/2, Cambuslang session minutes 1731–48, accounts 1700–1810, 31 January 1749, 59.

106 CH2/415/2, Cambuslang accounts, 29 August 1775, 370.

107 NRS CH2/242/14, presbytery of Linlithgow minutes 1742–72, 7 March 1750, 258.

Chapter 4

1 Wilkie, *Robert Burns*, p. 35.

2 May, *Chess Men*, p. 374.

3 *Acts of the General Assembly*, 1704, 342.

4 NRS CH2/247/3, presbytery of Lochmaben minutes 1730–43, 6 May 1740, 211.

5 'Daviot', *OSA*, vol. 6, p. 87.

6 NRS CH2/532/8, presbytery of Ayr minutes 1768–96, 29 November 1770, 29. See similar reports in the same volume for ordinations at Barr (8 March 1780, 177) and Sorn (13 May 1790, 479).

7 Whytock, *Educated Clergy*, pp. 101, 111.

8 Shepherd, 'Arts curriculum', p. 147.

9 Withers, *Burt's Letters*, p. 91.

10 Mullan, *Narratives*.

11 Edgar, *Church Life, vol. 1*, p. 99.

12 Steuart, *Collections*, p. xi.

13 Edgar, *Church Life, vol. 1*, pp. 21, 68, 231.

14 Clark, *History of Church Discipline*, p. 112.

15 Suderman, *Orthodoxy and Enlightenment*, p. 228.

16 *Overtures*, 1696, p. 4.

17 *Fasti*, vol. 6, p. 174

18 CH2/166/6, presbytery of Garioch, 8 April 1767, 214.

19 'Sale notice for effects of late Thomas Tait at Ellon Manse', *Aberdeen Journal*, 12 September 1810, p. 1.

20 *Fasti*, vol. 6, p. 162.

21 NRS CH2/4/4, Aberlady session minutes 1758–83, 7 January 1765, 49.

22 Edgar, *Old Church Life, vol. 1*, p. 3.

23 For example Hugh Ramsey, schoolmaster in Gladsmuir, ordained elder in 1788: CH2/169/3/1, Gladsmuir, 17 February 1788, 168.

24 NRS CH2/389/2, Humbie session minutes 1715–34, 22 February, 223; 12 April 1730, 231; 26 April 1730, 236; 8 June 1730, 241; 21 June 1730, 243; 26 July 1730, 246; 8 August 1730, 249; 10 January 1731, 266.

25 NRS CH2/556/7, Bothwell session accounts 1749–1827, 21 May 1761, 28.

26 Graham, *Social Life*, p. 366.

27 CH2/393/3, presbytery of Hamilton, 26 February 1740, 350; 26 July 1740, 359.

28 Fawcett, *Cambuslang Revival*, notes, 'their almost anarchic defiance of authority', p. 47.

29 *Acts of the General Assembly*, 1704, p. 342.

30 Ibid., p. 342.

31 Henderson, *Ruling Elder*, p. 222.

32 CH2/526/4, presbytery of Kirkcudbright, 5 August 1740, 422.

33 NRS CH2/86/5, Dalmeny session minutes 1757–1816, 28 July 1776, 139.

34 *Acts of the General Assembly*, 1784, p. 822.

35 Although a similar Act was eventually passed in 1816.

36 Inglis, 'Impact of Episcopacy', pp. 35–61.

37 CH2/527/3, Chapel of Garioch, 2 June 1771, 59. In Insch in 1777 'the paucity of their number & that some of them are aged & infirm': CH2/189/4, Insch, 8 June 1777, 39.

38 CH2/201/2, Keithhall, 1 June 1729, 206.

39 NRS CH2/549/1, Daviot session minutes 1731–99, 12 June 1796.

40 CH2/201/2, Keithhall, 21 April 1723, 127, 8 June 1729, 209; CH2/201/3 1744–78, 27 July 1747, 28; 13 November 1748, 36.

41 NRS CH2/266/3, Midcalder session minutes 1714–43, 8 February 1730, 95; 4 July 1734, 159; 7 December 1741, 216; 18 December 1741, 217.

42 CH2/247/2, presbytery of Lochmaben, 26 July 1710, 119.

43 CH2/527/3, Chapel of Garioch, 30 June 1771, 60.

44 NRS CH2/685/3, New Monkland session minutes 1737, 1744–52 and 1760–97, 8 March 1776, 147, 30 April 1776, 148.

45 NRS CH2/322/5, Saltoun session minutes and accounts 1719–39, 20 October 1723, 115.

46 CH2/322/7, Saltoun, 8 August 1762, 12.

47 NRS CH2/527/1, Chapel of Garioch session minutes 1714–41, 31 July 1720, 62.

48 CH2/392/2, Dailly, 16 September 1725, 63.
49 CH2/322/5, Saltoun, 21 May 1721, 70; 14 April 1723, 105.
50 *Acts of the General Assembly*, 1704, p. 347.
51 NRS CH2/87/2, Dalrymple session minutes 1726–83, 11 August 1730, 35; 19 July 1740, 80.
52 Steuart, *Collections*, p. 45.
53 *Acts of the General Assembly*, 1723, p. 562.
54 NRS CH2/224/5, presbytery of Kirkcaldy minutes 1713–24, 27 September 1721, 283.
55 CH2/82/5, presbytery of Cupar, 22 March 1720, 196.
56 CH2/526/4, presbytery of Kirkcudbright, 6 August 1740, 410.
57 CH2/392/3, Dailly, 31 March 1770, 57. In Rothesay a new minister had recorded that, 'ever since his admission to the work of the ministrie in this place he never could perceive there was any deacons among them according to the practice of this Church'. Accordingly ten were ordained in 1703 and their attendance was recorded until 1737. However, when another batch of elders was ordained in 1734 there was no mention of deacons and acknowledgement of their existence simply disappears after June 1737: Paton, *Session Book of Rothesay*, 8 June 1703, p. 167; 29 May 1734, p. 427; 2 June 1737, p. 435.
58 Inglis, 'Impact of Episcopacy', pp. 42–8.
59 NRS GD345/1109, Grant of Monymusk, papers concerning tenants of Monymusk, including articles of roup and lists of customs, Assessment for army and navy 1796.
60 CH2/169/3/1, Gladsmuir, 17 May 1795, 255.
61 CH2/310/5, Rayne, title page. Dalrymple, as Lord Drummore, was heavily involved in church politics. His connection with Rayne was through his wife Anne Horn of the local Logie estate. Drummore's main base was in the Lothians; his Rayne connection was probably useful in securing him attendance at the General Assembly. See Whitley, *Great Grievance*, p. 233.
62 NRS CH2/223/2, Kintore session minutes 1738–61, frontispiece.
63 CH2/549/1, Daviot, 20 October 1765, 120.
64 NRS CH2/169/2, Gladsmuir session minutes 1737–79, 17 April 1763, 115.
65 CH2/169/3/1, Gladsmuir, 6 July 1780, 17.
66 Ibid., 8 August 1780, 22; 27 March 1785, 99.
67 Ibid., 22 March 1789, 228.
68 *Fasti*, vol. 1, p. 367.
69 Cunningham, *Robert Burns*, p. 156.
70 NRS CH2/167/1, Garvald session minutes 1721–89, 1 May 1754, 113; 29 July 1764, 132; 5 August 1773, 149; 4 January 1789.
71 CH2/392/2, Dailly 1711–59; CH2/392/3, Dailly session minutes 1761–98.
72 *Overtures*, 1696, p. 1.
73 Withers, *Burt's Letters*, p. 13.
74 NRS CH2/1157/20, Dirleton session accounts 1752–72, 26 May 1769, 239; 4 June 1769, 240; February 1770, 244.
75 CH2/1399/2, Monymusk, 22 January 1797, 163.

76 Clark, *Church Discipline*, p. 179.

77 Wilkie, *Robert Burns*, p. 83.

78 Edgar, *Old Church Life*, vol. *1*, p. 179.

79 Schmidt, *Holy Fairs*, p. xxvii.

80 CH2/532/6, presbytery of Ayr, 6 March 1750, 58.

81 Wilkie, *Robert Burns*, p. 86.

82 CH2/310/5, Rayne, 15 July 1750, 71.

83 Ibid., 19 July 1750, 71; 21 July 1750, 71; 22 July, 72; 23 July 1750, 72.

84 NRS CH2/242/10, presbytery of Linlithgow minutes 1710–1713, 18 February 1713, 311.

85 CH2/167/1, Garvald, 3 October 1725, 27.

86 NRS CH2/223/1, Kintore session minutes 1713–38, 23 August 1730, 132.

87 CH2/169/3/1, Gladsmuir, 25 May 1783, 44.

88 CH2/87/2, Dalrymple, 11 August 1730, 35; 12 August 1730, 35.

89 Henderson, *Ruling Elder*, 48.

90 NRS CH2/799/6, Haddington session minutes 1711–26, 5 July 1711, 7.

91 NRS CH2/322/4, Saltoun session minutes 1714–18, 21 October 1717, 108.

92 CH2/169/2, Gladsmuir, 30 May 1740, 5. Other parishes in which lists were examined were: CH2/167/1, Garvald, 26 May 1730, 42; CH2/1157/2, Dirleton minutes and accounts 1703–37, 5 April 1719, 177; CH2/223/2, Kintore, 24 July 1760, 220; CH2/1146/15, Meldrum session minutes 1724–52, 25 April 1730, 136; CH2/86/2, Dalmeny session minutes 1691–1710, 20 July 1710, 242; CH2/87/2, Dalrymple, 11 August 1730, 35; NRS CH2/78/1, Culsalmond session minutes 1735–48, 7 July 1743, 83.

93 Todd, *Perth Sessions*, p. 158.

94 Steuart, *Collections*, p. 138.

95 CH2/341/3, presbytery of Stranraer, 8 March 1720, 106.

96 NRS CH2/799/7, Haddington session minutes 1781–1835, 1 July 1787, 102.

97 CH2/169/1, Gladsmuir, 24 June 1703, 101.

98 *Fasti*, vol. 1, p. 360; vol. 3, p. 474.

99 CH2/799/7, Haddington, 25 June 1782, 65.

100 CH2/1146/15, Meldrum, 25 April 1730, 136.

101 NRS CH2/87/5, Dalrymple session accounts 1725–71, 8 August 1732, 36.

102 NRS CH2/331/3, Slamannan session minutes 1716–51, 28 June 1730, 57.

103 CH2/86/5, Dalmeny, 21 June 1776, 138.

Chapter 5

1 Fawcett, *Cambuslang Revival*, p. 165.

2 Mitchison, 'The making', p. 88.

3 Cage, 'Debate', p. 117.

4 Mitchison, *Old Poor Law*, p. 65.

5 Ibid., p. 66.

6 Calvin, *Institutes*, p. 330.

7 Knox, *History*, p. 392.

8   Ibid., pp. 394, 395.
9   Kirk, *Stirling Presbytery*, p. 106.
10 Todd, *Perth Session*, p. 319.
11 Ibid., p. 446.
12 McCallum, *Reforming the Scottish Parish*, p. 66.
13 *Acts of the General Assembly*, 1704, p. 347.
14 Steuart, *Collections*, p. 51.
15 For more detail on these, see Alistair Mutch, 'Data mining', pp. 78–94.
16 NRS CH2/37/3, Bolton session minutes 1683–1745; CH2/37/4, Bolton session minutes 1744–1802, accounts 1744–1801.
17 NRS CH2/1157/3, Dirleton session minutes 1737–74, 3 February 1752, 71.
18 NRS CH2/229/7, Kirkliston session accounts 1731–52; CH2/229/11 accounts 1703–31; CH2/229/12 accounts 1751–81; CH2/229/13 accounts 1781–1821.
19 James Aho, *Confession and Bookkeeping*, p. 64.
20 NRS CH2/542/6, Kemnay session minutes 1745–52, 7 January 1750, 33.
21 NRS CH2/527/2, Chapel of Garioch session minutes 1741–66, 7 January 1750, 409.
22 The parishes examined and the coding structures employed are given in appendices 6 and 7.
23 Appendix 8 gives the full details of the analysis, supported by the coding structure used.
24 CH2/242/9, presbytery of Linlithgow, 25 June 1707, 279.
25 CH2/82/4 presbytery of Cupar 1708–14, 16 May 1710, 65.
26 Ibid., 23 August 1710, 80.
27 CH2/415/2, Cambuslang session accounts, 29 August 1775, 370.
28 NRS CH2/1146/17, Meldrum session accounts 1747–97, 16 November 1767, 144.
29 Alistair Mutch, 'Systemic accountability', pp. 45–65.
30 For the parishes examined, see Appendix 6.
31 CH2/310/5, Rayne, 25 July 1750, 71.
32 CH2/169/2, Gladsmuir, 16 April 1760, 93.
33 CH2/37/4, Bolton, *passim*.
34 The parishes examined are given in appendix 6. Parishes selected were conditioned by the availability of complete sets of accounts.
35 CH2/322/7, Saltoun, 18 May 1777, 47.
36 Hanham, *Sinners of Cramond*, p. 178.
37 NRS CH2/86/3, Dalmeny session minutes 1710–1728, 10 December 1710, 4.
38 CH2/169/2, Gladsmuir, 26 September 1739, 7.
39 Graham, *Social Life*, p. 239.
40 CH2/835/9, Abercorn, October 1751, 211.
41 NRS CH2/415/1, Cambuslang session minutes and collections 1658–1788, 1749, 235.
42 Ibid., 229.
43 NRS CH2/4/2, Aberlady session minutes 1697–1718, 27 October 1700, 12.
44 NRS CH2/169/9, Gladsmuir session accounts 1768–91.

45 NRS CH2/527/3, Chapel of Garioch session minutes 1766–1804, 22 March 1778, 135.
46 NRS CH2/4/6, Aberlady accounts 1758–83, 17 December 1780, 146.
47 CH2/1157/2, Dirleton, 6 November 1726, 254. Culsalmond possessed both a 'meikle' box and a little box: CH2/78/1, Culsalmond, 13 July 1741, 65 ('meikle' being 'muckle', that is, great or large). In Aberlady the record that money was placed in 'the little box' suggests that there was a larger box: CH2/4/3, Aberlady session accounts 1711–58, 10 July 1729. See also Bolton, Garvald and Saltoun.
48 NRS CH2/1399/1, Monymusk session minutes and accounts, 1678–1729, 22 May 1728. In Midcalder a reserved sum of money was, 'put into the little end of the Box': NRS CH2/266/9, Midcalder session accounts 1692–1729, 23 March 1725. At Ecclesmachen, reference is made to papers being kept in the inner box and reference to the ordinary collection at Slamannan being 'put in the box by the hol in the Lid' both suggest a segmentation of one box: NRS CH2/623/7, Ecclesmachen session minutes 1762–86, 15 June 1762; CH2/331/3, Slamannan, 29 November 1724.
49 CH2/799/6, Haddington, 16 October 1722. Cf NRS CH2/1157/2, Dirleton session minutes and accounts 1703–37, 16 March 1718, 102 for another local order. The evidence of new boxes is clustered in the early years of the century, with none of the eleven examples occurring after 1730. In 1716, the session of Chapel of Garioch recorded that it was 'needful to make a new Kirk Box the old one being so rotten that it was useless', CH2/527/1, Chapel of Garioch, 29 June 1716, 14. Cf CH2/201/2, Keithhall, 9 February 1711.
50 CH2/167/1, Garvald, 13 April 1727, 29.
51 CH2/527/1, Chapel of Garioch, 8 March 1730, 156.
52 CH2/4/5, Aberlady, 17 October 1737, 73.
53 CH2/37/3, Bolton, 6 July 1718, 188.
54 CH2/189/4, Insch, 14 May 1784, 155; CH2/167/1, Garvald, 30 September 1731, 52.
55 CH2/167/1, Garvald, 24 September 1754, 115; CH2/169/2, Gladsmuir, 15 October 1746, 46.
56 CH2/527/2, Chapel of Garioch, 26 July 1757, 505.
57 NRS CH2/542/5, Kemnay session minutes 1709–34, 13 June 1720, 85.
58 CH2/87/5, Dalrymple session accounts 1725–71, *passim*.
59 CH2/322/7, Saltoun, 28 October 1779, 172.
60 Ibid., 5 January 1793, 240.
61 Hazlett, 'Scots Confession', p. 57.
62 NRS CH2/169/9, Gladsmuir session accounts 1768–91, 21 February 1790, 216.
63 CH2/167/1, Garvald, 27 February 1782, 172.
64 CH2/322/7, Saltoun, 5 January 1793, 240.
65 CH2/197/4, presbytery of Irvine, 7 July 1730, 2.
66 CH2/242/13, presbytery of Linlithgow, 28 May 1740, 323.
67 Cage, *Scottish Poor Law*, p. 8.
68 CH2/722/13, presbytery of Stirling, 5 March 1740, 125.

69   CH2/546/10, presbytery of Dumbarton, 3 March 1741, 30; 21 January 1742, 113; 2 November 1742, 144.
70   CH2/415/2, Cambuslang, 17 November 1748, 155.
71   CH2/389/2, Humbie, 22 February 1730, 223; 1 March 1730, 226; 12 April 1730, 231; 19 April 1730, 234; 26 April 1730, 236; 8 June 1730, 241; 26 July 1730, 246; 30 August 1730, 249.
72   CH2/415/2, Cambuslang, session accounts 17 February 1749, 221.
73   Ibid., 20 July 1750, 238.
74   Mitchison, 'Scottish Poor Law: a rejoinder', p. 121.

Chapter 6

1   Skoczylas, Simson's Knotty Case, pp. 118–19.
2   Steuart, Collections, pp. 60–1.
3   Clark, History of Church Discipline, p. 130.
4   Graham, Aikenhead, p. 24
5   Todd, Perth Kirk Session, p. 33.
6   Macgregor, Scottish Presbyterian Polity, p. 136.
7   Hindle, State and Social Change, p. 23.
8   NRS CH2/835/5, Abercorn session minutes 1734–1803, 12 February 1794, 201.
9   CH2/392/3, Dailly, 26 August 1798, 272; Cf another Ayrshire parish at the same time: CH2/87/3, Dalrymple session minutes 1743–1846, 8 October 1797, 122.
10   Wallace, 'Presbyterian moral economy', pp. 54–72.
11   CH2/322/7, Saltoun session minutes, 20 October 1768, 29.
12   CH2/87/3, Dalrymple, 3 August 1797, 121.
13   NRS CH2/104/3, Dundonald session minutes 1731–81, 14 February 1779, 265.
14   Ian Carter, 'To roose the countra'.
15   Ian Carter, Farm Life, p. 2.
16   Buckle, Scotch Intellect.
17   Ibid., p. 90.
18   Ibid., p. 240.
19   Bowie, 'New perspectives', p. 313. See also Mann, Scottish Book Trade, p. 33: '[by] 1660 a Scottish society, which before had been primarily besotted with religion, elite politics, kings and faction, was gradually being infused with a new sense of polite culturalism, and mainly because it was reading more'.
20   Stair, Institutions of the Laws of Scotland.
21   Cairns, 'Lawyers from Holland', p. 152.
22   Steuart, Collections, p. iv.
23   Ford, Law and Opinion, p. 85.
24   Harvie, Travelling Scot, p. 59.
25   Parratt, Written Pleadings, p. ix. See also Walker, Legal History, p. 384.
26   Anderson, 'Lad of Parts'; Houston, Scottish Literacy; Smout, 'Cambuslang', p. 127; Withrington, 'Scottish Enlightenment', p. 15.
27   Holmes, 'Scottish agricultural books', pp. 45–78.

28 Of Samuel Crockett, minister, author and product of this system Donaldson
    comments:
    there is no hint that Crockett ever questioned the merit of a system which
    makes Latin and Greek the only escape routes for clever boys – and for
    girls no escape at all. Crockett is no rebel in this; he accepts what he has
    known. There is no suggestion that country children should be given an
    education more suited to country life. Future farmers, future ploughmen
    and future wives are all subjected to the same mechanical unimaginative
    educational grind not at all adapted to their lives on the land. It is because
    of this, perhaps that Scottish literature is so full of mothers longing for
    their sons to be ministers. It was the easiest way out – easier than
    medicine or the law.
    Donaldson, *Samuel Rutherford Crockett*, p. 214.
29 NRS CH2/295/10, presbytery of Peebles minutes 1734–52, 3 September 1740,
    275.
30 'Innerleithen', *OSA*, vol. 19, p. 602.
31 Mann, *Scottish Book Trade*, p. 31.
32 Strawhorn, *Ayr Academy*, p. 19.
33 Ibid., p. 28.
34 Ibid., p. 20.
35 Mepham, 'Scottish Enlightenment'.
36 Edgar, *Old Church Life, vol. 1*, p. 348.
37 NRS CH2/393/5, presbytery of Hamilton minutes 1785–99, 22 February 1791,
    132.
38 Drummond, *Kirk and Continent*, p. 146
39 Shepherd, 'Arts curriculum', p. 147
40 Emerson, 'Aberdeen professors', p. 163.
41 Devine, *Clearance and Improvement*, p. 8.
42 Hamilton, *Life and Labour*.
43 Shepherd, *Aberdeenshire*, pp. 141–2.
44 McKean, *Banff*, p. 123.
45 CH2/1399/2, Monymusk, 27 May 1792.
46 A fuller account of the twists and turns of the case, and of local tensions, is
    given in Mutch, 'Presbyterian governance', pp. 1–34.
47 CH2/166/6, Presbytery of Garioch, report of revisers of registers of
    Monymusk, 1 December 1790, 444.
48 Ibid.
49 NRS CS44/74/73, Court of Session, Decreet Presbytery of Garioch, Extract
    minute of presbytery 3 May 1761.
50 NRS CS44/74/73, Objections from SSPCK to accounts 1796.
51 Simpson, *Education*, p. 209.
52 NRS CS44/74/73, Petition of SSPCK, 23 February 1798.
53 Kidd and Jackson, 'Grant, Sir Francis'.
54 Cited in Kidd and Jackson.
55 Steuart, *Collections*, p. 54.

56   R. H. Campbell, 'Grant, Sir Archibald'.
57   Grant, *Particular and Inventory*.
58   Spalding Club, *Miscellany*, p. 97.
59   Campbell, 'Archibald Grant'.
60   Cited in Soper, 'Monymusk', p. 70.
61   NRS CS44/74/73, Petition of Society against interlocutor, 31 May 1810.
62   NRS CS44/74/73, Answers of Society to objections, 17 December 1808.
63   NRS CS44/74/73, Lord Newton minutes, 28 February 1807.
64   NRS CS44/74/73, Answers for Grant to petition of Presbytery, 5 December 1810.
65   NRS CS44/74/73, Minute in process, 7 June 1823; Heads of a plan for management, 1823; Minute in process, 5 March 1824; Minute of process to approve setting up of fund and plan of management, 23 February 1825.
66   NRS GD240/15/1, Records of Bruce & Kerr, WS, Information for Grant, 19 October 1797.
67   Scott, *Fasti*, vol. 6, p. 176.
68   NRS GD345/1096, extract of minutes, 9 February 1784.
69   NRS CH2/1399/2, Monymusk, 22 January 1797, 162.
70   NRS GD345/1096, Letter to Mr Alex Grant from Archibald Grant, 5 November 1797.
71   Suderman, *Orthodoxy and Enlightenment*, p. 4.
72   Campbell, *Lectures*.
73   Published by A. Brown, Aberdeen, 1811.
74   'Scottish intelligence', *Glasgow Herald*, 10 May 1822.
75   Ibid.
76   CH2/166/6, Presbytery of Garioch, replies for Sir Archibald Grant, 1 December 1790, 446–7.
77   NRS GD345/1096, Grant of Monymusk papers, Copy letter from Isaac Grant to Skene Keith, 7 October 1789.
78   NRS CH2/1399/2, Kirk Session of Monymusk, 24 June 1792, 120.
79   NRS CS44/74/73, Letter from Alexander Duff to Reverend Dr Kemp, Secretary to SSPCK, 28 September 1795.
80   NRS GD345/1096, Lewis Duff account of damages and expenses, July 1799.
81   He also supplied the account of the parish for the *Statistical Account*. Its lack of glowing commentary on the current heritor, as opposed to his praise for the first Sir Archibald, may reflect the tensions in the parish. 'Monymusk', *OSA*, vol. 3, pp. 66–76.
82   NRS CH2/166/8, presbytery of Garioch 1803–34, 31 August 1814, 188.
83   NRS CS44/74/73, Letter from Alexander Duff to Reverend Dr Kemp, Secretary to SSPCK, 28 September 1795.
84   NRS CH2/1399/4, Monymusk session minutes 1824–44, 16 May 1824, 7.
85   Scott, *Fasti*, vol. 6, pp. 149–84.

Chapter 7

1   Keith, *General View*, p. 177.
2   Ibid., p. 179. This was not strictly true of all of Scotland. In January 1764 the minutes of the parish of Aberlady record, 'After examining Accts the Session Dined': CH2/4/4, Aberlady, 7 January 1764, 49. This, however, was the only example in the records examined. Similarly, in the East Lothian parish of Abercorn there was, from 1775, a payment of 15 shillings to the 'elemosynar' (treasurer), which continued until the end of the century. Again, this was an exception in the records examined. CH2/835/10, Abercorn, 18 January 1775, 163.
3   Hindle, *On the Parish?*
4   On the eighteenth-century church see W. M. Jacob, *Lay People*; Spaeth, *Church in an Age of Danger*; Gregory, *Restoration, Reformation and Reform*; Gregory and Jeffrey *National Church*; Snape, *Church of England*.
5   Nottinghamshire Record Office (NRO), PR15483, Hickling.
6   Chambers, *Nottinghamshire*; Fowkes, *Progress*.
7   Chapman, *Hosiery and Knitwear*.
8   Beckett *Centenary History*, pp. 351 et seq.
9   See the more detailed discussion in Alistair Mutch, 'Personal accountability', pp. 69–88.
10 Hindle, *State and Social Change*, p. 29.
11 Wiltshire Family History Society, *Compleat Parish*.
12 Spaeth, *Age of Danger*, pp. 64–72; Gregory and Chamberlain, *National Church*, p. 41.
13 Stokes, *William Cole*, p. 34.
14 University of Nottingham Manuscripts and Special Collections (UoN), Archdeaconary of Nottingham, AN/PB 324/1–51, Presentment books, 1740.
15 UoN AN/PB323/154–178, Bingham presentment bills, October 1733.
16 Jacob, *Lay People*, p. 11.
17 Hill, *East Bridgford*, p. 94.
18 Vaisey, *Thomas Turner*.
19 Ayres, *Paupers*, p. 80.
20 Ibid., p. 262.
21 Stokes, *William Cole*, pp. 29, 204.
22 Linnell, *Benjamin Rogers*, p. 85.
23 Woodforde, *Diaries*, *Vol. 1 1776–7* (second edition) *and Vols 8–17*.
24 Woodforde, *Diaries*, *Vol. 1 1776–7* (second edition), p. 121.
25 Woodforde, *Diaries*, *Vol. 9 1780–1*, p. 30.
26 Woodforde, *Diaries*, *Vol. 10 1782–4*, p. 244.
27 Ibid., p. 261.
28 Woodforde, *Diaries*, *Vol. 12 1788–9*, p. 112.
29 For example, the only mention of parish business by George Woodward indicates grudging and limited engagement: Gibson, *Parson*, p. 94.
30 Woodforde, *Diaries*, *Vol. 8 1778–9*, p. 34.
31 Tate, *Parish Chest*.
32 Henstock, 'Parish divided', p. 96.

33   NRO PR15640, Stanton on the Wolds; PR19566, Flintham.
34   Spaeth, *Age of Danger*, p. 100.
35   Vaisey, *Thomas Turner*, p. 95.
36   Pitman, 'Tradition and exclusion', pp. 27–45.
37   Vaisey, *Thomas Turner*, p. 95.
38   Ayres, *William Holland*, p. 262.
39   Vaisey, *William Turner*, p. 95.
40   NRO PR6916, Langar, 14 June 1762.
41   Gregory, 'For all sorts', p. 42; Spaeth, *Age of Danger*, p. 182; Hunt, 'Lord's Supper', pp. 39–83; Haigh, 'Communion and community', pp. 721–40.
42   Spaeth, *Age of Danger*, p. 181.
43   NRS CH2/322/11, Saltoun session accounts 1795–1847, 31 January 1800, 31.
44   NRO PR2865, Shelford, 30 May 1705.
45   Hutton, *Merry England*, notes 'hundreds of sets of accounts' in which 'only summary totals of income and expenditure are noted': p. 263.
46   NRO PR789, Wysall, 24 January 1800.
47   UoN AN/A 82/1, Southwell Archdeaconry Act Books, 21 January 1777.
48   NRO PR15483, Hickling, 31 May 1800.
49   NRO PR19469, Orston, 5 May 1783.
50   Vaisey, *Thomas Turner*, p. 143.
51   NRO PR2590, Edwalton, 1725.
52   NRO PR799, Willoughby on the Wolds, 29 September 1786.
53   Vaisey, *Thomas Turner*, p. 67.
54   Ibid., p. 204.
55   Ibid., p. 290.
56   Hill, *East Bridgford*, p. 151.
57   Hindle, *On the Parish*, p. 223.
58   Ayres, *Paupers*, p. 36
59   White and Willock, *Scottish Legal System*, p. 29.
60   Whetstone, *Scottish County Government*, p. 39.
61   Jacob, *Lay People*, p. 34.
62   Winstanley, *Parson Woodforde*, p. 52
63   Buchan, *Capital of the Mind*, p. 123
64   McLean, *Adam Smith*, p. 38.
65   Hindle, *On the Parish*, p. 230.
66   Ashton, *Industrial Revolution*, p. 14.
67   Suderman, *Orthodoxy and Enlightenment*, p. 259.
68   Schmidt, *Holy Fairs*, p. xxvii.
69   Devine, *Clearance and Improvement*, p. 8.
70   Cooke, *Scottish Cotton Industry*, p. 176.
71   CH2/393/3, presbytery of Hamilton, 10 April 1750, 497.
72   CH2/185/10, presbytery of Haddington, 4 February 1702, 93.
73   CH2/835/4, Abercorn, 6 April 1721, 47.
74   CH2/86/3, Dalmeny, 26 February 1721, 103.
75   CH2/835/5, Abercorn, 20 December 1770, 170.

76 CH2/86/5, Dalmeny, 8 February 1780, 147.

77 NRS CH2/196/2, Inverurie session minutes 1716–51, 29 January 1721, 35.

78 NRS CH2/196/3, Inverurie session minutes 1751–72, 25 October 1763, 86.

79 CH2/527/2, Chapel of Garioch, 7 May 1758, 515.

80 CH2/189/3, Insch, 10 April 1768, 273.

81 CH2/189/4, Insch, 16 January 1779, 67.

82 NRS CH2/78/2, Culsalmond session minutes 1748–66, 15 June 1753, 24; 6 August 1756, 45.

83 NRS CH2/78/3, Culsalmond session minutes 1769–89, 4 August 1770, 4.

84 CH2/37/4, Bolton session minutes 1744–1802, 14 March 1761, 38; 8 January 1762, 41.

85 CH2/169/2, Gladsmuir, February 1753, 58; 30 December 1756, 63.

86 CH2/37/4, Bolton session minutes 1744–1802, 23 August 1753, 24; 4 January 1760, 34; 5 January 1770, 63.

87 CH2/37/4, Bolton session accounts 1744–1801, 3 January 1782, 112.

88 CH2/1157/3, Dirleton, 25 September 1761, 91.

89 CH2/322/7, Saltoun, 2 October 1769, 33.

90 CH2/104/3, Dundonald, 1 December 1760, 230; 19 November 1778, 264; 25 July 1779, 269.

91 CH2/415/2, Cambuslang, 2 February 1737, 50; 10 March 1743, 53.

92 Ibid., 15 May 1747, 57.

93 Ibid., 22 May 1749, 348; 13 February 1776, 246.

94 Ibid., 23 May 1758, 362.

95 Devine, *Tobacco Lords*.

96 Ambrose, *Prima, Media & Ultima*, 'Printed for Mr James Cullen, Preacher, Archibald Ingram, James Dechman, John Hamilton and John Glasford, Merchants in Glasgow, 1737'.

97 CH2/415/2, Cambuslang session accounts 1700–1810, May 1762, 363; 25 May 1768, 365; CH2/415/40, Cambuslang session accounts 1778–1838, 15 May 1787, 226; 15 May 1789, 230; 19 May 1797, 244.

98 Smout, 'Scottish sugar houses', pp. 240–53.

99 NRS CH2/461/1, Old Monkland session minutes and account 1684–1742, 29 November 1727, 110; November 1735, 117.

100 NRS CH2/461/7, Old Monkland accounts 1743–51, 17 June 1743, 7.

101 NRS CH2/461/8 Old Monkland accounts 1743–88, 14 November 1755, 152; 15 August 1751, 64; 14 November 1755, 79.

102 Devine, *Scotland's Empire*, p. 87.

103 Murray, *Chapters*, p. 20.

104 Ibid., p. 316.

105 Ibid., p. 321.

106 Ibid., p. 342.

107 Ibid., pp. 348, 271.

108 Miller, *First Impressions*, p. 69.

109 Hamilton, *Scotland*, p. 206.

110 Spraakman and Margret, 'Management accounting practices', pp. 101–19.

111   Johnstone, 'Work journals', pp. 38–51.
112   Richards and Clough, *Cromartie: Highland Life*, p. 324.
113   Spring, *English Landed Estate*.
114   Parker, *Coke of Norfolk*; Richards, *Leviathan of Wealth*.
115   Spring, *English Landed Estate*, p. 93.
116   Stevenson, *Diary of a Canny Man*, p. 41.
117   Ibid., p. 3.
118   Brown, *Diary of George Brown*, p. 277.
119   NRS CH2/297/6, Penicuik session minutes 1812–56, 16 May 1830, 129.
120   Ibid., 16 December 1832, 147.
121   Ibid., 16 June 1833, 148.
122   NRS CH2/1543/12, Crail session accounts 1782–1824, 11 October 1782, 12.
123   Cited in Parker, *Coke of Norfolk*, p. 134.
124   He was also elected 'preses', or chair, of a parish meeting to debate patronage: NRS CH2/752/5, Bowden session minutes 1775–1817, 29 January 1784, 9.
125   Holmes, 'Scottish agricultural books'; Raffe, *Culture of Controversy*, p. 21.
126   Mepham, *Accounting*, p. 2.
127   Sheldahl, 'America's earliest recorded text', p. 7; cf McCusker and Menard, *Economy*, p. 345.
128   Cooke, *Scottish Cotton Industry*, p. 179.
129   Chandler (ed.) *Precursors*; Gantman, *Capitalism*, p. 24.
130   Jeremy, 'Montgomery'.
131   Ganter and Walgenbach, 'Middle managers', p. 171.
132   Jeremy, *Capitalists and Christians*, p. 112.
133   Liverpool Record Office (LRO) 347 JUS Licensing Registers 1/1/3, 1845–6.
134   Moynihan, 'Walkers Ales', pp. 9–16.
135   Mutch, 'Public houses', pp. 1–19.
136   Mutch, 'Magistrates', pp. 325–42.
137   Peter Walker & Son, *Walker's Warrington Ales*.
138   Mutch, 'Shaping the public house', pp. 179–200.
139   See, for example, LRO, Peter Walker & Son, 380PWK/2/1/12a Statements for Canning Place Vaults 1858–66; 380PWK/2/10a–j Bundle of ms statements 1860–6; 380/1/4/12, Papers of David Walker 1865–6; 380PWK/1/4/15, Papers of David Walker 1865–6.
140   See the detailed account given for a later period in Peter Walker & Son, *Walker's Warrington Ales*.
141   Derbyshire Record Office, D1849, Walker-Okeover Papers, Box 2 bundle 19 'miscellaneous', Share certificate, St Andrew's Church, 15 December 1866; for Walker's regular attendance, LRO 380PWK/1/8 Appendix A Bundle 11 in-letters 1890, 10 March 1890, A. Wilson, Chester.
142   Gaskell, *Lancashire Leaders Social*, n.p.
143   Murdoch, *Scotland and America*, p. 134.
144   Schmidt, *Holy Fairs*, p. 208.
145   Tiedemann, 'Presbyterianism', p. 337.
146   Coldwell, 'Religious observance'.

147   Spooner, *Cases Argued:* George Smith vs. John Nelson, pp. 528–31.
148   Published by John Niven, Glasgow, 1840.
149   NRS CH2/916/2, Blantyre session minutes 1809–45, 7 September 1809.
150   Wall, *Andrew Carnegie*, p. 224.
151   Ibid., p. 160.
152   Hall, *Nonprofit*, p. 33.
153   Herman, *Scottish Enlightenment*; for notes of caution see Barr, *Stranger Within*,
      p. 5; Devine, *To the Ends of the Earth*, p. 12.

Chapter 8

1   Hall, *Nonprofit*, p. 143.
2   Foucault, *Security, Territory, Population*, pp. 123–90.
3   Elden, 'Problem of confession', pp. 23–41.
4   Lea, *Auricular Confession*, p. v.
5   Quattrone, 'Accounting for God', p. 666.
6   Tillotson, 'Yorkshire nunneries', pp. 1–21.
7   Bigoni, Gallardo and Fennell, 'Rethinking the sacred', p. 581.
8   Ibid., p. 584.
9   Espejo, Manjón and Sánchez-Matamoros, 'Accounting', pp. 129–50.
10   Weber, *Economy and Society*; cf Gorski, 'The little divergence', p. 165.
11   Demerath and Farnsley, 'Congregations resurgent', p. 202.
12   Ibid., p. 202.
13   Ali, *Islamic Perspectives*.
14   Devine, *Scotland's Empire*, p. xxvii.
15   Withrington, 'Scottish Enlightenment', p. 16.
16   Whytock, *Educated Clergy*, p. 233.
17   Nollen, *Jethro Tull*, p. 58.
18   A mistake made by this author: Mutch, 'National identity', pp. 116–29. In
      similar vein, David Armitage observes, in his consideration of the achievements
      of the Scottish diaspora, 'every achievement (or indeed every crime) of every
      Scot abroad should not be attributed solely to their Scottishness: as the duke
      of Wellington put it in another context, "Just because one is born in a stable
      does not make one a horse"' (Armitage, 'Scottish diaspora', p. 275). As Angela
      McCarthy points out, émigrés from many backgrounds pick out similar traits,
      such as hard work, as being distinctive traits in their own cultures, when they
      might be common attributes of the aspiring (McCarthy, 'Scottish diaspora since
      1815', p. 525).
19   Baltzell, *Puritan Boston and Quaker Philadelphia*, p. 37.
20   Campbell, 'Enlightenment', pp. 14–15.
21   McLean, *Adam Smith*, p. 142.
22   McCrone, 'Cultural capital', p. 74.
23   Philip, *Higher Tradition*. A Higher Certificate for Book-keeping and Commercial
      Arithmetic was available in the 1890s and this focus on commercial arithmetic
      appears to have shaped later examinations: pp. 22, 82.

24 Murray, *Chapters*, p. 310.
25 Clark, *Spiritual Merchant*, p. vii.
26 Ibid., p. 149.
27 Clark, *Presbyterial Government*.
28 Whatley, *Diary of John Sturrock*, p. 29.
29 Jamie, *Old Church Life*, p. i.
30 Biographical sketch of Hew Scott, DD, in *Fasti*, vol. 1, pp. xi–xvi.
31 Dickson, *Kirk and its Worthies*, p. 42.
32 Donaldson, 'Alexander'.
33 Donaldson, *Samuel Rutherford Crockett*, p. 53. See also Brown, 'Rotavating the kailyard', pp. 150–4.
34 Morton, *Unionist Nationalism*.
35 Kidd and Coleman, 'Mythical Scotland', p. 77.
36 Kelly, *Scott-land*.
37 Devine, *To the Ends of the Earth*, p. 282.
38 McHugh, 'Review', p. 583.
39 McLean, *Adam Smith*, p. 38.
40 Carter, *Ancient Cultures*.
41 Aspinwall, *Portable Utopia*, p. 14.

Bibliography

Primary sources

National Records of Scotland, Edinburgh

Church of Scotland records

KIRK SESSION RECORDS

Presbytery of Ayr

Ayr	CH2/751/28	Accounts 1730–49
Coylton	CH2/810/1	Minutes 1723–39,1748–1814
		Accounts 1723–31
Old Cumnock	CH2/81/5	Accounts 1754–87
	CH2/81/6	Accounts 1788–99
Dailly	CH2/392/2	Minutes 1711–59
	CH2/392/3	Minutes 1761–98
	CH2/392/4	Minutes and accounts 1799–1823
Dalrymple	CH2/87/2	Minutes 1726–83
	CH2/87/3	Minutes 1743–1846
	CH2/87/5	Accounts 1725–71
	CH2/87/6	Accounts 1771–1826
Dundonald	CH2/104/2	Minutes 1702–1809
	CH2/104/3	Minutes 1731–81
Galston	CH2/1335/18	Accounts 1710–56
	CH2/1335/19	Accounts 1754–68
Mauchline	CH2/896/3	Minutes 1695–1760
		Accounts 1734–55
Monkton	CH2/809/6	Minutes 1688–1726
	CH2/809/7	Minutes 1762–1812
	CH2/809/16	Accounts 1749–63
	CH2/809/17	Accounts 1763–85
	CH2/809/18	Accounts 1786–1817
Muirkirk	CH2/272/7	Accounts 1799–1826
Ochiltree	CH2/778/1	Minutes 1695–96, 1725–9, 1764–90, 1822–39

		Accounts 1695–97, 1725–27, 1763–92
	CH2/778/5	Accounts 1792–1819
St Quivox	CH2/319/2	Accounts 1737–83
	CH2/319/3	Accounts 1783–1803
Sorn	CH2/403/8	Accounts 1752–90
Symington	CH2/728/1	Minutes 1689–1787
		Accounts 1715–84
	CH2/728/4	Accounts 1787–1818
Tarbolton	CH2/825/11	Accounts 1799–1836

Presbytery of Dalkeith

Penicuik	CH2/297/6	Minutes 1812–56

Presbytery of Galloway

Kells	CH2/202/2	Minutes 1731–73

Presbytery of Garioch

Chapel of Garioch	CH2/527/1	Minutes 1714–41
	CH2/527/2	Minutes 1741–66
	CH2/527/3	Minutes 1766–1804
Culsalmond	CH2/78/1	Minutes 1735–48
	CH2/78/2	Minutes 1748–66
	CH2/78/3	Minutes 1769–89
	CH2/78/4	Minutes 1789–99
Daviot	CH2/549/1	Minutes 1731–99
	CH2/549/3	Accounts 1731–1820
Insch	CH2/189/2	Minutes 1720–32
		Accounts 1720–28
	CH2/189/3	Minutes 1732–71
	CH2/189/4	Minutes 1771–92, 1814–15
Inverurie	CH2/196/2	Minutes 1716–51
	CH2/196/3	Minutes 1751–72
	CH2/196/4	Minutes 1779–98
Keithhall	CH2/201/2	Minutes 1709–44
	CH2/201/3	Minutes 1744–78
Kemnay	CH2/542/5	Minutes 1709–34
	CH2/542/6	Minutes 1745–52
	CH2/542/7	Minutes 1758–1818
Kintore	CH2/223/1	Minutes 1713–38
	CH2/223/2	Minutes 1738–61
	CH2/223/3	Minutes 1761–1809

Meldrum	CH2/1146/15	Minutes 1724–52
	CH2/1146/16	Minutes 1752–72
	CH2/1146/17	Accounts 1747–97
Monymusk	CH2/1399/1	Minutes 1678–1729
	CH2/1399/2	Minutes 1763–99
	CH2/1399/3	Minutes 1799–1823
	CH2/1399/4	Minutes 1824–44
Oyne	CH2/293/4	Minutes 1776–1826
Rayne	CH2/310/3	Minutes 1705–26
	CH2/310/4	Minutes 1726–44
	CH2/310/5	Minutes 1744–70
	CH2/310/6	Minutes 1772–1800

Presbytery of Haddington

Aberlady	CH2/4/2	Minutes 1697–1718
	CH2/4/5	Accounts 1711–58
	CH2/4/4	Minutes 1758–83
Bolton	CH2/37/3	Minutes 1683–1745
	CH2/37/4	Minutes 1744–1802
		Accounts 1744–1801
Dirleton	CH2/1157/2	Minutes and accounts 1703–37
	CH2/1157/3	Minutes 1737–74
	CH2/1157/20	Accounts 1752–72
	CH2/1157/21	Accounts 1772–1801
Garvald	CH2/167/1	Minutes 1721–89
	CH2/167/2	Minutes and accounts 1694–1712, 1718–21
	CH2/167/3	Accounts 1761–1819
Gladsmuir	CH2/169/1	Minutes 1692–1711
	CH2/169/2	Minutes 1737–79
	CH2/169/3/1	Minutes 1775–1804
	CH2/169/8	Accounts 1746–68
	CH2/169/9	Accounts 1768–91
	CH2/169/10	Accounts 1791–1803
Haddington	CH2/799/6	Minutes 1711–26
	CH2/799/7	Minutes 1726–9, 1781–1835
Humbie	CH2/389/2	Minutes 1715–34
	CH2/389/3	Minutes 1734–50
Pencaitland	CH2/296/3	Minutes 1732–54
		Accounts 1728–1802
Prestonpans	CH2/307/10	Accounts 1744–68
Saltoun	CH2/322/3	Minutes and accounts 1685–1713
	CH2/322/4	Minutes 1714–18

	CH2/322/5	Minutes 1717–39
		Accounts 1719–39
	CH2/322/6	Minutes 1740–8
	CH2/322/7	Minutes 1760–95
		Accounts 1759–94
	CH2/322/11	Accounts 1795–1847
Yester	CH2/377/3	Minutes 1708–72
		Accounts 1708–1880

Presbytery of Hamilton

Blantyre	CH2/916/1	Minutes 1693–1711
		Accounts 1750–54
	CH2/916/2	Minutes 1809–45
Bothwell	CH2/556/1	Minutes 1707–49
	CH2/556/2	Minutes 1754–89
		Accounts 1749–51
	CH2/566/7	Accounts 1749–1827
Cambuslang	CH2/415/1	Minutes and collections 1658–1788
	CH2/415/2	Minutes 1731–48
		Accounts 1700–1810
	CH2/415/40	Accounts 1778–1838
Cambusnethan	CH2/48/8	Accounts 1772–1816
Dalserf	CH2/1013/6	Accounts 1737–59
Dalziell	CH2/462/1	Minutes and accounts 1723–1816
Hamilton	CH2/465/21	Accounts 1778–1802
East Kilbride	CH2/1485/1	Minutes 1720, 1746–55, 1809–25, 1831–3
		Accounts 1780–1800
New Monkland	CH2/685/2	Accounts and Minutes 1702–33
	CH2/685/3	Minutes 1737, 1744–52, 1760–97
	CH2/685/4	Minutes 1797–1825
Old Monkland	CH2/461/1	Minutes and accounts 1684–1742
	CH2/461/7	Accounts 1743–51
	CH2/461/8	Accounts 1743–88
Shotts	CH2/460/2	Minutes and accounts 1697–1793

Presbytery of Linlithgow

Abercorn	CH2/835/2	Minutes 1700–07
	CH2/835/4	Minutes 1718–33
	CH2/835/5	Minutes 1734–1803
	CH2/835/9	Accounts 1700–57
	CH2/835/10	Accounts 1758–99
Bo'ness	CH2/540/16	Accounts 1715–25

	CH2/540/19	Accounts 1795–1818
Midcalder	CH2/266/2	Minutes 1691–1761
	CH2/266/3	Minutes 1714–43
	CH2/266/4	Minutes 1743–52
	CH2/266/9	Accounts 1692–1729
West Calder	CH2/366/10	Accounts 1768–85
	CH2/366/12	Accounts 1794–1811
Carriden	CH2/61/10	Accounts 1714–57
	CH2/61/12	Accounts 1798–1806
Dalmeny	CH2/86/2	Minutes 1691–1710
	CH2/86/3	Minutes 1710–28
	CH2/86/4	Minutes 1729–57
	CH2/86/5	Minutes 1757–1816
Ecclesmachan	CH2/623/4	Minutes 1734–84
	CH2/623/7	Minutes 1762–86
Kirkliston	CH2/229/7	Accounts 1731–52
	CH2/229/11	Accounts 1703–31
	CH2/229/12	Accounts 1751–81
	CH/229/13	Accounts 1781–1821
Livingston	CH2/467/13	Accounts 1719–82
Muirvanside	CH2/712/3	Accounts 1740–58
	CH2/712/4	Accounts 1758–1805
Slamannan	CH2/331/3	Minutes 1716–51
Torphichen	CH2/503/7	Accounts 1743–54
	CH2/503/8	Accounts 1753–79
	CH2/503/9	Accounts 1779–1808

Presbytery of Selkirk

Bowden	CH2/752/5	Minutes 1775–1817

Presbytery of St Andrews

Crail	CH2/1543/12	Accounts 1782–1824

PRESBYTERY MINUTES

Synod of Aberdeen

Garioch	CH2/166/2	1697–1705
	CH2/166/3	1708–21
	CH2/166/4	1718–32
	CH2/166/5	1732–52
	CH2/166/6	1752–92

	CH2/166/7	1792–1803
	CH2/166/8	1803–34

Synod of Angus and Mearns

Arbroath	CH2/15/2	1704–13
	CH2/15/3	1712–21
	CH2/15/4	1721–34
	CH2/15/5	1734–75
Brechin	CH2/40/5	1706–10
	CH2/40/6	1710–17
	CH2/40/7	1717–21
	CH2/40/9	1729–38
	CH2/40/10	1738–49
Dundee	CH2/103/6	1706–10
	CH2/103/9	1717–25
	CH2/103/10	1725–31
	CH2/103/12	1739–57
Fordoun	CH2/157/13	Minutes of presbytery visitations 1677–88
	CH2/157/3	1700–10
	CH2/157/4	1710–21
	CH2/157/5	1722–39
	CH2/157/6	1739–51
Forfar	CH2/159/2	1717–27
	CH2/159/3	1727–43
Meigle	CH2/263/4	1708–13
	CH2/263/6	1718–22
	CH2/263/8	1728–34
	CH2/263/9	1734–40
	CH2/263/10	1740–49

Synod of Dumfries

Dumfries	CH2/1284/4	1701–10
	CH2/1284/6	1726–39
	CH2/1284/7	1739–43
Lochmaben	CH2/247/2	1708–18
	CH2/247/3	1730–43
Penpont	CH2/298/2	1714–25
	CH2/298/3	1725–36
	CH2/298/4	1736–45

Synod of Fife

Cupar	CH2/82/4	1708–14
	CH2/82/5	1715–23
	CH2/82/6	1723–30
	CH2/82/7	1730–36
Dunfermline	CH2/105/3	1696–1704
	CH2/105/4	1704–17
	CH2/105/5	1718–29
	CH2/105/6	1729–45
Kirkcaldy	CH2/224/4	1705–13
	CH2/224/5	1713–24
	CH2/224/6	1724–42
St Andrews	CH2/1132/1	1705–13
	CH2/1132/2	1714–23
	CH2/1132/3	1723–32
	CH2/1132/4	1733–40

Synod of Galloway

Kirkcudbright	CH2/526/2	1708–20
	CH2/526/3	1720–33
	CH2/526/4	1734–41
Stranraer	CH2/341/2	1702–16
	CH2/341/3	1716–26
	CH2/341/4	1726–36
	CH2/341/5	1736–59
Wigtown	CH2/373/2	1709–34
	CH2/373/3	1734–52

Synod of Glasgow and Ayr

Ayr	CH2/532/2	1687–1705
	CH2/532/3	1705–19
	CH2/532/4	1719–32
	CH2/532/6	1746–56
	CH2/532/7	1757–68
	CH2/532/8	1768–96
Dumbarton	CH2/546/6	1704–14
	CH2/546/7	1714–20
	CH2/546/9	1729–39
	CH2/546/10	1740–47
Glasgow	CH2/171/8	1707–13
	CH2/171/9	1720–23
	CH2/171/11/1	1733–43

Hamilton	CH2/393/2	1695–1719
	CH2/393/3	1719–57
	CH2/393/4	1757–79
	CH2/393/5	1785–99
Irvine	CH2/197/3	1710–30
	CH2/197/4	1730–43
	CH2/197/5	1743–59
Lanark	CH2/234/5	1709–17
	CH2/234/6	1718–24
	CH2/234/7	1724–31
	CH2/234/8	1732–49
Paisley	CH2/294/7	1707–22
	CH2/294/8	1722–35
	CH2/294/9	1735–52

Synod of Lothian and Tweeddale

Biggar	CH2/35/5	1701–11
	CH2/35/6	1711–20
	CH2/35/7	1720–34
	CH2/35/8	1734–53
Dalkeith	CH2/424/9	1705–11
	CH2/424/11	1719–26
	CH2/424/12	1726–42
Dunbar	CH2/99/4	1704–20
	CH2/99/5	1720–34
	CH2/99/6	1734–66
Edinburgh	CH2/121/6	1705–8
	CH2/121/7	1708–11
	CH2/121/10	1718–21
	CH2/121/12	1726–32
	CH2/121/14	1739–42
Haddington	CH2/185/10	1698–1716
	CH2/185/11	1718–30
	CH2/185/12	1730–96
Linlithgow	CH2/242/8	1694–1701
	CH2/242/9	1701–10
	CH2/242/10	1710–13
Peebles	CH2/295/7	1699–1716
	CH2/295/8	1716–26
	CH2/295/9	1726–34
	CH2/295/10	1734–52

Synod of Merse and Teviotdale

Chirnside	CH2/516/2	1702–21
	CH2/516/3	1721–34
	CH2/516/4	1734–56
Duns	CH2/113/4	1707–16
	CH2/113/5	1716–26
	CH2/113/6	1726–39
	CH2/113/7	1739–49
Jedburgh	CH2/198/7	1708–21
	CH2/198/8	1721–32
	CH2/198/9	1733–43
Earlston	CH2/118/2	1704–16
	CH2/118/3	1716–30
	CH2/118/4	1730–48
Selkirk	CH2/327/3	1706–16
	CH2/327/4	1716–25
	CH2/327/5	1725–36
	CH2/327/6	1736–55

Synod of Perth and Stirling

Dunblane	CH2/723/6	1709–16
	CH2/723/7	1716–22
	CH2/723/9	1729–42
Dunkeld	CH2/106/2	1706–12
	CH2/106/4	1717–24
	CH2/106/5	1724–31
	CH2/106/6	1731–46
Perth	CH2/299/7	1705–10
	CH2/299/10	1719–22
	CH2/299/12	1726–30
	CH2/299/14	1736–41
Stirling	CH2/722/9	1701–12
	CH2/722/11	1719–27
	CH2/722/12	1728–38
	CH2/722/13	1738–45

SYNOD MINUTES

Aberdeen	CH2/840/2	1706–21
	CH2/840/3	1722–34
	CH2/840/4	1752–87
	CH2/840/5	1787–1816

Edinburgh	CH2/252/12	1747–61
	CH2/252/13	1746–80
	CH2/252/14	1762–1800
Galloway	CH2/165/3	1713–46
Glasgow	CH2/464/3	1715–60
	CH2/464/4	1761–1803

Court of Session

CS44/74/73   Decreet Presbytery of Garioch 1845
Extract minute of presbytery 3 May 1761
Letter from Alexander Duff to Reverend Dr Kemp, Secretary to Society in Scotland for the Propagation of Christian Knowledge (SSPCK), 28 September 1795
Objections from SSPCK to accounts 1796
Petition of SSPCK, 23 February 1798
Lord Newton minutes, 28 February 1807
Answers of SSPCK to objections, 17 December 1808
Petition of SSPCK against interlocutor, 31 May 1810
Answers for Grant to petition of Presbytery, 5 December 1810
Minute in process, 7 June 1823
Heads of a plan for management, 1823
Minute in process, 5 March 1824
Minute of process to approve setting up of fund and plan of management, 23 February 1825

Records of Bruce & Kerr, WS

GD240/15/1   Informations for Alexander Duncan, WS, treasurer of the SSPCK, pursuer, and for Sir Archibald Grant of Monymusk and the kirk session of Monymusk, defenders, regarding mortification by deceased Sir Francis Grant of Cullen, senator of College of Justice.

Grant of Monymusk

GD345/1096   Papers concerning Lord Cullen's mortification to kirk session of Monymusk 1784–1800

GD345/1109   Grant of Monymusk, papers concerning tenants of Monymusk, including articles of roup and lists of customs, Assessment for army and navy 1796

Nottinghamshire Record Office

Parish records

Edwalton	PR2590	1725–99
Flintham	PR19566	1781–1800
Hickling	PR15483	1758–1800
Langar	PR6916	1710–1803
Orston	PR19469	1701–90
Shelford	PR2865	1691–1780
Stanton on the Wolds	PR15640	1768–78
Willoughby on the Wolds	PR799	1786–1815
Wysall	PR789	1747–1870

University of Nottingham, Manuscripts and Special Collections

AN/PB323/154–78, Bingham presentment bills, October 1733
ANPB324/1–51 Archdeaconry of Nottingham   Presentment books 1740
AN/A82/1 Archdeaconary of Southwell   Act Books 1777

Liverpool Record Office

347 JUS 1/1/3 Licensing registers 1845–6
380 PWK Peter Walker &Son
380 PWK/1/4/12, Papers of David Walker 1865–6
380 PWK/1/4/15, Papers of David Walker 1865–6
380 PWK/1/8 Appendix A Bundle 11 in-letters 1890
380 PWK/2/1/12a Statements for Canning Place Vaults 1858–66
380 PWK/2/10a–j Bundle of ms statements 1860–6

Derbyshire Record Office

D1849 Walker-Okeover Papers

Printed primary sources

Ambrose, Isaac, *Prima, Media & Ultima: The First, Middle and Last Things* (Glasgow: Alexander Miller, 1737).

Anon, *Overtures Concerning the Discipline and Method of Proceeding in the Ecclesiastick Judicatories in the Church of Scotland* (Edinburgh: George Mossman, 1696).

Ayres, Jack, *Paupers and Pig Killers: The Diary of William Holland a Somerset Parson 1799–1818* (Gloucester: Alan Sutton, 1984).

Brown, George, *Diary of George Brown, Merchant in Glasgow 1745–1753* (Thomas Constable: Edinburgh, 1856).

Calvin, Jean, *Institutes of the Christian Religion* (Grand Rapids, MI: Eerdmans Publishing, 1983 [1559]).

Campbell, George, *Lectures on Ecclesiastical History* (Aberdeen: A. Brown, 1800).

Church Law Society, *Acts of the General Assembly of the Church of Scotland 1638–1842* (Edinburgh: Church Law Society, 1843).

Clark, James, *Presbyterial Government as now Established in the Church of Scotland Methodically Described* (Edinburgh: James Wardlaw, 1701).

Clark, James, *The Spiritual Merchant: or, the Art of Merchandizing Spiritualized* (Glasgow: Robert Sanders, 1703).

Gibson, Donald, *A Parson in the Vale of White Horse: George Woodward's Letters from East Hendred, 1753–1761* (Gloucester: Alan Sutton, 1982).

Grant, Archibald, *A True and Exact Particular and Inventory of all and Singular the Lands, Tenements and Hereditaments, Goods, Chattels, Debts and Personal Estate Whatsoever, Which I Sir Archibald Grant, ... Was Seized or Possessed of or Intitled unto in my Own Right* (London: S. Buckley, 1732).

Hazlett, Ian, 'A new version of the Scots Confession, 1560', *Theology in Scotland*, 17(2) (2010), pp. 41–66.

Keith, George Skene, *General View of the Agriculture of Aberdeenshire* (Aberdeen: A. Brown, 1811).

Kirk, James, *Stirling Presbytery Records 1581–1587* (Edinburgh: Scottish History Society, 1981).

Knox, John, *The History of the Reformation of Religion in Scotland by John Knox; with which are included Knox's Confession and The Book of Discipline* (London: Melrose, 1905 [c. 1571]).

Linnell, C., *Diary of Benjamin Rogers 1720–1771*, (Streatley: Bedfordshire Records Society, 30, 1950).

Montgomery, James, *A Practical Detail of the Cotton Manufacture of the United States of America and the State of the Cotton Manufacture of that Country Contrasted and Compared with that of Great Britain* (Glasgow: John Niven, 1840).

Paton, Henry, *The Session Book of Rothesay 1658–1750* (Rothesay: Marquis of Bute, 1941).

Scott, Hew, *Fasti Ecclesiae Scotticanae*, seven volumes (Edinburgh: Oliver and Boyd, 1915–28).

Spalding Club, *The Miscellany of the Spalding Club, volume 2* (Aberdeen: Spalding Club, 1842).

Spooner, J. *Reports of Cases Argued and Determined in the Supreme Court of the State of Vermont* (Woodstock: Vermont Printing Company, 1847).

Stair, Viscount of, James, *The Institutions of the Laws of Scotland, Deduced from its Originals and Collated with the Civil, Canon and Feudal Laws, and with the Customs of Neighbouring Nations*, edited by David M. Walker (Glasgow and Edinburgh: Universities of Glasgow and Edinburgh, 1981 [1681]).

Statistical Account of Scotland (OSA) (Edinburgh, 21 volumes, 1791–99).

Stevenson, David, *The Diary of a Canny Man 1818–1828: Adam Mackie Farmer, Merchant and Innkeeper in Fyvie* (Aberdeen: Aberdeen University Press, 1991).

Stevenson, William (ed.) *The Presbytrie Booke of Kirkcaldie (1630–1653)* (Kirkcaldy: James Burt, 1900).

Steuart, Walter, *Collections and Observations Methodiz'd; Concerning the Worship, Discipline, and Government of the Church of Scotland* (Edinburgh: Andrew Anderson, 1709).

Stokes, Francis Griffin, *The Blecheley Diary of the Rev. William Cole, 1765–67* (London: Constable, 1931).

Todd, Margo, *The Perth Kirk Session Books, 1577–1590* (Woodbridge: Boydell, 2012).

Vaisey, David (ed.), *The Diary of Thomas Turner, 1754–1765* (Oxford: Oxford University Press, 1984).

Whatley, Christopher, *The Diary of John Sturrock, Millwright, Dundee, 1864–65* (East Linton: Tuckwell, 1996).

Wiltshire Family History Society, *The Compleat Parish Officer* (Devizes: Wiltshire Family History Society, 1996 [1734]).

Withers, C., *Burt's Letters from the North of Scotland* (Edinburgh: Birlinn, 1998).

Wodrow, Robert, *Analecta, or Materials for a History of Remarkable Providences, Volume 1* (Edinburgh, Maitland Club, 1842–3).

Woodforde, James, *The Diary of James Woodforde, Vol. 1 and Vols 8–17* (Wymondham: Woodforde Society, 1991–2007).

Secondary sources

Aho, James, *Confession and Bookkeeping: The Religious, Moral and Rhetorical Roots of Modern Accounting* (Albany: State University of New York Press, 2005).

Ali, Abbas J., *Islamic Perspectives on Management and Organization* (Cheltenham: Edward Elgar, 2005).

Anderson, Robert, 'In search of the "Lad of Parts": the mythical history of Scottish education', *History Workshop*, 19(1) (1985), pp. 82–104.

Armitage, David, 'The Scottish diaspora', in Jenny Wormald (ed.) *Scotland: A History* (Oxford: Oxford University Press, 2005), pp. 272–303.

Asad, Talal, *Genealogies of Religion: Discipline and Reasons of Power in Christianity and Islam* (Baltimore: Johns Hopkins University Press, 1993).

Ashton, T. S., *The Industrial Revolution, 1760–1830* (Oxford: Oxford University Press, 1968).

Aspinwall, Bernard, *Portable Utopia: Glasgow and the United States, 1820–1920* (Aberdeen: Aberdeen University Press, 1983).

Baltzell, E. Digby, *Puritan Boston and Quaker Philadelphia: Two Protestant*

Ethics and the Spirit of Class Authority and Leadership (New York: Free Press, 1979).

Barr, Jean, *The Stranger Within: On the Idea of an Educated Public* (Rotterdam: Sense Publishers, 2008).

Beckett, John (ed.), *A Centenary History of Nottingham* (Chichester: Phillimore, 2006).

Beckford, James and N. J. Demerath, *The Sage Handbook of the Sociology of Religion* (London: Sage, 2007).

Bigoni, Michele, Enrico Deidda Gallardo and Warwick Fennell, 'Rethinking the sacred and secular divide: accounting and accountability practices in the Diocese of Ferrara (1431–1457)', *Accounting, Auditing and Accountability Journal*, 26(4) (2013), pp. 567–94.

Black, Jeremy, 'Confessional state or elect nation? Religion and identity in eighteenth-century England', in Tony Claydon and Ian McBride (eds) *Protestantism and National Identity: Britain and Ireland, c. 1650–c. 1850* (Cambridge: Cambridge University Press, 1998), pp. 53–74.

Bowie, Karin, 'New perspectives on pre-Union Scotland', in T. M. Devine and Jenny Wormald (eds) *The Oxford Handbook of Modern Scottish History* (Oxford: Oxford University Press, 2012), pp. 303–19.

Brown, Callum G., 'The costs of pew-renting: church management, church-going and social class in nineteenth-century Glasgow', *Journal of Ecclesiastical History*, 38(3) (1987), pp. 347–61.

Brown, Callum G., *Religion and Society in Scotland Since 1707* (Edinburgh: Edinburgh University Press, 1997).

Brown, Callum, 'Rotavating the kailyard: re-imagining the Scottish "meenister" in discourse and the parish state since 1707', in Nigel Aston and Matthew Cragoe (eds), *Anticlericalism in Britain c. 1500–1914* (Stroud: Sutton Publishing, 2000), pp. 136–58.

Buchan, James, *Capital of the Mind: How Edinburgh Changed the World* (London: John Murray, 2003).

Buckle, Henry Thomas, *On Scotland and the Scotch Intellect* (Chicago: University of Chicago Press, 1970).

Cage, R. A., 'Debate: the making of the old Scottish poor law', *Past & Present*, 69 (1975), pp. 113–18.

Cage, R. A., *The Scottish Poor Law 1745–1845* (Edinburgh: Scottish Academic Press, 1981).

Cairns, John, 'Importing our lawyers from Holland: Netherlands influences on Scots law and lawyers in the eighteenth century', in Grant Simpson (ed.) *Scotland and the Low Countries 1124–1994* (East Linton: Tuckwell, 1996), pp. 136–53.

Camic, Charles, *Experience and Enlightenment: Socialization for Cultural Change in Eighteenth-Century Scotland* (Chicago: University of Chicago Press, 1983).

Campbell, R., 'The Enlightenment and the economy', in R. H. Campbell and Andrew Skinner (eds) *The Origins and Nature of the Scottish Enlightenment* (Edinburgh: John Donald, 1982), pp. 8–25.

Campbell, R. H., 'Grant, Sir Archibald, of Monymusk, second baronet (1696–1778)', *Oxford Dictionary of National Biography* (Oxford: Oxford University Press, 2004) [www.oxforddnb.com/view/article/65016, accessed 13 May 2010].

Campbell, Colin, 'Do today's sociologists really appreciate Weber's essay *The Protestant Ethic and the Spirit of Capitalism?*', *Sociological Review*, 54(2) (2006), pp. 207–23.

Carter, Ian, 'To roose the countra fae the caul' morality o' a deid moderatism: William Alexander and Johnny Gibb of Gushetneuk', *Northern Scotland*, 2 (1974–7), pp. 145–62.

Carter, Ian, *Farm Life in Northeast Scotland 1840–1914: The Poor Man's Country* (Edinburgh: John Donald, 1979).

Carter, Ian, *Ancient Cultures of Conceit: British University Fiction in the Post-War Years* (London: Routledge, 1990).

Chalcraft, David, 'Bringing the text back in: on ways of reading the iron cage metaphor in the two editions of The Protestant Ethic', in Mike Reed and Larry Ray (eds) *Organizing Modernity: New Weberian Perspectives on Work, Organization and Society* (London: Routledge, 1994).

Chambers, J. D., *Nottinghamshire in the Eighteenth Century: A Study of Life and Labour Under the Squirearchy* (London: Frank Cass, 1966 [1932]).

Chandler, Alfred, *Precursors of Modern Management: A Reprint of Montgomery, Carding and Spinning Master's Assistant and Major James Dalliba, Armory at Springfield* (New York: Arno Press, 1979).

Chapman, Stanley, *Hosiery and Knitwear: Four Centuries of Small-Scale Industry in Britain c. 1589–2000* (Oxford: Oxford University Press, 2002).

Clark, Anne, 'Testing the two modes theory: Christian practice in the later Middle Ages', in H. Whitehouse and Luther H. Martin (eds) *Theorizing Religions Past: Archaeology, History, and Cognition* (Walnut Creek, CA: AltaMira Press, 2004), pp. 125–42.

Clark, Ivo Mcnaughton, *A History of Church Discipline in Scotland* (Aberdeen: W. & W. Lindsay, 1929).

Clark, J. C. D., 'Protestantism, nationalism and national identity, 1660–1832', *Historical Journal*, 43(1) (2000), pp. 249–76.

Coldwell, Chris, 'The religious observance of Christmas and "Holy Days" in American Presbyterianism', *The Blue Banner*, 8 (1999) [www.fpcr.org/blue_banner_articles/americanxmas.htm, accessed 18 February 2014].

Colley, Linda, *Britons: Forging the Nation 1707–1837*, (New Haven, CT: Princeton University Press, 2005) (second edition).

Cooke, Anthony, *The Rise and Fall of the Scottish Cotton Industry 1778–1914: The Secret Spring* (Manchester: Manchester University Press, 2010).

Craig, Carol, *The Scots' Crisis of Confidence* (Glendurael: Argyll Publishing, 2011) (second edition).

Cunningham, Alan, *The Life of Robert Burns*, (London: James Cochrane, 1835).

Davidson, John, *Inverurie and the Earldom of the Garioch: A Topographical and Historical Account of the Garioch from the Earliest Times to the Revolution Settlement* (Edinburgh: David Douglas, 1878).

Demerath, N. and Terry Schmitt, 'Transcending sacred and secular: mutual benefits in analyzing religious and nonreligious organizations', in N. Demerath, Peter Hall, Terry Schmit and Rhys Williams (eds) *Sacred Companies* (New York: Oxford University Press, 1998), pp. 381–92.

Demerath, N., Peter Hall, Terry Schmit and Rhys Williams, *Sacred Companies: Organizational Aspects of Religion And Religious Aspects of Organizations* (New York: Oxford University Press, 1998).

Demerath, N. J. and Arthur E. Farnsley, 'Congregations resurgent', in James Beckford and N. J. Demerath (eds) *The Sage Handbook of the Sociology of Religion* (London: Sage, 2007), pp. 193–204.

Devine, Tom, *The Tobacco Lords: A Study of the Tobacco Merchants of Glasgow and their Trading Activities, c. 1740–90* (Edinburgh: John Donald, 1975).

Devine, Tom, *Scotland's Empire 1600–1815* (London: Penguin, 2003).

Devine, Tom, *Clearance and Improvement: Land, Power and People in Scotland 1700–1900* (Edinburgh: John Donald, 2006).

Devine, Tom, *To the Ends of the Earth: Scotland's Global Diaspora, 1750–2010* (London: Penguin, 2012).

Dickson, Nicholas, *The Kirk and its Worthies* (Edinburgh: T. N. Foulis, 1914).

Donaldson, Islay Murray, *The Life and Work of Samuel Rutherford Crockett* (Aberdeen: Aberdeen University Press, 1989).

Donaldson, William, 'Alexander, William (1826–1894)', *Oxford Dictionary of National Biography* (Oxford: Oxford University Press, 2006) [www.oxford dnb.com/view/article/39241, accessed 28 February 2014].

Drummond, Andrew L., *The Kirk and the Continent* (Edinburgh: Saint Andrews Press, 1956).

Drummond, Andrew L. and James Bulloch, *The Scottish Church 1688–1843: The Age of the Moderates* (Edinburgh: Saint Andrew Press, 1973).

Durkheim, Emil, *The Elementary Forms of Religious Life* (Oxford: Oxford University Press, 2001 [1912]).

Edgar, Andrew, *Old Church Life in Scotland: Lectures on Kirk-Session and Presbytery Records, volume 1* (Paisley: Alexander Gardner, 1885).

Edgar, Andrew, *Old Church Life in Scotland: Lectures on Kirk-Session and Presbytery Records, volume 2* (Paisley: Alexander Gardner, 1886).

Elden, Stuart, 'The problem of confession: the productive failure of Foucault's History of Sexuality', *Journal for Cultural Research*, 9(1) (2002), pp. 23–41.

Emerson, Roger, 'Aberdeen professors 1690–1800: two structures, two professoriates, two careers', in Jennifer Carter and Joan Pittock (eds) *Aberdeen and the Enlightenment* (Aberdeen: Aberdeen University Press, 1987), pp. 155–67.

Espejo, Concha Álvarez-Dardet, Jesus Manjón and Juan Baños Sánchez-Matamoros, 'Accounting at the boundaries of the sacred: the regulation of the Spanish Brotherhoods in the eighteenth century', *Accounting History*, 11 (2006), pp. 129–50.

Fawcett, Arthur, *Cambuslang Revival: The Scottish Evangelical Revival of the Eighteenth Century* (Edinburgh: Banner of Truth Trust, 1971).

Feldman, Martha, 'Organizational routines as a source of continuous change', *Organization Science*, 11(6) (2000), pp. 611–29.

Feldman, Martha and Brian Pentland, 'Reconceptualizing organizational routines as a source of flexibility and change', *Administrative Science Quarterly*, 48(1) (2003), pp. 94–118.

Ford, J. D., *Law and Opinion in Scotland During the Seventeenth Century* (Oxford: Hart, 2007).

Foucault, Michel, *Discipline and Punish: The Birth of the Prison* (London: Penguin, 1991).

Foucault, Michel, *Abnormal: Lectures at the Collège de France 1974–1975* (New York: Picador, 1999).

Foucault, Michel, *Security, Territory, Population: Lectures at the Collège de France 1977–1978* (Basingstoke: Palgrave Macmillan, 2009).

Fowkes, D. V., *The Progress of Agrarian Change in Nottinghamshire c. 1720–1830* (PhD: University of Liverpool, 1971).

Fox, Kate, *Watching the English: The Hidden Rules of English Behaviour* (London: Hodder & Stoughton, 2005).

Friedland, Roger, 'Institution, practice and ontology: towards a religious sociology', *Research in the Sociology of Organizations*, 27 (2009), pp. 45–83.

Fry, Michael, *The Union: England, Scotland and the Treaty of 1707* (Edinburgh: Birlinn, 2007).

Gallagher, Tom, *The Illusion of Freedom: Scotland under Nationalism* (London: Hurst & Co., 2009).

Ganter, Hans-Dieter and Peter Walgenbach, 'Middle managers: differences between Britain and Germany', in M. Geppert, D. Matten and K. Williams (eds) *Challenges for European Management In A Global Context* (Basingstoke: Palgrave Macmillan, 2002), pp. 165–88.

Gantman, Ernesto, *Capitalism, Social Privilege and Managerial Ideologies* (Aldershot: Ashgate, 2005).

Gardner, Ginny, *The Scottish Exile Community in the Netherlands, 1660–1690* (East Linton: Tuckwell, 2004).

Gaskell, Ernest, *Lancashire Leaders Social and Political* (London: Queenhithe Printing and Publishing Co., c. 1906).

Gerth, H. and C. Wright Mills, *From Max Weber: Essays in Sociology* (London: Routledge & Kegan Paul, 1948).

Gorski, Philip, *The Disciplinary Revolution: Calvinism and the Rise of the State in Early Modern Europe* (Chicago: University of Chicago Press, 2003).

Gorski, Philip, 'The little divergence: the Protestant Reformation and economic hegemony in early modern Europe', in W. Swatos and L. Kaelber (eds) *The Protestant Ethic Turns 100: Essays on the Centenary of the Weber Thesis* (Boulder, CO: Paradigm Publishers, 2005), pp. 165–91.

Graham, Henry, *The Social Life of Scotland in the Eighteenth Century* (London: Adam & Charles Black, 1899).

Graham, Michael, *The Blasphemies of Thomas Aikenhead: Boundaries of Belief on the Eve of the Enlightenment* (Edinburgh: Edinburgh University Press, 2008).

Gregory, Jeremy, '"For all sorts and conditions of men": the social life of the Book of Common Prayer during the long eighteenth century: or, bringing the history of religion and social history together', *Social History*, 34 (2009), pp. 29–54.

Gregory, Jeremy, *Restoration, Reformation and Reform, 1660–1828: Archbishops of Canterbury and their Diocese* (Oxford: Oxford University Press, 2000).

Gregory, Jeremy and Jeffrey Chamberlain, *The National Church in Local Perspective: The Church of England and the Regions, 1660–1800* (Woodbridge: Boydell, 2003).

Haigh, Christopher, 'Communion and community: exclusion from communion in post-Reformation England', *Journal of Ecclesiastical History*, 51(4) (2000), pp. 721–40.

Hall, Peter Dobkin, *Inventing the Nonprofit Sector and Other Essays on Philanthropy, Voluntarism and Nonprofit Organizations* (Baltimore: Johns Hopkins University Press, 1992).

Hall, Peter Dobkin, 'Religion and the organizational revolution in the United States', in N. Demerath, Peter Hall, Terry Schmit and Rhys Williams, *Sacred Companies* (New York: Oxford University Press, 1998), pp. 99–115.

Hamilton, Henry, *Life and Labour on an Aberdeenshire Estate, 1735–1750* (Aberdeen: Third Spalding Club, 1946).

Hamilton, Douglas, *Scotland, the Caribbean and the Atlantic World 1750–1820* (Manchester: Manchester University Press, 2005).

Hanham, Alison, *Sinners of Cramond: The Struggle to Impose Godly Behaviour on a Scottish Community, 1651–1851* (Edinburgh: John Donald, 2005).

Harvie, Christopher, *Travelling Scot: Essays on the History, Politics and Future of the Scots* (Glendaruel, Argyll: Argyll, 1999).

Henderson, G. D., *The Scottish Ruling Elder* (London: James Clarke & Son, 1935).

Hennis, Wilhelm, *Max Weber: Essays in Reconstruction* (London: Allen & Unwin, 1988).

Henstock, Adrian, 'A parish divided: Bingham and the Rev. John Walter 1764–1810', *Transactions of the Thoroton Society*, 85 (1981), pp. 90–101.

Herman, Arthur, *The Scottish Enlightenment: The Scots' Invention of the Modern World* (London: Fourth Estate, 2003).

Hill, Arthur Du Boulay, *East Bridgford, Notts: The Story of an English Village* (Oxford: Oxford University Press, 1932).

Hindle, Steve, *The State and Social Change in Early Modern England 1550– 1640* (Basingstoke: Palgrave Macmillan, 2000).

Hindle, Steve, *On the Parish? The Micro-politics of Poor Relief in Rural England c. 1550–1750* (Oxford: Oxford University Press, 2004).

Holmes, Heather, 'The circulation of Scottish agricultural books during the eighteenth century', *Agricultural History Review*, 54 (2006), pp. 45–78.

Houston, Robert, *Scottish Literacy and the Scottish Identity: Illiteracy and Society in Scotland and Northern England, 1600–1800* (Cambridge: Cambridge University Press, 1985).

Hunt, Arnold, 'The Lord's Supper in early modern England', *Past & Present*, 161(1) (1998), pp. 39–83.

Hutton, Ronald, *The Rise and Fall of Merry England: The Ritual Year, 1400– 1700* (Oxford: Oxford University Press, 2001).

Inglis, Bill, 'The impact of Episcopacy and Presbyterianism before and after 1690, on one parish: a case study of Dunblane kirk session minutes', *Records of the Scottish Church History Society*, 33 (2003), pp. 35–61.

Jackson, Clare, *Restoration Scotland, 1660–1690: Royalist Politics, Religion and Ideas* (Woodbridge: Boydell, 2003).

Jacob, W. M., *Lay People and Religion in the Early Eighteenth Century* (Cambridge: Cambridge University Press, 1996).

Jamie, David, *Old Church Life in Ballingry (Being the history of a Fifeshire parsh, based chiefly on its old session records)* (Kinross: George Barnet, 1890).

Jeremy, David, 'Important questions about business and religion in modern Britain', in David Jeremy (ed.) *Business And Religion in Britain* (London: Gower, 1988), pp. 1–26.

Jeremy, David, *Capitalists and Christians: Business Leaders and the Churches in Britain, 1900–1960* (Oxford: Clarendon, 1990).

Jeremy, David, 'Montgomery, James (1794–1880)', *Oxford Dictionary of National Biography* (Oxford: Oxford University Press, 2004) [www.oxford dnb.com/view/article/39066, accessed 6 May 2014].

Johnstone, Muir, 'Work journals as historical evidence: the Burrell journals, 1763–1820', *Scottish Archives*, 18 (2012), pp. 38–51.

Kelly, Stuart, *Scott-land: The Man who Invented a Nation* (Edinburgh: Polygon, 2010).

Kidd, Colin and James Coleman, 'Mythical Scotland', in T. M. Devine and Jenny Wormald (eds) *The Oxford Handbook of Modern Scottish History* (Oxford: Oxford University Press, 2012), pp. 62–77.

Kidd, Colin and Clare Jackson, 'Grant, Sir Francis, first baronet, Lord Cullen (1658x63–1726)', *Oxford Dictionary of National Biography* (Oxford: Oxford University Press, 2004) [www.oxforddnb.com/view/article/11256, accessed 4 February 2014].

Kirk, James, *The Second Book of Discipline* (Edinburgh: Saint Andrew Press, 1980).

Kirk, James, *Patterns of Reform: Continuity and Change in the Reformation Kirk* (Edinburgh: T. & T. Clark, 1989).

Kyle, R., 'The nature of the church in the thought of John Knox', *Scottish Journal of Theology*, 37(4) (1984), pp. 485–501.

Lea, Henry Charles, *A History of Auricular Confession and Indulgences in the Latin Church* (Philadelphia: Lea Brothers & Co, 1896).

Lewis, Samuel, *A Topographical Dictionary of Scotland* (London: S. Lewis & Co., 1846) at British History Online [www.british-history.ac.uk/source.aspx?pubid=308, accessed 11 October 2013].

Lindsay, Jean, *The Scottish Poor Law: Its Operation in the North East from 1745 to 1845* (Ilfracombe: Stockwell, 1975).

McCallum, John, *Reforming the Scottish Parish: The Reformation in Fife, 1560–1640* (Farnham: Ashgate, 2010).

McCarthy, Angela, 'The Scottish diaspora since 1815', in T. M. Devine and Jenny Wormald (eds) *The Oxford Handbook of Modern Scottish History* (Oxford: Oxford University Press, 2012), pp. 510–32.

McCrie, Thomas, *Life of Andrew Melville* (Edinburgh: William Blackwood, 1856).

McCrone, David, *Understanding Scotland: The Sociology of a Nation* (London: Routledge, 2001).

McCrone, David, 'Cultural capital in an understated nation: the case of Scotland', *British Journal of Sociology*, 56(1) (2005), pp. 65–82.

McCrone, David, 'A new Scotland? Society and culture', in T. M. Devine and Jenny Wormald (eds) *The Oxford Handbook of Modern Scottish History* (Oxford: Oxford University Press, 2012), pp. 671–86.

MacCulloch, Diarmaid, *Reformation: Europe's House Divided 1490–1700* (London: Penguin, 2004).

McCusker, John and Russell Menard, *The Economy of British North America, 1607–1789* (Chapel Hill, NC: North Carolina University Press, 1985).

Macgregor, Janet, *The Scottish Presbyterian Polity: A Study of its Origins in the Sixteenth Century* (Edinburgh: Oliver and Boyd, 1926).

McHugh, F., 'Review of *The Church of Scotland: An Economic Survey*', *Economic Journal*, 91 (1981), pp. 583–4.

McIlvanney, Liam, *Burns the Radical: Poetry and Politics in Late Eighteenth-Century Scotland* (East Linton: Tuckwell, 2002).

McInnes, Alan, *Charles I and the Making of the Covenanting Movement, 1625–1641* (Edinburgh: John Donald, 1991).

McIntosh, John, *Church and Theology in Enlightenment Scotland: The Popular Party 1740–1800* (East Linton: Tuckwell, 1998).

McKean, Charles, *Banff & Buchan* (Edinburgh: Mainstream Publishing, 1990).

McKinstry, Sam and Ying Yong Ding, 'Alex Cowan & Sons Ltd, Papermakers, Penicuik: a Scottish case of Weber's Protestant work ethic', *Business History*, 55(5) (2013), pp. 721–39.

MacLaren, A. Allan, *Religion and Social Class: The Disruption Years in Aberdeen* (London: Routledge & Kegan Paul, 1974).

McLean, Iain, *Adam Smith, Radical And Egalitarian: An Interpretation for the 21st Century* (Edinburgh: Edinburgh University Press, 2006).

McPherson, J. M., *The Kirk's Care of the Poor, With Special Reference to the North-East of Scotland* (Aberdeen: John Avery, 1945).

McWilliam, Colin, *The Buildings of Scotland: Lothian* (Harmondsworth: Penguin, 1978).

Mann, Alastair, *The Scottish Book Trade 1500–1720: Print Commerce and Print Control in Early Modern Scotland: An Historiographical Survey of the Early Modern Book in Scotland* (East Linton: Tuckwell, 2000).

Marshall, Gordon, *Presbyteries and Profits: Calvinism and the Development of Capitalism in Scotland, 1560–1707* (Oxford: Clarendon Press, 1980).

May, Peter, *The Chess Men* (London: Quercus, 2013).

Megill, Alan, *Historical Knowledge, Historical Error: A Contemporary Guide to Practice* (Chicago: University of Chicago Press, 2007).

Mepham, Michael, *Accounting in Eighteenth Century Scotland* (New York: Garland, 1988).

Mepham, M. J., 'The Scottish Enlightenment and the development of accounting', in R. H. Parker and B. Yarney (eds) *Accounting History: Some British Contributions* (Oxford: Oxford University Press, 1994), pp. 268–93.

Miller, Hugh, *First Impressions of England and its People* (Edinburgh: Johnstone and Hunter, 1853).

Mitchison, Rosalind, 'The making of the old Scottish poor law', *Past & Present*, 63 (1974) 58–93.

Mitchison, Rosalind, 'The making of the old Scottish poor law: a rejoinder', *Past & Present*, 69 (1975) 119–21.

Mitchison, Rosalind, *The Old Poor Law in Scotland: The Experience of Poverty, 1574–1845* (Edinburgh: Edinburgh University Press, 2000).

Mitchison, Rosalind and Leah Leneman, *Sexuality and Social Control: Scotland 1660–1780* (Oxford: Blackwell, 1989).

Morton, Graeme, *Unionist Nationalism: Governing Urban Scotland 1830–1860* (East Linton: Tuckwell, 1999).

Moynihan, Peter, 'Walker's Ales', *Journal of the Brewery History Society*, 46 (1985), pp. 3–8.

Moynihan, Peter, 'Walker's Ales', *Journal of the Brewery History Society*, 47 (1986), pp. 9–16.

Mullan, David George, *Narratives of the Religious Self in Early-Modern Scotland* (Farnham: Ashgate, 2010).

Munro, J. Forbes, *Maritime Enterprise and Empire: Sir William MacKinnon and his Business Network, 1823–1893* (Woodbridge: Boydell, 2003).

Murdoch, Alexander, *Scotland and America c. 1600–c. 1800* (Basingstoke: Palgrave Macmillan, 2010).

Murray, James, *Kilmacolm: A Parish History, 1100–1898* (Paisley: Alexander Gardner, 1898).

Murray, David, *Chapters in the History of Bookeeping, Accountancy & Commercial Arithmetic* (Glasgow: Jackson, Wylie & Co., 1930).

Mutch, Alistair, 'Magistrates and public house managers, 1840–1914: another case of Liverpool exceptionalism?', *Northern History*, 40 (2003), pp. 325–42.

Mutch, Alistair, 'Shaping the public house 1850–1950: business strategies, state regulation and social history', *Cultural and Social History*, 1(2) (2004), pp. 179–200.

Mutch, Alistair, 'Public houses as multiple retailing: Peter Walker & Son 1846–1914', *Business History*, 48(1) (2006), pp. 1–19.

Mutch, Alistair, 'National identity and popular music: questioning the "Celtic"', *Scottish Studies Review*, 8(1) (2007), pp. 116–29.

Mutch, Alistair, 'Custom and personal accountability in eighteenth century south Nottinghamshire church governance', *Midland History*, 36(1) (2011), pp. 69–88.

Mutch, Alistair, 'Data mining the archives: the emergence of separate books of account in the Church of Scotland 1608–1800', *Scottish Archives*, 18 (2012), pp. 78–94.

Mutch, Alistair, 'Systemic accountability and the governance of the Kirk: the Presbytery of Garioch in the eighteenth century', *Northern Scotland*, 3 (2012), pp. 45–65.

Mutch, Alistair, 'Presbyterian governance in practice: Monymusk 1790–1825', *Records of the Scottish Church History Society*, 42 (2013), pp. 1–34.

Nollen, Scott Allen, *Jethro Tull: A History of the Band, 1968–2001* (Jefferson, NC: McFarland & Co., 2002).

Parker, R. A. C., *Coke of Norfolk: A Financial and Agricultural Study 1707–1842* (Oxford: Clarendon, 1975).

Parratt, David R., *The Development and Use of Written Pleadings in Scots Civil Procedure* (Edinburgh: Stair Society, 2006).

Patrick, Derek, 'The Kirk, Parliament and the Union 1706–7', *Scottish Historical Review*, 87 (2, Supplement) (2008), pp. 94–115.

Pentland, Brian and Martha Feldman, 'Organizational routines as a unit of analysis', *Industrial and Corporate Change*, 14(5) (2005), pp. 793–815.

Peterkin, Alexander, *A Compendium of the Laws of the Church of Scotland* (Edinburgh: Edinburgh Printing and Publishing, 1840).

Philip, Henry, *The Higher Tradition: A History of Public Examinations in*

Scottish Schools and how they Influenced the Development of Secondary Education (Dalkeith: Scottish Examination Board, 1992).

Pitman, Jan, 'Tradition and exclusion: parochial officeholding in early modern England, a case study from north Norfolk 1580–1640', *Rural History*, 15 (2004), pp. 27–45.

Quattrone, Paulo, 'Accounting for God: accounting and accountability practices in the Society of Jesus (Italy, XVI–XVII centuries)', *Accounting, Organizations and Society*, 29(7) (2004), pp. 647–83.

Raffe, Alasdair, 'Presbyterianism, secularization, and Scottish politics after the Revolution of 1688–1690', *Historical Journal*, 53(2) (2010), pp. 317–37.

Raffe, Alasdair, *The Culture of Controversy: Religious Arguments in Scotland, 1660–1714* (Woodbridge: Boydell, 2012).

Raffe, Alasdair, 'Scotland restored and reshaped: politics and religion', in T. M. Devine and Jenny Wormald (eds) *The Oxford Handbook of Modern Scottish History* (Oxford: Oxford University Press, 2012), pp. 251–67.

Ranson, Stewart, Alan Bryman and Bob Hinings, *Clergy, Ministers and Priests* (London: Routledge & Kegan Paul, 1977).

Reid, Harry, *Reformation: The Dangerous Birth of the Modern World* (Edinburgh: Saint Andrew Press, 2010).

Richards, Eric, *The Leviathan of Wealth: The Sutherland Fortune in the Industrial Revolution* (London: Routledge & Kegan Paul, 1973).

Richards, Eric and Monica Clough, *Cromartie: Highland Life 1650–1914* (Aberdeen: Aberdeen University Press, 1989).

Ryrie, Alec, *The Origins of the Scottish Reformation* (Manchester: Manchester University Press, 2006).

Schmidt, Leigh Eric, *Holy Fairs: Scotland and the Making of American Revivalism* (Grand Rapids, MI: Eerdmans Publishing Co., 2001).

Sheldahl, Terry, 'America's earliest recorded text in accounting: Sarjeant's 1789 book', *Accounting Historians Journal*, 12(2) (1985), pp. 1–42.

Shepherd, Christine, 'The Arts curriculum at Aberdeen at the beginning of the eighteenth century', in Jennifer Carter and Joan Pittock (eds) *Aberdeen and the Enlightenment* (Aberdeen: Aberdeen University Press, 1987), pp. 146–54.

Shepherd, Ian, *Aberdeenshire: Donside and Strathbogie* (Edinburgh: Rutland Press, 2006).

Simpson, Ian, *Education in Aberdeenshire before 1872* (London: University of London Press, 1947).

Skoczylas, Anne, *Mr. Simson's Knotty Case: Divinity, Politics, and Due Process in Early Eighteenth-century Scotland* (Montreal: McGill-Queen's University Press, 2001).

Smith, William Robertson, *Lectures on the Religion of the Semites* (London: Routledge, 1997 [1889]).

Smout, T Christopher, 'The early Scottish sugar houses, 1660–1720', *Economic History Review*, 14(2) (1961), pp. 240–53.

Smout, T., *A History of the Scottish People 1560–1830* (London: Collins, 1969).

Smout, T., 'Born again at Cambuslang: new evidence on popular religion and literacy in eighteenth-century Scotland', *Past & Present*, 97 (1982), pp. 114–27.

Snape, M. F., *The Church of England in Industrialising Society: The Lancashire Parish of Whalley in the Eighteenth Century* (Woodbridge: Boydell, 2003).

Snell, K. D. M., *Parish and Belonging: Community, Identity and Welfare in England and Wales, 1700–1950* (Cambridge: Cambridge University Press, 2006).

Soper, T. P., 'Monymusk: a study of the economic development of a Scottish estate' (PhD: University of Aberdeen, 1954).

Spaeth, Donald, *The Church in an Age of Danger: Parsons and Parishioners, 1660–1740* (Cambridge: Cambridge University Press, 2000).

Spraakman, Gary and Julie Margret, 'The transfer of management accounting practices from London counting houses to the British North American fur trade', *Accounting, Business and Financial History*, 15(2) (2005), pp. 101–19.

Spring, David, *The English Landed Estate in the Nineteenth Century: Its Administration* (Baltimore: Johns Hopkins University Press, 1963).

Stephen, Jeffrey, *Scottish Presbyterians and the Act of Union, 1707* (Edinburgh: Edinburgh University Press, 2007).

Stephen, Jeffrey, *Defending the Revolution: The Church of Scotland 1689–1716* (Farnham: Ashgate, 2013).

Stevenson, David, *The Scottish Revolution, 1637–1644* (Newton Abbott: David & Charles, 1973).

Stevenson, David, *Revolution and Counter-Revolution in Scotland, 1644–1651* (Newton Abbott: David & Charles, 1978).

Stinchcombe, Arthur, 'Social structure and organizations', in James G. March (ed.) *Handbook of Organizations* (Chicago: Rand McNally, 1965), pp. 142–93.

Strawhorn, John, *750 Years of a Scottish School: Ayr Academy 1233–1983* (Ayr: Alloway Publishing, 1983).

Struthers, Gavin, *History of the Relief Church* (Glasgow: A. Fullarton, 1843).

Suderman, Jeffrey, *Orthodoxy and Enlightenment: George Campbell in the Eighteenth Century* (Montreal: McGill-Queen's University Press, 2001).

Tate, W. E., *The Parish Chest: A Study of the Records of Parochial Administration in England* (Chichester: Phillimore, 1983).

Taylor, Alan, 'SRB Interview: James Robertson', *Scottish Review of Books*, 9(2) (2013), pp. 4–6.

Tiedemann, Joseph, 'Presbyterianism and the American Revolution in the Middle Colonies', *Church History*, 74 (2005), pp. 306–44.

Tillotson, John, 'Visitation and reform of the Yorkshire nunneries in the fourteenth century', *Northern History*, 30 (1994), pp. 1–21.

Todd, Margo (ed.), *The Culture of Protestantism in Early Modern Scotland* (New Haven: Yale University Press, 2002).

Veyne, Paul, *Writing History: Essay on Epistemology* (Manchester: Manchester University Press, 1984).

Walker, Peter & Son, *Walker's Warrington Ales* (Warrington: Peter Walker & Son, 1896).

Walker, David M., *A Legal History of Scotland, Volume V: The Eighteenth Century* (Edinburgh: T. & T. Clark, 1998).

Walker, Graham, 'The religious factor', in T. M. Devine and Jenny Wormald (eds) *The Oxford Handbook of Modern Scottish History* (Oxford: Oxford University Press, 2012), pp. 585–601.

Wall, Joseph Frazier, *Andrew Carnegie* (New York: Oxford University Press, 1970).

Wallace, Valerie, 'Presbyterian moral economy: the Covenanting tradition and popular protest in Lowland Scotland, 1707–c. 1746', *Scottish Historical Review*, 89(1) (2010), pp. 54–72.

Weatherhead, James, *The Constitution and Laws of the Church of Scotland* (Edinburgh: Church of Scotland, 1997).

Weber, Max, *Economy and Society, vol. 1* (Berkeley: University of California Press, 1968 [1922]).

Weber, Max, *The Protestant Ethic and the Spirit of Capitalism* (London: Allen & Unwin, 1976 [1905]).

Whatley, Christopher, *Scottish Society 1707–1830: Beyond Jacobitism, Towards Industrialisation* (Manchester: Manchester University Press, 2000).

Whatley, Christopher, 'Reformed religion, regime change, Scottish Whigs and the struggle for the "soul" of Scotland, c. 1688–c. 1788', *Scottish Historical Review*, 92(1) (2013), pp. 66–99.

Whatley, Christopher and Derek Patrick, *The Scots and the Union* (Edinburgh: Edinburgh University Press, 2006).

Whetstone, Ann, *Scottish County Government in the Eighteenth and Nineteenth Centuries* (Edinburgh: John Donald, 1981).

White, Robin and Ian Willock, *The Scottish Legal System* (Haywards Heath: Tottel, 2006) (fourth edition).

Whitehouse, Harvey, *Modes of Religiosity: A Cognitive Theory of Religious Transmission* (Walnut Creek, CA: AltaMira Press, 2004).

Whitley, Laurence, *A Great Grievance: Ecclesiatical Lay Patronage in Scotland until 1750* (Eugene, OR: Mipf and Stock, 2013).

Whytock, Jack, *'An Educated Clergy': Scottish Theological Education and Training in the Kirk and Secession, 1560–1850*, (Milton Keynes: Paternoster, 2007).

Wilkie, George Scott, *Understanding Robert Burns* (Glasgow: Neil Wilson, 2002).

Winstanley, Roy, *Parson Woodforde – The Life and Times of a Country Diarist* (Bungay: Morrow & Co., 1996).

Withrington, Donald, 'What was distinctive about the Scottish Enlightenment?', in Jennifer Carter and Joan Pittock (eds) *Aberdeen and the Enlightenment* (Aberdeen: Aberdeen University Press, 1987), pp. 9–19.

Withrington, Donald, 'Constructing a new university tradition: the curious emergence of "Democratic Intellectualism" as the distinctive mark of the Scottish Universities in the 19th century', 19th International Congress of Historical Science, Oslo, 6–13 August (2000) [www.oslo2000.uio.no/ AIO/AIO16/group%204/Withrington.pdf, accessed 10 July].

Jenny Wormald, 'Reformed and Godly Scotland?', in T. M. Devine and Jenny Wormald (eds) *The Oxford Handbook of Modern Scottish History* (Oxford: Oxford University Press, 2012), pp. 62–77.

Wuthnow, Robert, *Communities of Discourse: Ideology and Social Structure in the Reformation, the Enlightenment, and European Socialism* (Cambridge, MA: Harvard University Press, 1989).

Yates, JoAnne and Wanda Orlikowski, 'Genres of organizational communication: a structurational approach to studying communication and media', *Academy of Management Review*, 17(2) (1992), pp. 299–326.

Yates, Nigel, *Preaching, Word and Sacrament: Scottish Church Interiors 1560– 1860* (London: T. & T. Clark, 2009).

Zahniser, Keith, *Steel City Gospel: Protestant Laity and Reform in Progressive-era Pittsburgh* (New York: Routledge, 2005).

Index